THE SHROPSHIRE & MONTGOMERYSHIRE LIGHT RAILWAY

UNDER MILITARY CONTROL

1940-1960

© Michael Christensen and Lightmoor Press 2011
Designed by Ian Pope
British Library Cataloguing-in-Publication Data. A catalogue record for this book
is available from the British Library
ISBN 13: 978 1899889 54 9
All rights reserved. No part of this publication may be reproduced, stored in a
retrieval system or transmitted in any form or by any means,
electronic, mechanical, photocopying, recording or otherwise, without the written
permission of the publisher.

Lightmoor Press

Lightmoor Press is an imprint of Black Dwarf Lightmoor Publications Limited
144b Lydney Industrial Estate, Harbour Road
Lydney, Gloucestershire, GL15 4EJ
Printed and bound by T J International, Padstow, Cornwall

THE
SHROPSHIRE & MONTGOMERYSHIRE LIGHT RAILWAY

UNDER MILITARY CONTROL
1940-1960

Above: One of the newly-delivered Austerity tank locomotives paused during shunting on the Criggion Branch sidings at Kinnerley. The men sit in the sunshine taking their rest. The wagons on the right were for the stone traffic from the quarries at Criggion – those in the siding on the left were usually in for repairs.
Geoffrey Bannister, courtesy Andrew Bannister

Opposite: The S&M as it will be remembered by many enthusiasts. Austerity 0-6-0 Saddle Tank locomotive WD193 was photographed at Shrewsbury Abbey Station while working a special (hence the 'S' target disc) train for the Birmingham Locomotive Club trip on 26th June 1955.
Geoffrey Bannister, courtesy Andrew Bannister

Mike Christensen OBE

A scene typical of the Colonel Stephens era. One of the ex-L&NWR 'Collier' locomotives – the number too dirty to read but probably 8182 – took on water at Kinnerley while working a westbound train to Llanymynech. The wooden panelling on the coach had been patched up, but the paint was peeling off again. Coaches not needed were stabled in the bay platform on the left. Some shunting would be needed before the train could depart; a wagon had been left standing on the main line (visible beyond the bracket signal).

Lens of Sutton Association

CONTENTS

1 The Planning Phase 7
2 The Construction Phase 35
3 The War Department Runs The Railway 49
4 Local Railway Working Instructions 65
5 The Post-War Period 131
6 A Typical Day's Train Working in 1958 167

Appendices
A Photographs of some of the rolling stock 175
B Locomotives and rolling stock in November 1940 186
C Steam locomotives allocated to the S&M from 1941 to 1948 187
D Description of the Depot in 1946 188
E Operating Notices 189

Acknowledgements 191

TERMINOLOGY

The words used to describe railway equipment has changed over the years. Wagons that were constructed to protect the goods carried from the weather were known on the Midland Railway as Covered Goods Wagons, and the War Department (WD) sometimes used this term. More often the Army has used the term 'box wagon' and that is the origin of the designation currently in use – WGB (Wagon, Goods, Box). Generally in this book, the term most commonly used amongst the men – van – has been adopted.

To the Army, a 'tank' is a form of Armoured Fighting Vehicle, so wagons constructed to carry fluids are known as Cistern Wagons in WD parlance. Again, the word 'tank' was commonly used amongst railwaymen for these vehicles, and has been adopted in the text.

Whilst railwaymen may use the term locomotive to describe the motive power, the WD term has always been 'engine'. Since an engine might be a piece of equipment not used on a railway, the driver's designation makes it clear that he is on a railway – R.E.D. (Railway Engine Driver). Stevedores were employed on the railway – men trained in the loading and unloading of ships. Because of a shortage of manpower, men from Port Operating Companies were allocated to the Depot, and used on tasks for which they could quickly be trained such as keepers at level crossings. The term 'hook off' was used meaning to uncouple a vehicle from a train, by removing its coupling from the hook on the adjacent vehicle.

Even in 1947, the station buildings at Kinnerley still carried Shropshire & Montgomeryshire (S&M) notices about the acceptance of traffic – a reminder that although the WD ran the railway, it was still open for civilian freight traffic.

H. C. Casserley, reference 49036

THE SHROPSHIRE & MONTGOMERYSHIRE LIGHT RAILWAY UNDER MILITARY CONTROL 1940-1960

Meole Brace exchange sidings, seen from the nearby footbridge, looking south-west on 3rd September 1937 – a little over three years before the Army conducted its first survey of the line. The gates marking the boundary in the sidings between the GWR/LMS and the S&M are evident, as is the change of maintenance standards at this boundary. There was a scotch block on the S&M side of the boundary gate, plus trap points with an associated disc signal on the 'main line' side of the gate – a 'belt and braces' protection against any runaways because the gradient falling towards Shrewsbury is 1 in 120. *R. K. Cope, (RKC/B41) courtesy Roger Carpenter*

Shrewsbury West on 9th October 1931, looking north-east with the GWR/LMS Joint line on the left and the weed-overgrown single line of the Shropshire & Montgomeryshire Light Railway on the right. Passenger services were still being operated at this time – they were not withdrawn until 6th November 1933. Shrewsbury West Halt on the S&M, one of several built for the re-opening of the line as a Light Railway in 1911, was located underneath the road overbridge in the background. It was a simple, and very short, platform. No shelter was provided for the passengers – the bridge itself sufficed. *R. K. Cope, (RKC/B47) courtesy Roger Carpenter*

Chapter 1
THE PLANNING PHASE

The background to War Department control

In the months after the declaration of war on 3rd September 1939, the planning of the British and French military was that the ground war would (as in the Great War of 1914-18) take place around the border between France and Germany. The German Army had demonstrated its capacity for Blitzkrieg ('Lightning War') in the invasion of Poland in September 1939, but it was still expected that the war on the western flank of Germany would be different. There were substantial fortifications along France's border with Germany – the Maginot Line – and similar (if weaker) fortifications across the border between France and Belgium, stretching to the coast.

Following this assumption, Britain spent the early months of the war sending a large British Expeditionary Force (BEF) to northern France. By late spring of 1940, most of the British Army and its weapons were deployed in France. However, the German attack when it came on 10th May 1940 was not a frontal attack on the Maginot Line. Instead, the German Army violated the neutrality of Holland and Belgium and advanced swiftly through the lighter defences between France and Belgium. By 14th June 1940 the Germans were in Paris. The BEF retreated, in varying degrees of chaos, to the northern coast of France. It was imperative that as much as possible of the BEF should be saved, and 'Operation Dynamo' was initiated – an evacuation from the beaches near Dunkirk. By Monday 27th May large numbers of troops began to reach England. When 'Dynamo' was complete on 4th June, some 338,200 men had been brought out of France. It was seen as a minor 'miracle' – and it was certainly a most remarkable achievement to bring so many men away from capture. However, the fall of France – a treaty of surrender was signed on 22nd June 1940 – was a significant defeat. Whilst many men had been brought out of France, virtually all their equipment had been left behind. There were only 167 anti-tank artillery pieces available in the whole of Britain to defend against invasion, should the Germans now attempt to cross the Channel. In Britain another 'minor miracle' had happened. New factories for making ordnance had been planned for some time. In July 1935 the Cabinet had decided that the factory at Woolwich (very vulnerable to attack from the air) should be supplemented by a second factory at Chorley. Over the next two years further new munitions factories had been decided upon, at Tremains near Bridgend (March 1936) and at Glascoed (July 1937). Construction proceeded, though slowly. As a war in Europe became virtually inevitable, a major expansion programme was developed with five further factories authorised in August and December 1939 (Swynnerton, Risley, Kirkby, Aycliffe and Thorp Arch). Construction work on the '1939 Programme' factories proceeded with remarkable speed. Swynnerton (always associated primarily with the production of 20mm cannon rounds) was in limited production by August 1940 – only nine months after drawing board work had started. It was just as well. Lorries queued up at the factory to take the ammunition straight to the airfields of southern England.

In the event, the dreaded invasion was not pursued. The Battle of Britain, fought over the skies of southern England in the late summer of 1940, denied the German forces the air supremacy deemed necessary for an invasion across the English Channel. From late 1940 the German tactic became to bomb or (more likely) starve Britain into eventual submission.

Thus by the early Autumn of 1940 it was apparent that there would be a long period of re-building supplies of arms and ammunition before there was any prospect of an invasion force re-entering France. Few perhaps expected that the wait would last for nearly four years. In the meantime, the ammunition (and other armaments) would have to be stored. With the British ordnance factories gearing up to full production there was going to be a need for extensive ammunition depots to store the munitions until required for new offensives in the various theatres of war. Indeed, the need to make a start was urgent.

continued on page 27

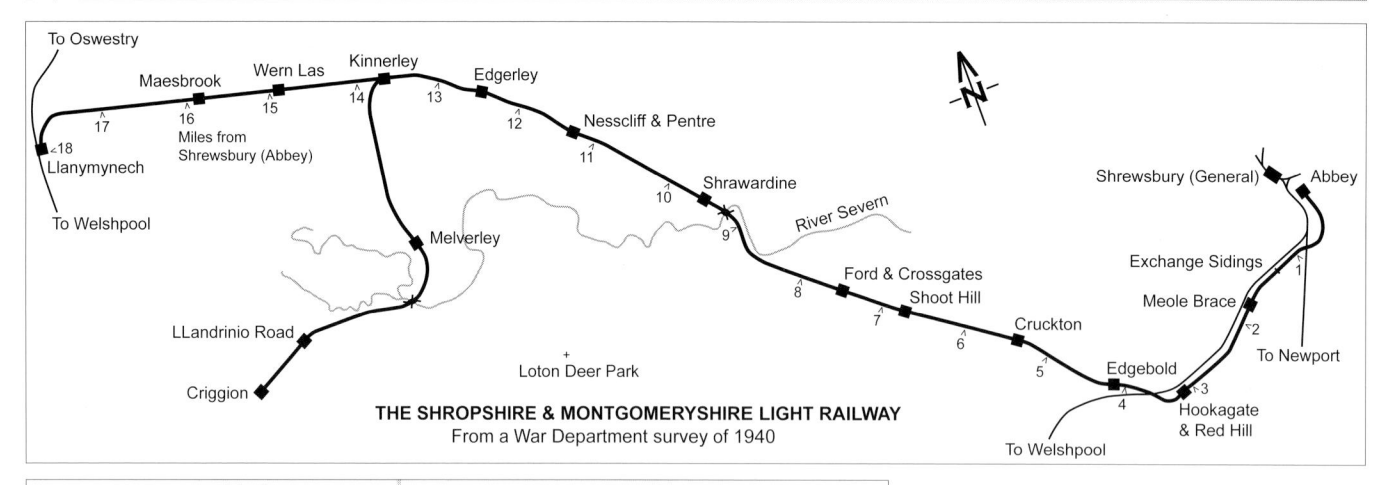

THE SHROPSHIRE & MONTGOMERYSHIRE LIGHT RAILWAY UNDER MILITARY CONTROL 1940-1960

THE SHROPSHIRE & MONTGOMERYSHIRE LIGHT RAILWAY
From a War Department survey of 1940

The daily goods train at Meole Brace, hauled by Locomotive No. 2 (LMS 8108), on 27th July 1940. The train consisted of an ex-Midland Railway passenger van No. 1 (painted green) and four empty wagons. As was by now common, the S&M train did not bother to marshall the brake van at the rear of the train. It was easier to shunt intermediate sidings without the van at the back. The locomotive had emerged from the workshops at Kinnerley in May 1939 after a heavy repair that had taken eighteen months to complete. It was painted in green (a shade described as 'Southern Green') lined with black edged in white with the number 2 in yellow on the cab side, and S&M on the tender. Soon after the WD took over the line, this locomotive was painted again – in a light green described as 'Camouflage Green'. It was also renumbered back to 8108, to keep the numbering consistent with the former LMS number (which was stamped on components such as the motion).

Graham Vincent

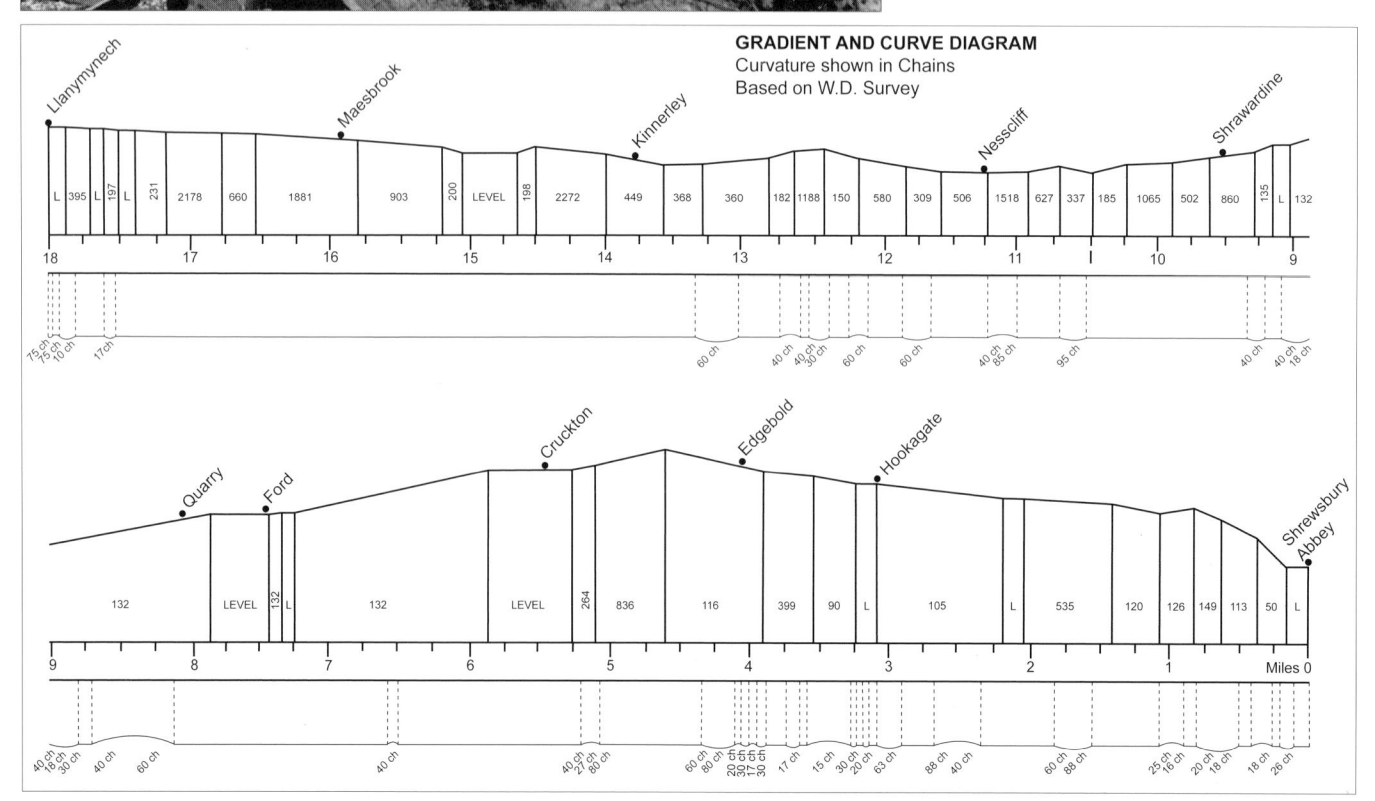

GRADIENT AND CURVE DIAGRAM
Curvature shown in Chains
Based on W.D. Survey

THE PLANNING PHASE

A view of the Meole Brace exchange sidings, from a train being backed into the sidings from the S&M line. A GWR locomotive waited to take the wagons forward. This set-up would have been quite inadequate for the potential War Department traffic.
R. K. Blencowe Negative Archive, number 21243

LMS 27752 shunting at Meole Brace exchange sidings on 31st July 1941. Notable was the size of the emergency coal stack.
Graham Vincent

Below: Looking north-eastwards towards the exchange sidings at Meole Brace on 2nd September 1937, with the GWR/LMS line on the left. The houses of the suburbs of Shrewsbury were close to the railway – there was no room for laying in new exchange sidings here, and the gradient (falling towards Sutton Bridge Junction at Shrewsbury) was unfavourable anyway. *R. K. Cope (RKC/B100) courtesy Roger Carpenter*

THE SHROPSHIRE & MONTGOMERYSHIRE LIGHT RAILWAY UNDER MILITARY CONTROL 1940-1960

Shrewsbury Abbey Station, in an undated photograph probably taken shortly before the withdrawal of regular passenger services in November 1933. A single passenger coach, and an ex-Midland Railway passenger brake van, would more than suffice for the traffic expected. *Lens of Sutton Association*

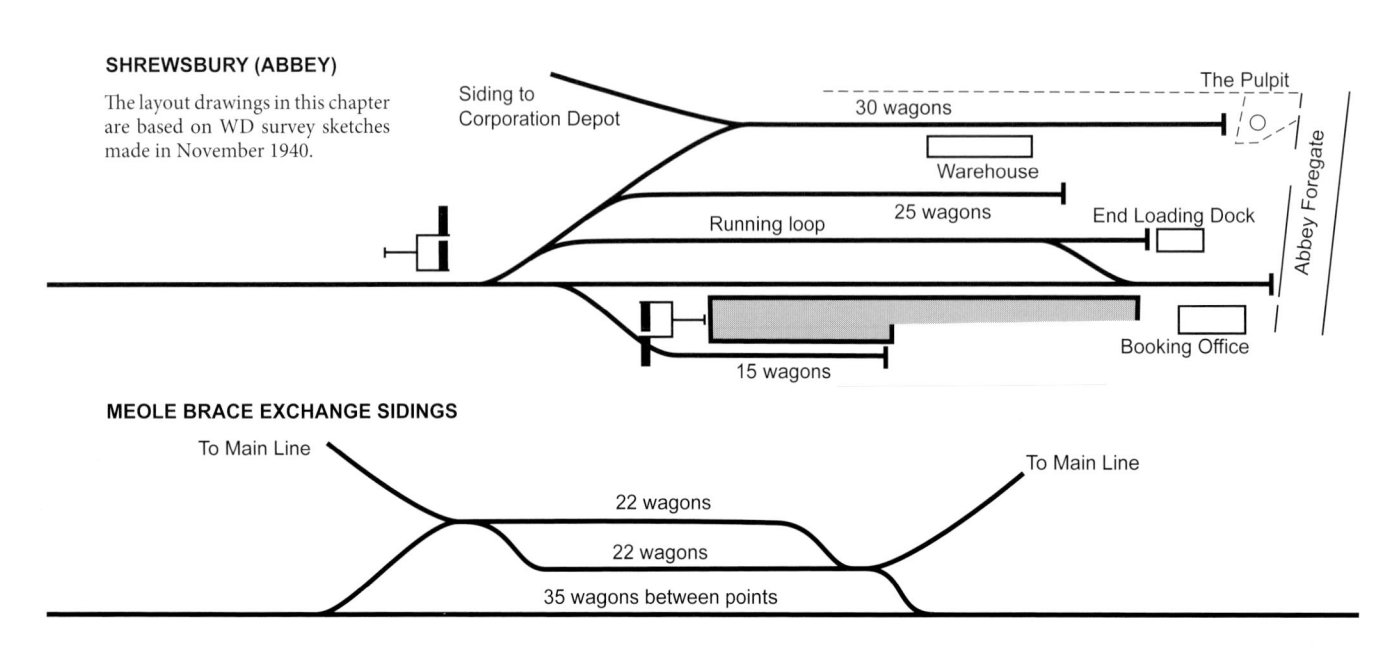

SHREWSBURY (ABBEY)

The layout drawings in this chapter are based on WD survey sketches made in November 1940.

- Siding to Corporation Depot
- 30 wagons
- The Pulpit
- Warehouse
- Running loop
- 25 wagons
- End Loading Dock
- Abbey Foregate
- 15 wagons
- Booking Office

MEOLE BRACE EXCHANGE SIDINGS

- To Main Line
- 22 wagons
- 22 wagons
- 35 wagons between points
- To Main Line

THE PLANNING PHASE

MEOLE BRACE STATION

Hand points locked by staff

Signal out of use (formerly used to protect trains standing at station for ticket inspection)

7 wagons

Small Office and store

To Shrewsbury

The platform at Meole Brace Station (opened in 1911) looking south-west towards Hookagate, with the short siding just beyond the platform and the GWR/LMS double track on the right. There was a small passenger shelter (partly protected by the road bridge) and a grounded van body in use as a store.
Photographer unknown

In slightly more prosperous days this view looks back towards Shrewsbury and shows the approach to the station. Notable was the absence of a buffer stop at the end of the siding (this was later added as seen in the photograph above).
Lens of Sutton Association

THE SHROPSHIRE & MONTGOMERYSHIRE LIGHT RAILWAY UNDER MILITARY CONTROL 1940-1960

REDHILL (HOOKAGATE)

Suggested new exit to Main Line

22 wagons — To Shrewsbury

Possible accommodation for laying 4 or 5 exchange sidings if bungalows are removed

Hookagate Station (more fully referred to by the S&M as Hookagate for Redhill) was another of the short platforms newly-constructed for the re-opening of the line as a Light Railway in 1911. It replaced an earlier station known as Redhill which had been some 100 yards nearer to Shrewsbury. This was the view looking west on 20th May 1929. The station remained unchanged, except for the fading of the paintwork, until the Army arrived. Even the simple disc signal, by which passengers indicated their need for the train to halt for them (painted red with a white band) was still in place in 1940. The short goods loop siding was west of the platform.
R. K. Cope (RKC/B9) courtesy Roger Carpenter

Looking west from Hookagate Station, showing the goods loop siding on the S&M, and part of the two lever ground frame that operated the points at the platform end of the loop. In the distance the level ground extended to the south of the S&M line and on this flat land several bungalows had been built. A few are visible. These were to be demolished to allow the War Department to use this flat area for the new exchange sidings.
R. K. Cope (RKC/B52) courtesy Roger Carpenter

EDGEBOLD

Coal depot and Creamery — To Shrewsbury
Small Office and store — 35 wagons — Bridge No. 16
Bridge No. 17 — Hand points, locked by staff — Bridge No. 15 Over LMS & GWR Joint Line

Some 200 yards on the Shrewsbury side of the passenger station at Edgebold was the connection that gave access to a steeply graded siding for the goods yard (and site of the later creamery). This 1937 view looking towards Kinnerley shows the condition into which the lightly laid track was deteriorating. The points and facing point lock (FPL) – a flimsy piece of apparatus, which can just be discerned amongst the weeds in the running line – were worked from the two-lever ground frame (supplied by Tyer & Co.) on the left. The FPL lever was unlocked by a key. *R. K. Cope (RKC/B162) courtesy Roger Carpenter*

THE PLANNING PHASE

The S&M station at Edgebold, looking south-east towards Shrewsbury on 9th October 1931, with the 'conditional stop' signal prominent on the platform. Photographs suggest that these signals were left permanently in the 'Stop' position. The railway here was above the level of the surrounding land, which is why this part of the line was deemed unsuitable for the construction of Explosive Store Houses. The multi-insulator telegraph line is believed to have been a GPO pole route run along the line of the railway for convenience – the railway requirement was just two wires! The S&M company had been undertaking some 'spot' replacement of sleepers using what was clearly untreated timber – yet the company was to complain bitterly when in the exigencies of war the War Department used sleepers that had not been treated with creosote.

R. K. Cope (RKC/B43) courtesy Roger Carpenter

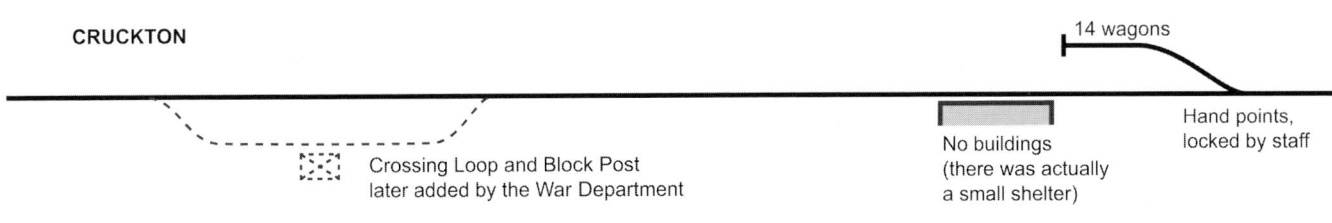

CRUCKTON

14 wagons

Crossing Loop and Block Post later added by the War Department

No buildings (there was actually a small shelter)

Hand points, locked by staff

The remote station at Cruckton with a small shelter on the platform, looking towards Llanymynech.

Lens of Sutton Association

THE SHROPSHIRE & MONTGOMERYSHIRE LIGHT RAILWAY UNDER MILITARY CONTROL 1940-1960

SHOOT HILL HALT

No buildings   House (occupied)

Water Tower for 1600 gallons   Level Crossing No. 1   To Shrewsbury
Fed by gravity from a spring
half a mile away
Takes 24 hours to fill
Out of order at present

The Birmingham Locomotive Club (BLC) special train on 30th April 1939, ready to depart and with some steam to spare in the tiny boiler. This view shows nicely the short length and relatively light weight of the rails on the S&M and the weather-beaten nameboard still in position long after ordinary passenger trains had ceased to run. The very limited protection afforded by the rear cab on **Gazelle** is apparent, as is the lightweight nature of the underframe of the coach.
courtesy John Ward collection

The S&M station (built for the 1911 re-opening) at Shoot Hill had a short platform substantially constructed in stone, but no shelter at all for the passengers. By the time this photo was taken in April 1939 the regular passenger trains had not run for six years, but the platform and its oil lamps were still well maintained. The S&M management ran occasional excursion traffic, and also special trains for enthusiasts (who already recognised the line's rare appeal and the unique nature of its locomotive **Gazelle**). This was a Birmingham Locomotive Club special train, consisting of **Gazelle** and one coach, taking water. The lineside water tank here just about sufficed the needs of this tiny locomotive, but contained only 1,600 gallons so it would not fill the tender of one Dean Goods locomotive (tender capacity 3,000 gallons) and would then take 24 hours to refill. The WD would need to make other arrangements to water its locomotives. *Lens of Sutton Association, 66047*

The S&M ran a special train for an annual outing for the boys from Shrewsbury School. This was **Gazelle** taking water at Shoot Hill on the occasion of the schoolboy's last annual special on 14th October 1939, just over a month after the outbreak of the war. Graham Vincent recorded in his diary that the train 'arrived from Kinnerley at Meole Brace at 1.30. The locomotive went into the siding and the coach was pushed past. The train left Meole Brace at 1.45 and the first stop was at Shoot Hill to take water. The rails here were wet and the hand brake had little effect, so we overshot the tank and had to reverse. Taking water is a complicated business. The pipe leading to the tank on the locomotive is only two inches diameter, so a funnel is necessary. One of the passengers had to mount the ladder to the top of the water tower as the chain was missing, and pull the lever slightly to allow a mere trickle of water to come down the pipe so as not to douse the engine driver who meantime holds the end of the pipe over the funnel held over the pipe on the locomotive. This procedure took 10 minutes'. No wonder that the Army's surveyors described the whole set-up as 'out of order'. *Graham Vincent*

THE PLANNING PHASE

FORD STATION

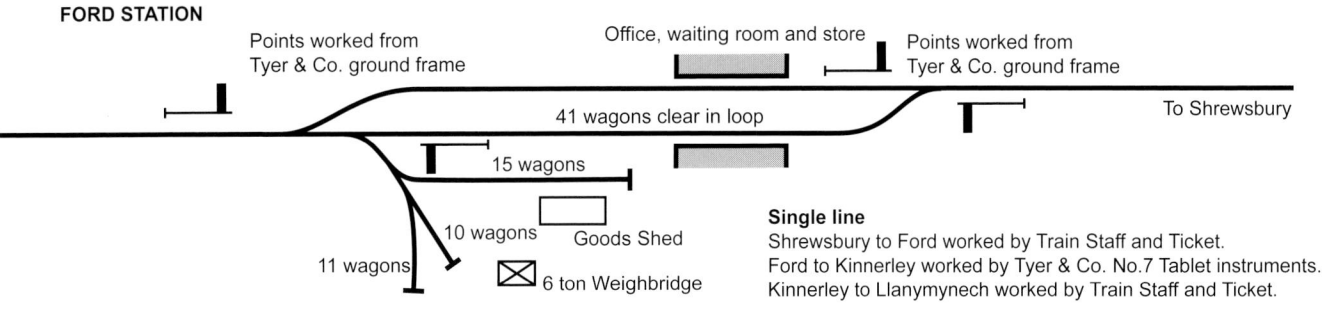

Points worked from Tyer & Co. ground frame — Office, waiting room and store — Points worked from Tyer & Co. ground frame

41 wagons clear in loop

To Shrewsbury

15 wagons

10 wagons — Goods Shed

11 wagons

⊠ 6 ton Weighbridge

Single line
Shrewsbury to Ford worked by Train Staff and Ticket.
Ford to Kinnerley worked by Tyer & Co. No.7 Tablet instruments.
Kinnerley to Llanymynech worked by Train Staff and Ticket.

Ford Station, referred to more fully in timetables as Ford & Crossgates, looking south-east towards Shrewsbury on 31st August 1937. This was the principal intermediate station between Shrewsbury and Kinnerley, with a substantial goods yard. It was a block post and was provided with a fully signalled passing loop. For years after the cessation of regular passenger services, the notice boards still carried posters, indeed the headings on the boards still dated from before 1924. The wooden railings on the bridge over the Shrewsbury road can be seen just beyond the platform ends. *R. K. Cope (RKC/B56) courtesy Roger Carpenter*

Ford Station, looking towards Kinnerley on 15th May 1938 with the Shrewsbury road bridge in the foreground and the platforms beyond. Passengers gained access to the station by a path up from the road on the right hand side, and got on to the Down (left hand) platform by crossing the line at the foot of the platform ramps, hence the lamp at the foot of the platform ramp. The raised part of the platforms, at the far end, allowed access to the guards van on the level for the loading of goods and any milk churns – the remainder of the platform was notably lower, and quite a step up into the carriages.

R. K. Cope (RKC/B246) from the 'Detachment Photograph Album'

THE SHROPSHIRE & MONTGOMERYSHIRE LIGHT RAILWAY UNDER MILITARY CONTROL 1940-1960

Looking towards Ford Station from Kinnerley on 5th October 1931, showing the steeply graded siding leading down to the goods yard. As at Edgebold, the railway was above the lie of the land here so the goods yard was constructed at a lower level than the running line.   *R. K. Cope (RKC/B16) courtesy Roger Carpenter*

The north-west end of the loop at Ford Station looking towards Kinnerley on 3rd October 1937. The lightweight track was pretty much worn out and the War Department had immediately to relay much of the S&M main line. The new marshalling sidings would be built on the land behind the hedges on the right hand side of this view. The signals, by Tyer & Co., were not retained – the WD introduced its (rather more flexible) flagboard signalling.   *R. K. Cope (RKC/B170) courtesy Roger Carpenter*

THE PLANNING PHASE

SHRAWARDINE

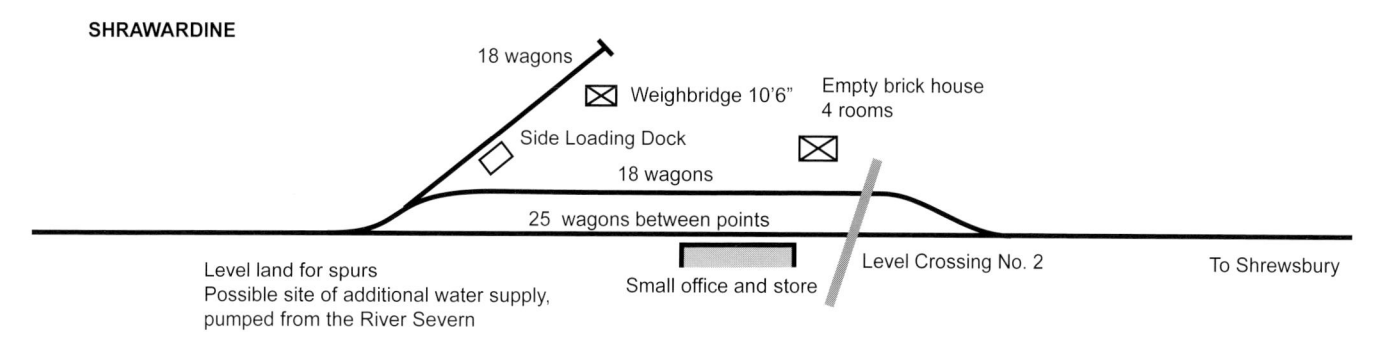

```
                              18 wagons
                                  ╲
                          ⊠ Weighbridge 10'6"    Empty brick house
                      ◇ Side Loading Dock           4 rooms
                                         ⊠
                              18 wagons
                        25 wagons between points
───────────────────────────────────────────────────────────────────
Level land for spurs                  ▬▬▬▬         │
Possible site of additional water supply,  Small office and store   Level Crossing No. 2          To Shrewsbury
pumped from the River Severn
```

Shrawardine Station, looking towards Kinnerley in 1939, a few months before the Royal Engineers arrived. Little had changed since 1930, though inevitably the paintwork had faded. Still intact were the oil lamps on the platform, and the 'conditional stop' signal as well as the station nameboard. By this time little freight traffic originated here, so the loop siding was used to hold empty wagons waiting until they were needed at the quarry at Criggion. *Lens of Sutton Association, 66258*

17

THE SHROPSHIRE & MONTGOMERYSHIRE LIGHT RAILWAY UNDER MILITARY CONTROL 1940-1960

NESSCLIFF

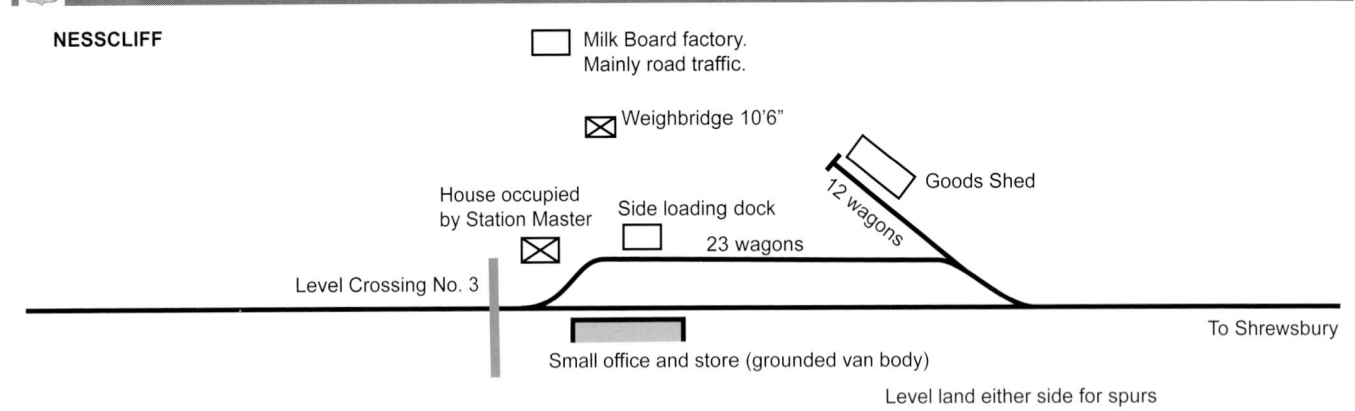

[Track diagram: Milk Board factory (mainly road traffic); Weighbridge 10'6"; House occupied by Station Master; Side loading dock (23 wagons); Goods Shed (12 wagons); Level Crossing No. 3; Small office and store (grounded van body); To Shrewsbury; Level land either side for spurs]

'Nesscliff & Pentre' Station, so its nameboard still proclaimed on 1st September 1938 nearly five years after closure to ordinary passenger traffic. The single platform, with its lamps and bench, was maintained for the passengers on the occasional summertime excursion trains. The goods loop and siding saw regular traffic, as witnessed by the number of wagons in the sidings. *R. K. Cope (RKC/B61) from the 'Detachment Photograph Album'*

On the end of the goods loading dock at Nesscliff was this veteran coach body, long since grounded and in use as a warehouse cum workshop. The coach was reputedly one of the vehicles acquired by the Potteries, Shrewsbury & North Wales Railway for its opening in 1866. The company had started with twenty-one coaches, but (ever short of money) it sold five within a year and another ten in 1877, leaving just six still owned when the line was forced to close in 1880. *Photo from the 'Detachment Photograph Album'*

The general state of repair of the storage sheds on the S&M when the WD took over is characterised by this second view of the grounded coach body on the goods loading dock at Nesscliff. The S&M was truly a railway in a desperately run down condition. *Photo from the 'Detachment Photograph Album'*

THE PLANNING PHASE

The short platform erected by the S&M Light Railway (opened in July 1927, some time after the re-opening in 1911) to try to attract passenger traffic at Edgerley, seen here looking north-west to Kinnerley. This was an over-optimistic venture because very few people lived within walking distance of this location. The WD did not use this platform, even though the Nesscliff District was fairly close by on the right in this view. The platform, photographed on the 4th October 1937, would have been hopelessly inadequate for military traffic, and new halts were built a short distance both east and west of this S&M platform.

R. K. Cope, from the 'Detachment Photograph Album'

The eastern approach to Kinnerley Station on the 1st September 1937, viewed from the road bridge looking towards Shrewsbury, showing the Tyer & Co. pattern signals used when the line re-opened in 1911. The land to the right of the line is nearest to the River Severn and is prone to flooding. That to the left of the line would be used for some of the Explosive Store Houses (Sheds) of Kinnerley District.

R. K. Cope (RKC/B64) courtesy Roger Carpenter

THE SHROPSHIRE & MONTGOMERYSHIRE LIGHT RAILWAY UNDER MILITARY CONTROL 1940-1960

The east end of Kinnerley Station, looking towards Shrewsbury, on 2nd October 1937. A rake of wagons carrying stone from the Criggion Branch had been set ready for working forward (but only just clear of the east end loop points). The nearest wagon still showed its ownership as 'Ceiriog' – the Ceiriog Granite Co. Ltd operated the quarries at Criggion from c1925 until the British Quarrying Co. Ltd took over as from 4th February 1929. A ganger's 'pump trolley' stood on the left hand platform. The road bridge was typical of the structures on the S&M – metal girders to carry the load but cheaper timberwork for the fencing to the roadway. Note the water tank, partly resting on the brick abutments of the bridge.
R. K. Cope (RKC/B1427) from the 'Detachment Photograph Album'

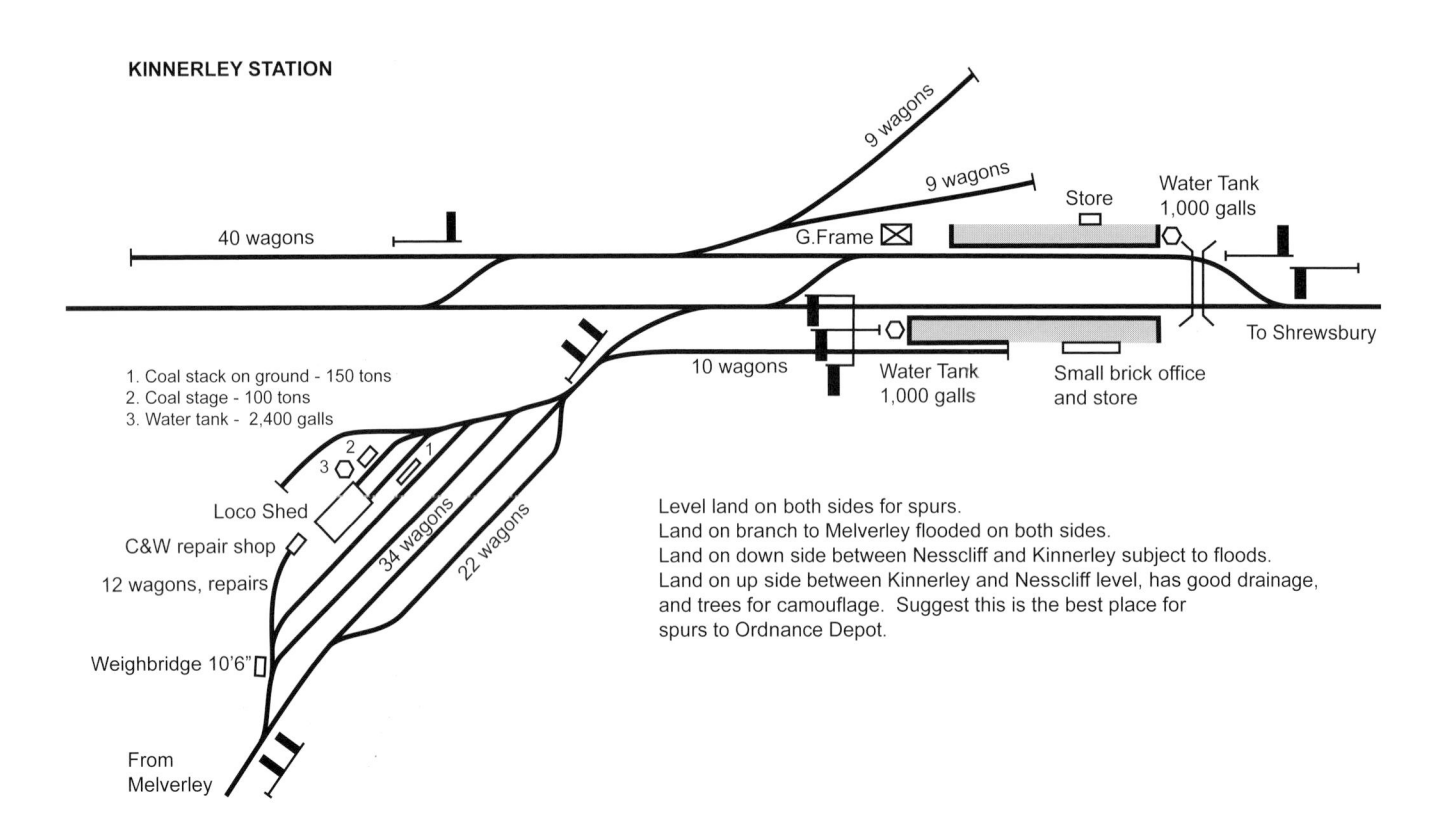

KINNERLEY STATION

1. Coal stack on ground - 150 tons
2. Coal stage - 100 tons
3. Water tank - 2,400 galls

Loco Shed
C&W repair shop
12 wagons, repairs
Weighbridge 10'6"
From Melverley

40 wagons
9 wagons
9 wagons
Store
Water Tank 1,000 galls
G.Frame
10 wagons
Water Tank 1,000 galls
Small brick office and store
To Shrewsbury
34 wagons
22 wagons

Level land on both sides for spurs.
Land on branch to Melverley flooded on both sides.
Land on down side between Nesscliff and Kinnerley subject to floods.
Land on up side between Kinnerley and Nesscliff level, has good drainage, and trees for camouflage. Suggest this is the best place for spurs to Ordnance Depot.

THE PLANNING PHASE

Looking east through the platforms at Kinnerley. The three-arm bracket signal was the finest piece of signalling on the line, though by now with some of its glasses missing. As was customary, the coaches not in use were stabled in the bay platform. There was no covered storage available for them. Standing out in all weathers, they were slowly rotting away. *Lens of Sutton Association*

Kinnerley was the principal centre of operations on the S&M, and had full signalling provided by Tyer & Co. The lever frame was protected, in part at least, by a shelter made from corrugated iron. On 11th April 1938 the Ilfracombe Goods class locomotive **Hesperus** was shunting the goods yard sidings on the north side of the station. The lightweight nature of the track – using 60lb rail with quite wide sleeper spacing – is evident. *R. K. Cope, from the 'Detachment Photograph Album'*

THE SHROPSHIRE & MONTGOMERYSHIRE LIGHT RAILWAY UNDER MILITARY CONTROL 1940-1960

The mainstay of the S&M locomotive power when the WD took over were three former L&NWR locomotives acquired by the S&M from the LMS in 1930-32. Here former LMS 8182, in black livery with yellow lettering, was shunting the goods yard sidings at Kinnerley on 4th October 1937.

R. K. Cope (RKC/B199) from the 'Detachment Photograph Album'

The shunting had been undertaken so that coach No. 6 could be brought out for the photographer. This former Midland Railway Brake/First/Third class coach (acquired for the re-opening of the line as a Light Railway in 1911) was one of the best that the S&M now had to offer. Even so the brown paintwork was showing clear signs of age and neglect.

R. K. Cope (RKC/B220) from the 'Detachment Photograph Album'

The S&M ran excursion trains in the summer for several years after the ordinary passenger services were withdrawn in November 1933. This was the scene at Shrewsbury Abbey on 5th August 1935, as picnic parties arrived to catch their train. The rearmost coach was the 'Royal Saloon'. This was a four-wheeled former Royal Saloon of the London & South Western Railway – sometimes know as the 'Adelaide Coach' or 'Queen Adelaide's coach' in the mistaken belief that it had been used for the first journey on the L&SWR by a member of the Royal Family. The seats may have been plush, but the ride characteristics of this four-wheel coach on the S&M's track were hardly smooth.

H. F. Wheeler, courtesy Roger Carpenter

THE PLANNING PHASE

A view of Kinnerley shed, taken in May 1938. This view is looking towards the main line junction, with the locomotive sheds and workshops on the left and some of the S&M's worn out coaches in the sidings to the right of the Criggion Branch running line. No wonder the first Army railwaymen posted here were aghast at what they found they had to work with.
Graham Vincent

S&M locomotive No. 3 **Hesperus** (on the left) and former LMS 8236, on shed at Kinnerley. The working conditions were hardly conducive to maintaining locomotives in good order.
Graham Vincent

THE SHROPSHIRE & MONTGOMERYSHIRE LIGHT RAILWAY UNDER MILITARY CONTROL 1940-1960

WERN LAS

```
                                                    Side
                                                    loading
                                  4 wagons          dock      No buildings
─────────────────────────────────────\──────────────▭──────────────────────────
                                  Points locked by staff  ⊠                    To Shrewsbury
                                                       House occupied
                                        Level Crossing No. 4
```

This photograph of the siding beside the level crossing at Wern Las on 1st September 1937 typifies the 'minimal' installations put in under the aegis of Col Stephens for the re-opening in 1911. The short siding was connected to the running line by points worked from a simple throw-over point lever, locked by a key. There was no facing point lock bolt, nor were there any gates at the level crossing, just a timber-built cattle grid. The re-opening had taken full advantage of the relaxation of requirements allowed for a Light Railway.

R. K. Cope (RKC/B86) courtesy Roger Carpenter

THE PLANNING PHASE

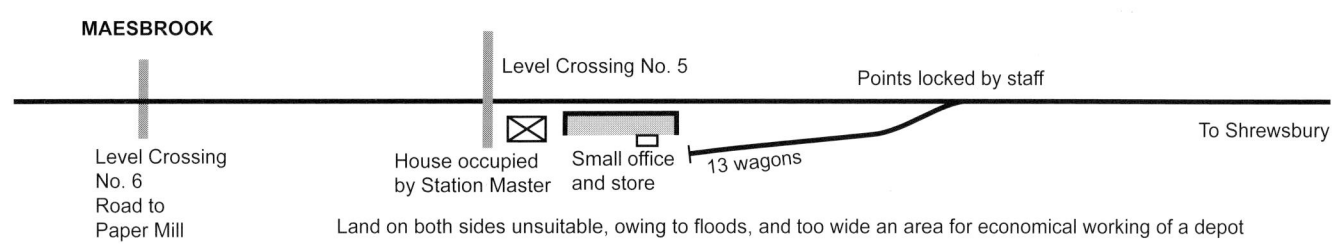

MAESBROOK

Level Crossing No. 5 — Points locked by staff

House occupied by Station Master — Small office and store — 13 wagons — To Shrewsbury

Level Crossing No. 6 Road to Paper Mill

Land on both sides unsuitable, owing to floods, and too wide an area for economical working of a depot

Above: Maesbrook Station, looking towards Kinnerley and Shrewsbury. The raised section of the platform at the far end enabled the loading of cattle from the adjacent pen. The 'conditional stop' signal was the last to survive on the S&M, and it features in photographs of trains in the last years of operation.
Lens of Sutton Association

The eastern approach to Llanymynech was protected by this bracket signal supplied by Tyer & Co. The signals indicated the route set not at the points just beyond the signal (they were worked locally by a hand lever) but at the points beyond that, where the running line split into two platform lines. When the WD laid in additional sidings, they were on the land to the left of the running line, involving the removal of much of the hedge and the acquisition of land the other side of it. 4th October 1937.
R. K. Cope (RKC/B191) courtesy Roger Carpenter

THE SHROPSHIRE & MONTGOMERYSHIRE LIGHT RAILWAY UNDER MILITARY CONTROL 1940-1960

LLANYMYNECH

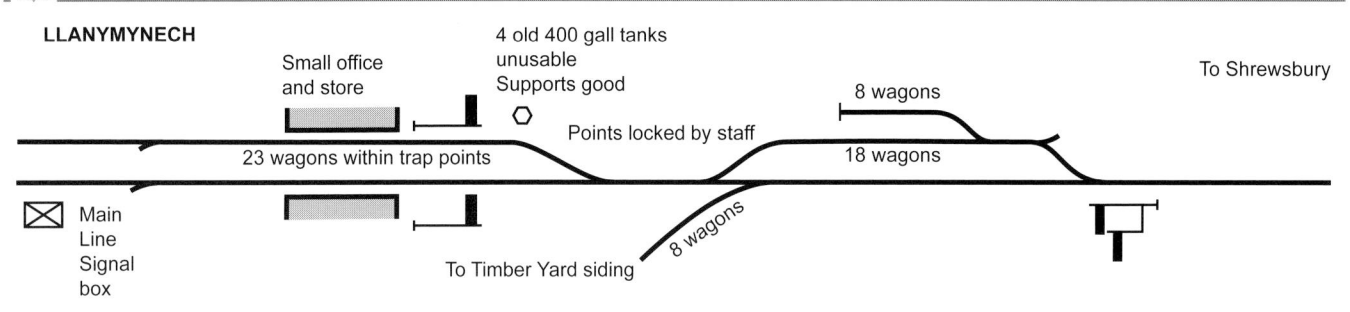

Diagram labels:
- Small office and store
- 4 old 400 gall tanks unusable Supports good
- Points locked by staff
- 8 wagons
- To Shrewsbury
- 23 wagons within trap points
- 18 wagons
- Main Line Signal box
- To Timber Yard siding
- 8 wagons

Llanymynech Station, viewed from the direction of Kinnerley, with the goods yard sidings centre and to the right. The single running line was to the left of centre with the siding to the timber yard diverging to the left through a pair of white gates. The WD removed the goods yard sidings.

R. K. Cope (RKC/B192) courtesy Roger Carpenter

Llanymynech, with the BLC special on 30th April 1939 stood in the platform adjacent to the GWR line. The S&M nameboard and oil lamp were still extant. In the right background can be seen the four water tanks, described in the WD survey as old and unusable.

Lens of Sutton Association

26

THE PLANNING PHASE

Llanymynech Station, viewed from the road bridge in May 1938, with the main line tracks in the foreground and the S&M platforms beyond. Years after the withdrawal of passenger services the advertising board still proclaimed that the S&M offered the 'Shortest route to Shrewsbury' – factually correct, but shortest may not be quickest – and 'Frequent trains Cheap fares'. This view shows the Tyer & Co. signals (worked from a six-lever frame) and a siding to the north of the running line – all of which were taken out of use by the War Department.
Graham Vincent

continued from page 7

In the Western Command area sites for such depots were considered at Wem in Shropshire and Nantwich in Cheshire. Either would be reasonably close to the new ordnance factories. The Nantwich plan was abandoned because of strong opposition from the Ministry of Agriculture to the taking of good quality agricultural land, and the site at Wem was unsuitable because of flooding risks. A third site considered was at Shrawardine in Shropshire – for a depot to hold 50,000 tons of ammunition, as a substitute for both Wem and Nantwich. It was proposed that this Depot be built along – and adjacent to – the Shropshire and Montgomeryshire Light Railway (S&M). 'A portion of this railway will be reconditioned, spurs and loops will be run from it where the ground alongside is sufficiently level, and sheds built on these' – (War Office Memorandum 1230, 14th January 1941). By using an existing line the amount of railway construction would be significantly reduced, and urgency to get started led to the adoption of this scheme.

The Condition of the S&M in 1940

A reconnaissance of the railway was undertaken on 4th and 5th November 1940 by Lt Col R. McCreary, Major D. McMullen of Tn3A at the War Office, Major Bostock with Lieutenant Duthie from No. 2 Railway Operating Group, and Captain Whale of 165 Railway Construction Company. They reported that the section of the line from Shrewsbury to Shrawardine was regarded as unsuitable for depot building because of the topography. The Shrawardine area was recommended since the area was flat and free from flooding. Fifty magazines to hold 1,000 tons each, located at least 200 yards apart, were envisaged.

The railway generally was found to be in a poor state, with sleepers rotting and bridges devoid of decking. The track consisted in part of 82½lb per yard bull head rail, but there were some lengths of 60lb rail laid in 1922. Approximately 25 per cent of the sleepers needed renewing. The axle loading on the line was as low as 11 tons. It was noted that 'the bridge over the River Severn at Shrawardine makes a good target and must be considered vulnerable'. So alternative access via Llanymynech was essential even though the land between Kinnerley and Llanymynech was liable to flooding and useless for military purposes.

Traffic on the line was mainly in coal, sugar beet (in season), timber and cattle food. One train a day was sufficient for all traffic. WD reports noted that traffic on the Criggion Branch had 'almost entirely ceased' because of the 'collapse' of the bridge over the River Severn at Melverley (it had been damaged by ice floes in the river during the hard winter of January 1940). The figures on page 29 show just how badly this had damaged the railway's traffic and income totals.

The existing exchange sidings at Meole Brace could only hold fifty wagons at most and the site did not allow for expansion, so a new exchange facility at Hookagate was recommended (though this would require the demolition of a row of bungalows), together with a triage (marshalling yard) between Hookagate exchange sidings and the Depot at Shrawardine. Accompanying the report were sketches of the existing layouts. It was expected that a minimum of five locomotives would be required to work the Depot. Only one (and that in doubtful condition) was available.

The existing staff consisted of seven men on the Permanent Way (ages 31 to 68), one driver (aged 58), one fireman (aged 19), one guard (aged 35) and three workshop staff (ages 30 to 60). The S&M had the atmosphere of being a family business. Of the thirteen men, three were from the Mansell family (respectively born in 1882, 1909 and 1921).

THE SHROPSHIRE & MONTGOMERYSHIRE LIGHT RAILWAY UNDER MILITARY CONTROL 1940-1960

By the time that the Army came to survey the line in November 1940, the bridge over the River Severn at Melverley had been out of use for months. It had been damaged in January, when ice floes on the river – it was an exceptionally hard winter – damaged the timber piles of slender piers. This view shows that even before some of the pier timbers had been carried away the bridge was a frail structure.
Graham Vincent

This close-up view of the bridge timbers shows how some had been snapped by the force of the ice in the river and large sections carried away. The structure was clearly unsafe and a barrier had been erected at the Kinnerley end of the bridge to prevent all traffic from crossing.
Graham Vincent

THE PLANNING PHASE

Traffic in tons	1938			1939			1940 (the first 7 months)		
Stations	Inward	Out	Total	Inward	Out	Total	Inward	Out	Total
Abbey	13,782	92	**13,874**	15,580	68	**15, 648**	7,360	53	**7,413**
Meole Brace	71	4	**75**	15	–	**15**	20	–	**20**
Redhill	57	28	**85**	104	5	**109**	43	2	**45**
Edgebold	23	–	**23**	141	–	**141**	63	–	**63**
Cruckton	15	–	**15**	11	–	**11**	–	8	**8**
Ford & Crossgates	1,121	437	**1,558**	1,248	378	**1,626**	815	357	**1,172**
Shrawardine	62	12	**75**	59	616	**675**	74	311	**385**
Nesscliff	629	9	**638**	849	10	**859**	451	13	**464**
Kinnerley	1,473	17	**1,490**	1,383	11	**1,394**	729	4	**733**
Maesbrook	345	6	**351**	346	2	**348**	255	5	**260**
Llanymynech	567	3	**570**	440	1	**441**	116	1	**117**
Criggion	929	13,785	**14,714**	549	10,005	**10,554**	18	360	**378**
Crew Green	78	–	**78**	17	–	**17**	20	–	**20**
Llandrinio Road	1	–	**1**	–	1	**1**	–	–	**–**
Melverley	2	3	**5**	8	–	**8**	20	–	**20**
Total	**19,155**	**14,397**	**33,552**	**20,750**	**11,097**	**31,847**	**9,992**	**1,106**	**11,098**
Average daily			92			88			53

From a War Office report dated 4th November 1940.

Proposed requisition by the War Department

A meeting was held at the Ministry of Transport (MoT) on 15th November 1940. G. S. Szlumper (the Railway Control Officer) was in the Chair. Three officers of the S&M Light Railway were in attendance – James Ramsay OBE (its Chairman and Managing Director since the death of Col Stephens, and a former officer of the Caledonian Railway), John Pike (a Director of the S&M, and one time Goods Commercial Manager of the LMS) and W. H. Austen (Director and Engineer). The Great Western Railway (GWR) – with which the S&M had been attempting to reach agreement for the working of its stone traffic from Criggion to the GWR at Llanymynech, and repairs to the damaged bridge at Melverley – was represented by Keith Grand. The War Department was represented by Colonel H. L. Woodhouse and Major D. McMullen.

It was agreed that the S&M would be de-controlled by the MoT (which had taken all but a handful of UK railways under Government control at the commencement of the war) and immediately requisitioned by the War Office, which would then be solely responsible for working all traffic. Regular passenger services over the line had been withdrawn from 6th November 1933. The War Office would enter onto the line immediately to begin bridge strengthening work, and when the Army took over all maintenance the S&M would withdraw its platelayers.

A detailed survey of the railway and its environs was undertaken between 21st-22nd November by a party including the officers commanding 162 Railway Construction Company and a detachment of 165 Railway Survey Company. They further developed the proposed scheme for connecting fifty Explosive Store Houses (ESHs, more commonly simply called 'Sheds') to the existing railway. Although the report of the reconnaissance of 4th-5th November suggested that the topography along the line between Shrewsbury and Shrawardine was unsuitable for the construction of sheds, the diagram showed that it was proposed to put in connections to fifteen sheds along this part of the railway. It was agreed that proposals for the layout of the storage sheds would be completed by the end of the month.

Plans for new construction

Planning meetings followed in quick succession. A meeting at the War Office on 3rd December 1940 concluded that the maximum traffic likely to be handled on one day was 2,000 tons, equivalent to 200-250 wagons. The exchange sidings at Meole Brace could not be expanded to handle this level of traffic. A new exchange yard at Hookagate was decided on, to have five double-ended exchange sidings and a small dead-end marshalling yard. The following day the draughtsmen prepared plans for a marshalling yard near the S&M station at Ford, a yard of exchange sidings at Hookagate, and a passing loop at Cruckton approximately halfway between the two. On 9th December a meeting was held at Paddington with the Assistant Superintendent of the Line on the GWR, to appraise him of the War Office requirement.

The objective on 3rd December 1940 was to have the first ammunition train in on 15th May 1941, with 30,000 tons stored by 1st June 1941 and 90,000 tons stored by 1st August – a timetable which was to prove excessively optimistic.

A meeting to discuss the availability of labour on 10th December concluded that billeting in the local area was not a practical proposition, either in Shrewsbury or near the site. Camps for 500 men could be provided in eight weeks, but civilians must not be in the same camps as soldiers, and civilians could not be carried on trains without Ministry of Transport approval. As many camping coaches as were available were to be sought. Some were known to be available at Conway, and most of the coaches obtained were ex-L&NWR in origin.

A meeting at Shrewsbury on 12th and 13th December concluded that the immediate need would be for 500 Transportation (Tn) Construction and 25 Tn Operating troops. When construction work was complete this would change to:

    50 Tn Construction (for maintenance)
    100 Tn Railway Operating
    40 Depot staff officers
    200 Ordnance personnel
    800 Labourers
    100 Police.

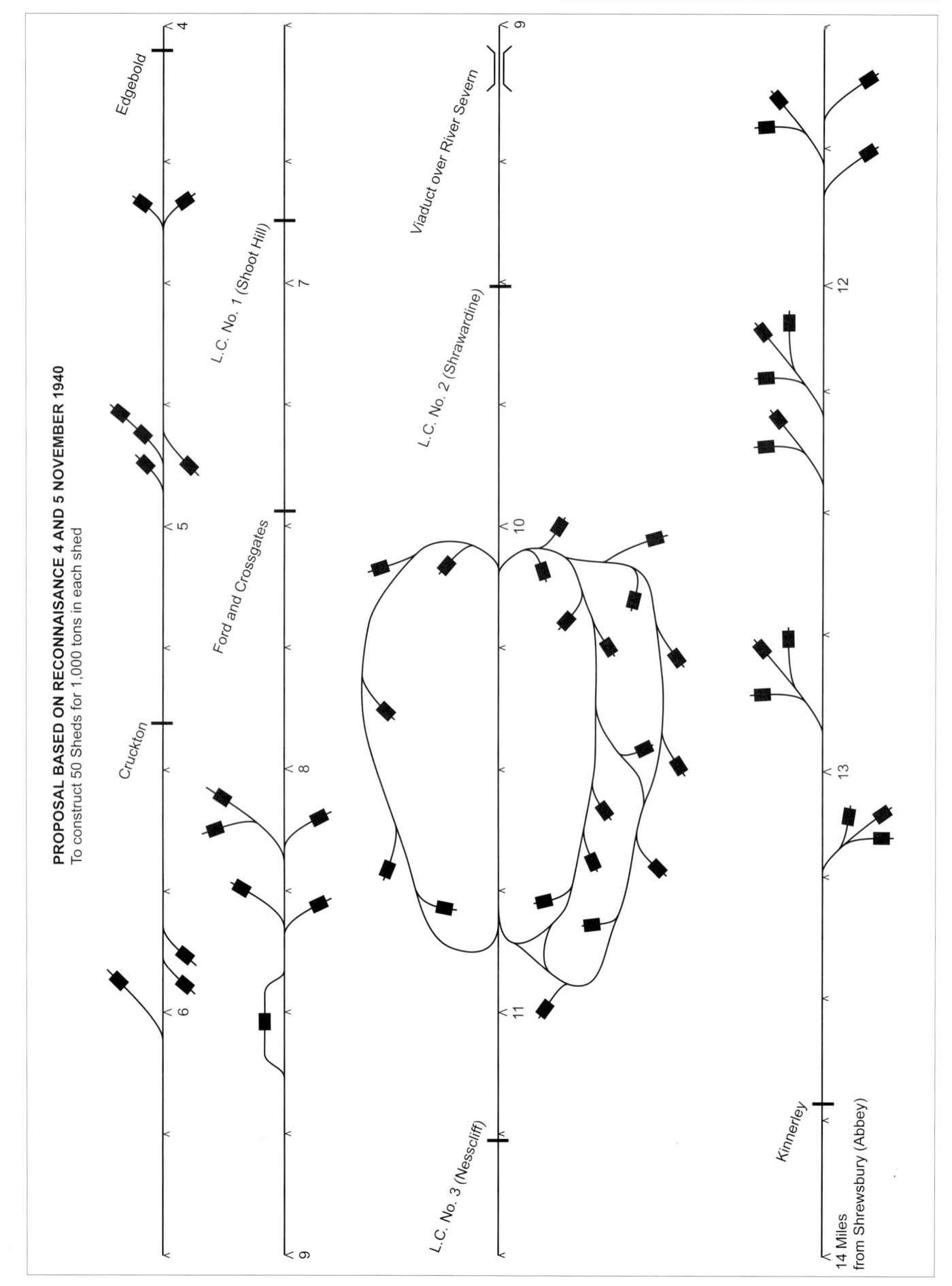

THE SHROPSHIRE & MONTGOMERYSHIRE LIGHT RAILWAY UNDER MILITARY CONTROL 1940-1960

PROPOSAL BASED ON RECONNAISSANCE 4 AND 5 NOVEMBER 1940
To construct 50 Sheds for 1,000 tons in each shed

Edgebold
L.C. No. 1 (Shoot Hill)
Viaduct over River Severn
L.C. No. 2 (Shrawardine)
Cruckton
Ford and Crossgates
L.C. No. 3 (Nesscliff)
Kinnerley
14 Miles from Shrewsbury (Abbey)

THE PLANNING PHASE

Much of the S&M freight stock was barely fit for traffic. Goods Brake van (No. 1) with its unusual verandah – lacking any corner posts – was photographed derelict on 11th January 1942, but had been used by the WD for several months after the WD took over the working of the line. *Graham Vincent*

This horsebox appeared to be derelict and beyond likely further use when photographed at Kinnerley on 5th May 1940, some six months before the arrival of the Army. It was, however, to be refurbished for traffic by the WD, used as a tool van by track/bridge reconstruction teams and then later as an 'Engineer's Department' van in the breakdown train – still in its S&M livery of blue and lettered 'S&MR 15'.
Graham Vincent

For work on strengthening Bridge 28 at Shrawardine (the work consisting of fitting additional cross beams), the WD troops had to make do with the tools to hand. These included the horsebox, and a small capacity hand-operated crane. The vehicles, with the 'crane runner' four-wheeled flat wagons, were photographed in the 'Civilian Yard' sidings at Shrawardine on 2nd March 1941. The jib on the crane looked new because it was, one of the first tasks tackled by the WD carpenters was to complete the fitting of the new wooden jib. This work was noted as being in progress on 1st December 1940. *Graham Vincent*

THE SHROPSHIRE & MONTGOMERYSHIRE LIGHT RAILWAY UNDER MILITARY CONTROL 1940-1960

Much of the rolling stock acquired by the WD was way past redemption, even by the determined carpenters that the Army brought in. These vehicles, if they could move at all, were placed in the back sidings at the Quarry end of Ford Yard, and eventually cut up as part of the drive for scrap metal to feed the war effort. This view shows Coach No. 14 (an ex-North Staffordshire Railway four compartment First/Third Composite), derelict at Ford on 11th January 1942 in the company of other coaches and wagons. On 10th May 1942, it was noted that scrapping of these derelict vehicles had begun. *Graham Vincent*

Also in the yard at Ford was Coach No. 10, ex-L&SWR Brake/Third. *Graham Vincent*

Passenger Brake van No. 2, ex-Midland Railway, can only have been moved to Ford Yard at some risk. *Graham Vincent*

Three engines in working order would be needed immediately. No. 2 – former LMS 8108 – was the only working engine available (see Appendix B for the state of the locomotives available at this time). The water storage capacity at Kinnerley had to be increased by 2,000 gallons, and additional water capacity would be needed at Ford Yard (5,000 gallons fed at 1,000 gallons per hour) and Hookagate (similarly, 5,000 gallons storage fed at 1,000 gallons per hour).

Overlapping with this detailed planning of the railway requirements, on 6th December the plans for the number of the store sheds had been changed, and 100 sheds in fifty pairs were now envisaged. Each was to be 14ft 6in. to the ridge, 13ft 6in. to the eaves, to allow stacking to eleven feet from the platform level. The sheds in each pair were to be a minimum of fifty feet apart, with 200 yards between pairs. Earth traverses (blast protection barriers) were to be put in only between the five pairs of sheds at Ford, which would be used for category C and E ammunition. Otherwise blast protection between the sheds would not be provided, on the basis that the adjacent walls between sheds would be of twelve inches reinforced concrete or eighteen inches if built in brick. D Tn (the Director of Transportation) staff would be responsible for pegging out the lines of the rails, and the sheds would be constructed around these pegs. Except at Ford, the sheds would be solely served by rail – there would be no road access to the sheds, essential to reducing visibility from the air.

By 16th December 1940 Treasury approval had been given for a depot for 50,000 tons of ammunition. Approval was still needed for the extension of capacity to 100,000 tons and for the requisitioning of the railway. But speed of construction was vital, and there could be no question of waiting for competitive quotations for contractors (which would in any event be problematic since the full scope of the works remained to be finalised). A memo of 20th December suggested that the contract be let quickly on the basis of cost plus a profit percentage.

The contractor most likely to carry out the work in the shortest time was named as Sir Alfred McAlpine & Sons Ltd (McAlpines). This company was stated to be well equipped with plant, to have a 'following' of skilled labour, and to be ready to undertake more work 'in their area' (the firm's base was in Liverpool). A meeting was held on 27th December with a Mr Shaw of McAlpines – the firm was prepared to work on cost plus basis, the estimated cost at this stage being £724,000. The contract was finally signed and sealed (though still considered to be in draft) on 19th February 1941, with a fixed sum remuneration for McAlpines set at £18,600 (two per cent) on the assumption that the costs would be £930,000 – which included £30,000 for railway earthworks that the civil contractors were now expected to construct. However, when the Treasury formally issued its letter of acceptance on 25th March 1941, it was on the simple basis of cost plus two per cent. The subsequent expansion of the works – including a substantial increase in the number of sheds required – resulted in an eventual cost (McAlpine's statement number 47 dated 26th January 1944) of £1,695,334 2s 8d. McAlpine's supervision fee included in this was just the £18,600 first proposed.

Although the S&M was in a poor state of repair, the men continued to provide a service of freight trains for its customers. Most of the traffic to Shrewsbury – where the goods yard, situated beside Telford's main road east of the river, was a convenient location for unloading freight – was coal. In 1939, over 15,500 tons of traffic was received here, but only 68 tons sent out. The uninviting entrance to the passenger station was through the gap to the left of the group of advertising hoardings.

Lens of Sutton Association

THE SHROPSHIRE & MONTGOMERYSHIRE LIGHT RAILWAY UNDER MILITARY CONTROL 1940-1960

Kinnerley Station, looking west, with passenger coaches rotting away in the bay platform. Only stone traffic from Criggion quarry kept the railway from terminal insolvency, so the loss of this traffic after the damage to the bridge over the River Severn at Melverley in January 1940 was bad news indeed. How much longer the railway would have survived, even with the wartime shortages of petrol and rubber that affected road vehicles, is open to doubt. In the event, the arrival of the Army would transform the whole run-down railway. *Lens of Sutton Association*

Whilst the surveyors for the WD were clearly unimpressed by the vehicles that provided the warehouse accommodation at Shrewsbury Abbey, the Army had no option but to carry on using them for the duration of the war. If the roof of a vehicle leaked (and most did), it was simply covered by a wagon sheet. This view shows No. 18 (a former North London Railway passenger luggage van) which the old S&M company had used as a grain store and the two passenger coaches No's 7 and 17.

Lens of Sutton Association

Chapter 2
THE CONSTRUCTION PHASE

The railway construction teams were on site before the end of 1940. Their intention to remove components from the bridge at Melverley to strengthen bridges on the main line brought a protest on 24th December 1940 from Lydden (the Deputy Chief Engineer [Roads] at the Ministry of Transport) to the effect that this would hamper his efforts to increase the output of the quarries at Criggion, which was much needed for the construction programme for roads and runways. It was agreed that the Criggion Branch would not be cannibalised to make good the main line. In the event, the MoT brokered a deal (confirmed at a meeting on 8th May 1941) that the GWR would make the necessary repairs to the bridge at Melverley. The quarry company agreed to pay one third of the cost up to a maximum of £500, and the Railway Executive Committee would pay the balance, subject to the quarry company agreeing to send two-thirds of its output by rail.

The placing of the civilian contract for the construction of what, at the time, was referred to as 'Army Depot No. 3' was proceeding, and on 10th January 1941 a meeting took place at which representatives of the contractors McAlpines were present. It was agreed that the contractors would do all the earthworks for the railway, except those required for doubling the line and the marshalling yards. The contractors were told that the railway would be available for the acceptance of materials in six weeks time. It was estimated that the civilian labour force for the construction of depot buildings would be 1,000, rising to 4,000. The military requirement in the construction period was put at two Railway Construction Companies and four companies of the Pioneer Corps.

In the event, availability of labour in this fairly remote part of Shropshire turned out to be a problem and the contractors had to consider paying premium rates of pay. Some relief came later in 1941 with the suggestion in a note of 17th July that Italian Prisoners of War be assigned to the work. They were housed in a camp adjacent to 'Kinnerley East' (about 2½ miles from the civilian labour camp), to do building work in 'Kinnerley West' where earthworks had been done by the military earlier in the year, which relieved the contractors to work in Kinnerley East, nearer to the contractor's main base at Shrawardine. The Royal Engineers (REs) had to provide guards – 126 men to guard the 625 prisoners – together with the necessary plant and technical supervision. Huts and barbed wire were on order and the first prisoners were expected from 7th September. The prisoners started work at the west end of Kinnerley West so as to be as far away as possible from the sheds at Kinnerley East which would be filled with stores as soon as they were completed. It was noted that if the sheds at Kinnerley East were filled sufficiently fast as to jeopardise the prisoners' safety, it would be necessary to remove them from their camp.

Not surprisingly, McAlpines did not object to part of the contract being transferred to the REs for construction. However, a WD internal memo of 30th November 1941 pointed out that the PoWs had been housed in huts costing the WD £40,000 and they were to build twenty-eight Explosive Store Houses (sheds), equivalent to about twenty per cent of the contract. It was suggested that McAlpine's 'supervision fee' should be reduced. Given the way in which the project had expanded in other respects, this suggestion was not pursued. It was just as well, because at the end of 1941 tensions with the contractors about the provision of locomotives for the construction work were about to boil over.

THE SHROPSHIRE & MONTGOMERYSHIRE LIGHT RAILWAY UNDER MILITARY CONTROL 1940-1960

Kinnerley Station on 24th May 1942, perforce photographed from some distance at that date since the area around Kinnerley Station was heavily guarded because of the presence of Italian Prisoners of War working in 'Kinnerley West depot'. This remarkable photo shows LNER Y7 class locomotive No. 982, in front of GWR 2425 (WD96). 982 had reached the S&M by a lengthy journey from the North East, but it was not very successful here and was soon transferred to a smaller depot where its inability to undertake long runs was not an issue. The bracket signal at the junction, provided by Tyer & Co. for the re-opening of the line in 1911 and not yet taken down by the WD, is prominent in this view – evidence that the new signalling at Kinnerley had not yet been brought into use. The armed guards around Kinnerley Station were withdrawn a few days later and making notes became a little easier.
Graham Vincent

Terms of the War Department lease

The advice of the Treasury Solicitor was that a working railway company could not be requisitioned, so the War Office had to enter into a leasing arrangement. A meeting with officers of the S&M on the afternoon of Tuesday 28th January 1941 concluded a written 'Heads of Agreement' for this lease. The terms included:

1. The WD was to recondition the line between Hookagate (Red Hill) and Llanymynech (and thereafter maintain the permanent way), and construct all additional railway connections and sidings required for WD traffic.
2. The WD would take over all existing operating facilities, operate all WD traffic on the railway, and operate a daily goods train from Llanymynech to Shrewsbury (Abbey) Station, placing and lifting wagons as required for civil traffic. Civilian traffic had to be placed for traders as far as possible by 2pm each day.
3. The WD would take over all engines, rolling stock, coaling and watering facilities.
4. The S&M would provide all facilities, clerical and other labour (except that required for actual train working) necessary for handling the civilian traffic on the line.
5. The S&M would take the whole of the receipts for civilian traffic, it being considered that the reconditioning of the line and the working of civilian traffic was sufficient rent for the use of the line, land and buildings by the WD and the hire of the company's locomotives and rolling stock.

Notably excluded from the proposed terms of the lease was the Criggion Branch from Kinnerley (which the War Office very wisely shunned completely). Additionally, although the WD would operate the railway from Hookagate to Shrewsbury (Abbey) it did not in the Heads of Agreement undertake to refurbish that part of the line. This was changed in the final lease document, in which the WD undertook to recondition and maintain the whole of the line from Abbey to Llanymynech.

The formal lease between the War Office and the S&M was not signed until 9th June 1942 (nearly 18 months later) but it was then deemed to run from 1st June 1941. An indemnity covering the S&M company during the operations of the War Office during the interim period was signed on 6th January 1941, having been drafted on 19th November 1940. The WD indemnified the S&M for costs arising from renewal or strengthening of track or bridges. The indemnity was to end in the event of the operation of the line being taken over by the WD.

In the lease agreement the WD undertook that at the end of its period of occupation, all permanent way, buildings and rolling stock would be returned to the S&M 'in as good a condition as they were when the use thereof was granted'; although, frankly, to have attempted to reduce the railway back to such a dilapidated condition would have been well-nigh impossible.

There were also a few agreements not included in the formal lease. One was that the WD would take into its employment the existing operating staff of the S&M. The S&M would continue to pay them and submit an account to the WD for the costs. So civilian staff continued to be engaged on the maintenance of the track and on the operation of trains (especially the 'Civilian Goods'). William Jones, known as 'Patsy', was nominally a Guard but fulfilled a number of office roles at Kinnerley as well, still wearing the uniform supplied to him in Col Stephens' day. George Beeston (born in 1910) continued to act as Assistant to Fitter C. Owen, in due time taking over as a driver when Frank King (born in 1882) left the railway – George was to remain with the S&M until driving the last enthusiasts' train on 20th March 1960.

Another side agreement was that eleven members of the staff of the S&M and their wives, who had passes allowing them to travel as passengers in the guard's van of the daily goods train (at their own risk), could continue to do so (War Office letter to Ramsay 23rd July 1941, following a letter from the S&M company indemnifying the WD against any claims that might arise from these passengers).

To allow the construction of the new yard at Hookagate, ten bungalows had to be requisitioned (and then demolished). The evacuation of the bungalows was completed by 31st March 1941.

THE CONSTRUCTION PHASE

Locomotive stock

The WD found that the problem of weak bridges on the main line restricted the maximum axle loading to 11 tons and required the use of light locomotives. From the S&M the WD took over:

- one 'Ilfracombe Goods', named **Hesperus**. It was quite beyond further use and was scrapped in the sidings at Abbey Station in November 1941. Sergeant Thorne said that it had been sold to Shrewsbury Council for scrap, which is why it was broken up in the Corporation Siding
- the lightweight locomotive **Gazelle**
- three ex-L&NWR Coal (often called 'Collier') 0-6-0 tender engines.

On 22nd March 1941 it was recorded that of the three ex-L&NWR locomotives, one had been overhauled, one was at Crewe for that purpose (this would have been 8236, seen at Crewe South Shed on 1st April 1941, painted in a 'battleship grey' and with W↑D markings) and the third would go there when the second had returned. The last of the three to be overhauled, 8018, went to Crewe Works in June 1941. Additional motive power would clearly be needed. To cover the immediate need until further WD locomotives could be brought in, two Coal engines were loaned by the LMS – 28204 from December 1941 (it was on the railway by 19th December) to 3rd March 1942 and then 28308 from April to 6th July 1942.

Freight train loading and speeds

Since most of the main line was level or nearly so, the standard loading of freight trains was up to thirty-three loaded wagons and an absolute maximum of fifty-five, reduced to twenty-five loaded or forty-five total on the down gradient from Hookagate to Ford. On the steeply graded section into Shrewsbury Abbey the rule was fifteen loaded or twenty-five total (but with a maximum of five loaded tank wagons included) into Abbey and ten loaded or twenty total from Abbey to Hookagate. The wording 'tank wagons' in this context meant wagons for carrying fuel oil (which the Army called cistern wagons, to distinguish them from wagons carrying tanks – armoured fighting vehicles).

Civilian traffic

The buildings available for the storage of civilian traffic remained rather primitive:

Shrewsbury	Goods warehouses No's 1, 2, 3.
	A building used as a cement store.
	Passenger van No. 18 (ex-NLR) used as a grain store.
	Passenger coaches No's 7 (ex-L&SWR) & 17 (ex-GER) stripped of seats and used for storage of grain. The grain store wagons were finally scrapped at Hookagate during a 'tidy up' operation in the 1950s.
	Box wagons No's 15, 16, 17, 18, 20, 21, 22, 23, 24.
	Cattle wagons No's 30, 31, 32, 33, 42, 43.
Meole Brace	Stationary (i.e. grounded) box wagon.
Ford & Crossgates	Four stationary box wagons.
Nesscliff	Building used as a goods store and a grounded coach.
Kinnerley	Goods warehouse on Up platform.

Progress on new work and formal takeover by the War Department

The work of putting the railway into good order continued, but with ongoing uncertainties. On 25th January 1941 it was minuted that the location of the crossing loop at Cruckton was in abeyance until the location of possible magazines in that area was known. If they were to be near Cruckton, then the block post layout might have to be fitted into the magazines layout. In the event no sheds were built near here, and it was noted by the War Department on 9th May 1941 that the earthworks for the passing loop at Cruckton 'will be put in hand shortly'.

Graham Vincent noted on 2nd February 1941 that the section of line from Hookagate to Kinnerley had been cleared of weeds, and pegs placed along the line in readiness for track renewal. Men were at work putting additional cross beams in place to strengthen the viaduct at Shrawardine and on strengthening other bridges.

By 8th April 1941 it was reported to the War Office that the essential resleepering was nearly complete, though it had been necessary to use untreated timber because creosoted sleepers were unobtainable. Ramsay, the Managing Director of the S&M, complained bitterly to the War Office about short term expediency.

Shortage of labour was a constant problem, and on 29th May 1941 it was suggested to McAlpines that advantage should be taken of the good weather to complete the formation for railway track for as much track as possible. If necessary, earthworks at Kinnerley could be done by military plant and men.

Work was sufficiently progressed for it to be agreed at a meeting on 5th May 1941 between officers of the S&M and of the War Office that the WD would formally take over all operations of the S & M as from 1st June 1941. On 31st May a full inventory of consumable stores was undertaken in preparation for the formal transfer the following day. Not that everything was ready – on 27th May detailed drawings for the railway HQ offices at Kinnerley were still being prepared.

Work continued through the summer. On 20th July a ballast train, consisting of four open wagons containing cinders, S&M coach No. 10 and locomotive 8108 (painted pale green and with W↑D on the tender), was observed working between Edgebold and Cruckton.

The meeting of 5th May 1941 also discussed the future of the Criggion Branch, which was not required for military traffic for any part of the depot. It was agreed that the quarry company locomotive would be put in order to work the traffic over the Criggion Branch and that the WD would marshal the traffic at the junction at Kinnerley at a cost calculated at an hourly hiring charge for locomotive and crew. The GWR had in hand the matter of reconstructing the damaged bridge over the River Severn at Melverley. The work was completed for the Criggion Branch to re-open as from 27th October 1941.

Telephones

The telephone circuits in existence at 4th November 1940 were:

- An omnibus circuit with connections at Abbey, Meole Brace Station, Edgebold, Ford, Shrawardine, Nesscliff, Kinnerley, Maesbrook and Llanymynech
- A block circuit from Ford to Kinnerley for the Tyer & Co. No. 7 Tablet instruments
- A local circuit from Abbey to Meole Brace Signal Box
- Post Office phone lines at Abbey and Kinnerley.

On 30th April 1941, it was noted that the LMS engineers who maintained the S&M telephone circuit on its main line reported that it was in poor condition and liable to fail at any time. The memo from 3 Railway Operating Group, RE recommended the immediate erection of new poles and wires, even if some of the buildings to be served had not yet been built. As a temporary measure, two leads had been taken from the omnibus circuit to the block posts at Hookagate and Shrawardine – the first six Ordnance sheds being scheduled for completion on 14th June 1941.

By 13th May 1941 half of the 42 Line Maintenance Section (25 other ranks) were ready to move on to the S&M to repair existing telephone circuits and install new ones. They were attached to 161 Railway Construction Company for administrative purposes.

Changes to Ammunition Depot plans

The plans for the number of sheds in the depot were regularly changed. On 25th January 1941 it was decided that another fifty sheds would be added to the 100 already planned. Then on 5th May 1941 it was reported to a site inspection meeting that there was a requirement to store an additional 10,000 tons of AA ammunition. A Sub-depot at Ford adjacent to the triage was considered to be the only practical option.

A significant new problem came to light at a meeting at Shrawardine on 1st July 1941. Colonel Lonsdale pointed out that the sheds being built to 150 feet x 90 feet dimensions would hold more ammunition than could safely be stored in sheds laid out in pairs and so could not be filled to more than two-thirds capacity. It was agreed that the fifteen sheds already started to these dimensions would be completed, but the other eighty-five sheds in the original layout would be constructed with a reduced length of 104 feet. The height of the walls would also be reduced to 10 feet at the eaves not 13ft 6inches, further reducing the stackage capacity to an acceptable quantity. The outcome of this was that sites for a further forty-two sheds and associated railway spurs had to be sought. Plans were prepared within a month, the additional sheds being at Kinnerley East (Nesscliff).

It was also agreed to lower the rails in the sheds by 3ft 6in. wherever possible (not to be done where the water table did not allow). The reduction in the height of the platforms and outer walls of the sheds thus achieved would amount to a saving of some twenty per cent on the cost of £700,000.

A meeting at the War Office on 5th March 1942 noted that by 1st April sheds 31-44 and 65-76 would be finished, completing the east end of Pentre and Shrawardine Sub-depot. Some were already in use. The west end of the Sub-depot was under construction. As finally built, the Depot consisted of four Sub-depots (Shed numbers 141 and 142 were not used):

- No. 1   Maesbrook and Argoed Districts, Sheds 143-206
- No. 2   Kinnerley and Nesscliff Districts, Sheds 77-140
- No. 3   Shrawardine and Pentre Districts, Sheds 11-76
- No. 4   Alberbury, comprising Sheds 1-10 in Ford District and the stacking area in Loton Deer Park.

Problems between War Department and S&M

The informal nature of the agreement under which the military took over the assets of the S&M was to cause endless problems, notably on the upkeep of land and buildings. The S&M company was constantly complaining of the state of the access roads leading to civilian goods yards.

The relaying of the S&M sidings at Llanymynech revealed that the WD had not been told of certain 'understandings' that the S&M company had entered into. Southerns Ltd, the proprietors of the local timber yard, had an 'understanding' that the S&M company would lay rails into their yard at no cost for the rails laid on S&M land and with Southerns paying for the track laid on their land (on the basis that the S&M would benefit from the revenue from the extra rail traffic). The WD, knowing nothing of this, told Southerns on 12th April 1941 that if they wished a connection, they would have to pay for it. For the WD things now got worse, because Southerns claimed in a letter of 12th May that they rented land from the S&M (on which the WD planned to lay sidings) for stacking timber, and produced a copy of a lease dated 21st March 1940 to this effect. If they had to, Southerns would give up the land, but they would then have to stack the timber in an adjacent field – to which siding access would then be desirable. The company was holding stocks of timber for the Ministry of Supply Timber Control under the Ministry's Timber Dispersal Scheme. The timber stacking regulations required large fire breaks between the stacks. Eventually Ramsay arranged a meeting on 17th May 1941, at which it was agreed to retain the siding into the sawmill 'after moving it westwards' and also to provide a connection at the east end of Southern's field that was rented from Bradford Estates. In the process the WD took over a small area of land on which to lay two of its additional loop sidings – an acquisition that was to be the subject of further correspondence years later.

The problems were again highlighted when the station house at Shrawardine, unoccupied when the WD took over and which was being used by the men of the Construction Companies for taking their midday meals, was gutted by fire on 1st November 1941. The S&M's insurance company naturally wanted to know details of the WD's tenancy and its possible obligations to repair the property, and was most reluctant to pay out on the S&M's policy. The WD wanted the property repaired quickly, since it planned to use the house as a police post for Shrawardine Sub-depot. Eventually it was agreed that the WD would undertake the reconstruction of the station house (at an estimated cost of £400, quite a large sum in those days) if the S&M company undertook to pay over any insurance proceeds received.

The WD was not a little surprised to receive a letter from Ramsay on 17th April 1941 about a bank guarantee. Lord Powis had heard that the WD had taken over the S&M line. He had sometime previously given a guarantee to Lloyds Bank to secure a loan of £800 from the Bank to the S&M company to 'assist in developing the line'. Powis now said that he saw no reason to continue the guarantee since the Government had now taken over the line. The War Office wrote back to Ramsay on 25th April saying that there was 'no question of the Government taking over the line completely and financially'.

Another surprise inheritance was 'The Pulpit'. Inside the grounds of the one-time Abbey that formed part of the station yard at Shrewsbury when the WD leased the railway was the Pulpit that had been within the refectory of the Abbey. It is attributed to the time of Nicholas Stevens, who was Abbot from 1361 to 1399. The WD had leased the land on which the Pulpit stood, but had no desire to look after its maintenance – after all, the S&M company owned it. The solution was that by a formal Deed (number 71886 of 29th September 1944) the powers conferred on the S&M company under the Ancient Monuments Acts of 1913 and 1931 were nominated to the Mayor, Aldermen and Burgesses of the Borough of Shrewsbury, who consented to become the Guardians of the monument. The Pulpit, together with the plot of land on which it stood (74ft by 40ft, tapering to 36ft 10in.) ceased to be a railway responsibility. Happily the Pulpit still stands.

Progress of new construction and signalling installation

A passenger service to take men to work sites was in operation by 19th October 1941, at which date a timetable was chalked up at Cruckton:

Llanymynech Depart	7.00am
Kinnerley	7.20
Ford	8.00
Abbey (Shrewsbury)	8.35

No Sunday Service.

Returning	
Abbey	4.00pm
Ford	4.35
Kinnerley	5.10
Llanymynech	5.50

On Wednesday 12th November the Down Workmens train was seen at Meole Brace at 4.10pm, consisting of the four LT&S coaches and S&M coach No. 12, hauled by WD 8182. The LT&S coaches were now the usual coaches for the workmen's train. They were seen again on this duty, this time with a 6-wheel Ferry van of Italian origin, on 25th November. Propelling empty coaches to and from Shrewsbury rather than running round there was a common practice. On Tuesday 26th August 1941, WD 8108 was seen at Shrewsbury West pushing six empty coaches towards Kinnerley, and on 25th November 8236 passed

Meole Brace at 4.05pm pushing the coaches towards Abbey (already late for the 4.00pm departure). SR pattern brake vans were available by late November 1941. The standard make-up of the workmens trains was then four LT&S coaches plus one SR pattern brake van, although two Italian vans (one 4-wheeled and one 6-wheeled) remained in use as additional brake vehicles.

On 19th October 1941, it was noted that the new passing loop had been laid in at Cruckton, breaking up the long single line section between Hookagate and Ford. With the tank at Shoot Hill unserviceable, the provision of water still remained a problem that delayed traffic. On 15th November, WD 8108 working a Down goods train was observed at Ford spending 15 minutes taking water from a pipe at the lineside.

Initially, transfer of construction materials to the S&M line (and outwards stone traffic from Criggion, typically eight or nine loaded wagons per day from October 1941) had to be through the existing exchange sidings at Meole Brace. It was not until 18th November 1941 that the work at Hookagate was sufficiently well advanced for detailed signalling plans to be sketched out at a meeting in Shrewsbury jointly between WD and GWR staff – the work was done by the GWR because that company had responsibility for operating the joint GWR/LMS line. The detailed plans were ready two days later. On 23rd December 1941 the War Office accepted the GWR's costing for the work at £512 plus a supervision fee at 7.5 per cent (i.e. £38) and the GWR was asked to carry out the work as quickly as possible. This was done. By 8th January 1942 the signal box and signals were complete except for the signal arms. The four-lever ground frame needed for Hookagate No. 1 Block Post on the WD line (later known as Hookagate East) was on order and it was expected that it would be installed between 9th and 12th January – the work to be done by the GWR. The locking in the new signal box was ready for inspection on 15th January 1942.

Progress on the construction of the sheds was proceeding steadily. It was noted on 17th September 1941 (rather over-optimistically) that rail access to sixty of the 'storehouses' at Shrawardine would be completed by the end of December. The decision was made that ordnance traffic would commence on 1st January 1942, although the hutted camp was likely to be occupied by the civilian construction labour force until June 1942.

Although formally ready to accept ammunition from 1st January 1942, the work of upgrading the railway was far from over. The plans for a station to serve the Camp at Nesscliff were not drawn up until December 1941 (the Tn plan is dated 8th December). The block posts at Kinnerley, Nesscliff No. 2 (later known as Nesscliff West), Shrawardine and Quarry were not completed, although they were due to be handed over on 10th February.

Locomotives available during the construction period

In 1939 and 1940 the WD acquired 108 of the Dean Goods engines still remaining on the GWR. Many were shipped to France with the BEF and lost with the fall of France, but some had remained in the UK. With an engine weight of 36t 16cwt on three axles (13 tons maximum axle load) and a tender capacity of 3,000 gallons, they were well suited to the weak bridges and long runs on the main line.

In response to the desperate need for additional locomotive power, arrangements were made in December 1941 for two Dean Goods and one diesel locomotive to come to the S&M. Dean Goods WD 200 (GWR 2552) arrived from Longmoor on 12th December 1941 and after minor repairs was put into traffic on the 18th, still fitted with the additional pannier tanks fitted by the War Office. Locomotive WD 97 (GWR 2442) arrived from Long Marston on the 15th December and was in traffic on the S&M the following day.

Since the line had a nominal axle load of 11 tons, the Dean Goods were limited to 5 miles per hour over Shrawardine Bridge, the bridge over the Welshpool line near Hookagate, and Bridge No. 41, near mile post 16¼ (one of the flood relief bridges near Maesbrook) – WD memo dated 7th December 1941. A further memo of 5th January 1942 authorised that the general speed limit on the line be raised to 20 miles per hour, subject to observing these three local speed restrictions.

An issue not quite so quickly resolved was that the S&M Light Railway Order of 1909 was considered still to be in force, including the restriction that no tender engine should exceed a speed of 15 mph when running tender first. To get round this problem, a formal Order had to be made, using the powers under the Defence (General) Regulations 1939. Known as the 'Shropshire & Montgomeryshire Light Railway (Relaxation of Speed Limit) Order 1943' – Statutory Instrument 948 of 1943 – the speed restriction relating to tender-first running was abolished.

The old S&M equipment was a source of some difficulty. On a visit by the Director of Transportation in the first week of November 1941, he noted that the Kinnerley Engine Shed area was 'very untidy'. The men on the ground replied to his aides that one factor was the scrap and old rolling stock belonging to the S&M company which was lying around because it was difficult to know what to do with it. It did not belong to the WD (the railway was only on lease) so it could not just be scrapped. It was agreed that it would be 'concentrated at one end of the yard'. Eventually the rolling stock was concentrated in sidings at the Quarry end of Ford Yard, and a decision taken to break it up for the metal.

Civilian construction work continued to demand the provision of motive power, three engines per day being regularly allocated. Complaints from the contractors about delays arising from non-availability of an engine were frequent. A report prepared in this connection on 30th January 1942 provides an insight into the motley collection of locomotives with which the operators were expected to cope:

In working order were:
  8108 and 8236, ex-L&NWR 'Colliers'
  28204, of the same class, on loan from the LMS
  WD 200 (ex-GWR Dean Goods 2552)
  Bagnall (this would have been WD 73)
  982 (LNER 0-4-0T on loan)
  Diesel 45 (0-4-0)
Under repair:
  8182 (the third ex-S&M 'Collier', hence the need for the loan of 28204)
  2442 (Dean Goods WD 97, at Oswestry for attention to a hot box)
  Diesel 40 (0-4-0, similar to 45 above, gear trouble, expected to be ready next week)
  Diesel 44 (returned to makers for repair)
Not available (and in the event neither ever did any serious work on the S&M):
  Yeovil (just arrived, very sharp flanges, unsuitable)
  Victory (delivered on a wagon, very bad condition including twenty-three broken stays).

Neither this list, nor other WD papers, make any mention of Dean Goods WD 96 (GWR 2425), though secondary sources state that this locomotive was on the S&M by the end of 1941.

Locomotive 982 was an interesting acquisition. A small 0-4-0 shunting engine of LNER class Y7, it was hired by the WD and had arrived on 29th December 1941 after a seventeen day journey from Tyne Dock via Knottingley, Chester and Wrexham. It did not stay long on the S&M – it departed in January 1943 via York (where it spent a month) to work in a US depot in the Fylde.

WD 73 was new from the makers and should, in theory, have been a most useful engine. It had, however, been built for an overseas order that had been cancelled, and was 'out of gauge'. In particular, the buffer beams were oversize for the UK and regularly took bits off the newly built platforms. It could be worked only by special crews who knew where the locomotive could, and could not, safely go. Added to this was the fact that the locomotive was fitted with grease axleboxes, designed for short distance trips. On the longer runs required on the S&M, the engine suffered overheated axleboxes. It was transferred in 1944 to a depot at Sinfin (Derby) where clearances allowed it to be used more safely.

Records suggest that **Yeovil** and **Victory** were too worn out to do any useful work on the S&M. **Victory** was seen on a wagon on 8th February 1942 in transit to Peckett's works for repairs – it did not return to the WD line. **Yeovil** was perforce pressed into occasional use.

0-4-0 diesel mechanical locomotives were tried on the S&M in the early years of the war. WD32 (built Drewry) and Barclay-built WD 40, WD 44, WD 45 and WD 48 were all delivered new to the S&M in 1941 and 1942. Although capable of light shunting, they were not a great success, and had departed for other depots or Longmoor by the end of 1943. It was hard for the men at Kinnerley to keep them in reliable working order, and they were unsuited to the long runs and quite heavy loads required on the S&M system. Not for the last time, the Army was to discover that what was needed on the lengthy rail system that made up this Central Ammunition Depot were locomotives capable of trip working, not yard shunters.

It is an indication of just how desperate the War Office (and its contractors) were at this time that in 1942 they accepted two ex-L&NWR 0-4-0 shunting locomotives 3014 and 3015. Whilst these engines may have been up to the work for which they were designed – of pottering around Crewe Works – they were unsuitable for the new task. Completely and utterly useless. These diminutive locomotives had such small boilers that they ran out of steam long before they reached whatever Explosive Store House they were going to. Worse still, they had ineffective hand brakes, so that they could not stop any weight of wagons when they did arrive at the shed doors. They were very quickly laid aside in the sidings at Quarry that were also home to the decaying remnants of the pre-war S&M company's rolling stock, and they went to A. R. Adams Ltd in Newport (Mon) in 1943.

The WD did manage to acquire one useful small tank engine. **Ashford** (an 0-6-0 saddle tank, built by Avonside in 1920 to works number 1872) had arrived by 24th May 1942. The WD used the works number as the WD number allocated – the engine thus becoming 71872 when all WD locomotives were renumbered with a 70XXX prefix during 1944 (to reduce the risk that WD numbers would clash with the numbers of locomotives captured as the Army advanced into Europe). The locomotive came to the S&M in 1942 via George Cohen & Sons Ltd, and was to remain on the line for the duration of the war – it went to Abelson & Co. (Engineers) Ltd of Birmingham in March 1949.

Two other small locomotives did some service on the S&M. Manning, Wardle 0-6-0 saddle tank, works number 654 built in 1877 arrived from Long Marston in April 1942. Numbered WD 92, it remained on the S&M until May 1945 when it went to Sinfin Lane. WD 202, an 0-4-0 saddle tank built by Avonside in 1889 as works number 1407 and carrying the name **Tartar**, came from Queensferry in 1942 and returned there the following year.

The arrival of the locomotive **Victory** was not met with enthusiasm – it was found that amongst other faults it had 23 broken stays in the firebox. The locomotive was photographed on 8th February 1942 at Hookagate, on its way to Peckett's works for repairs.
Graham Vincent

THE CONSTRUCTION PHASE

Most useless of all the locomotives sent to assist with the construction of the WD lines was the pair of ex-L&NWR shunters from Crewe Works. They had neither the steam-generating capacity to haul construction trains, nor the brake power to stop them. Altogether under-engineered for the new task – look at the lightweight nature of the side rods arrangement. They were soon sidelined to the sidings.

S. H. Pearce Higgins, reference 42/63

WD 1872, named **Ashford**, seen in the sidings at Kinnerley on 13th April 1947. It was quite in keeping with the rough treatment suffered by the locomotives in the construction phase that part of the top of the chimney was missing.

Photo from Geoffrey Banister's thesis, possibly taken by Graham Vincent

An ancient locomotive that did an honourable amount of work on the S&M was the 0-6-0ST known simply as '654' seen here at Kinnerley on 24th May 1942. 654 was the Manning, Wardle works number for this elderly locomotive, built in 1877. The locomotive came late in the construction phase on the S&M, having arrived only a month before this picture was taken. It was to stay until May 1945.

Graham Vincent

Passenger coaches

Accommodation for the construction troops was an early problem. Until hutted camps could be provided, the War Office sought to hire Camping Coaches from the main line companies. The LMS was able to provide vehicles fully equipped for camping purposes. On a visit to Kinnerley on 2nd March 1941 it was noted that there were seventeen Camping Coaches, of which five were of the clerestory roof type, apparently of Midland Railway origin. Eight were in the sidings by the locomotive shed, the remainder in the bay platform siding. By October the number had increased, with nine now beside the locomotive shed, and several more in the new siding leading to what would become Argoed yard. As building work progressed to Districts further from Kinnerley, the Camping Coaches were moved around – there were none at Kinnerley by 14th May 1942, although formal return to the LMS did not take place until 1944.

Some of the construction troops had to make do with less well appointed vehicles. In the platform at Ford on 11th January 1942 there were two large vans simply fitted out with bunks for eight men (these vehicles had been designed for continental traffic, and carried the legend 'Not to be used between Baker St and Finchley Road on the Met & Dist Rly nor between Tonbridge and West St. Leonards nor on the Whitstable Harbour Branch of the SR'). There were some more of the same vans in the yard together with three Camping Coaches of GWR origin – and also some tents.

The provision of passenger rolling stock for the workmens trains was a developing problem. Many of the coaches taken over from the S&M were really only fit for use as warehouses, but for a while they would have to do. Amongst the first troops to arrive, on 20th March 1941, were men able to patch up the more robust of the available coaches – and an NCO to supervise arrived on the 24th March. Coaches 14, 13, 3, 9 and 6 (see appendix B) were noted in the platform at Kinnerley on 22nd June 1941. A separate report in September 1941 confirmed that three of the ex-Midland Railway coaches, one from the North Staffordshire Railway and one from the L&SWR were still in service, despite the arrival of some replacement coaches in July.

Some of the troops engaged on construction work had the relative luxury of sleeping in LMS Camping Coaches which had been converted for civilian camping holidays before the war. This view shows a rake of these coaches standing on the Criggion Branch line at Kinnerley. 9th March 1941. Graham Vincent

The Camping Coaches on the Criggion Branch at Kinnerley, looking towards the station on 9th March 1941. To the left of the Camping Coaches was the Criggion Loop (in practice kept clear as the running line towards Criggion). Barely visible amongst the grass were the locomotive shed sidings – with some of the S&M's almost unusable coaches not yet consigned to the scrap line but simply stabled amongst the wagons. One of the original Tyer & Co. signals is just visible in the distance. Graham Vincent

THE CONSTRUCTION PHASE

By 11th May 1941, construction work on the new exchange sidings at Hookagate had reached the stage where most of the new sidings had been roughly laid in, though not yet lined and levelled. The wagons in the sidings were for unloading the ash that would form the 'ballast' under most of the sidings. The former S&M main line is in the centre of this view, looking towards Shrewsbury from the half-way point within the yard. The GWR/LMS Joint line was on the left. *Graham Vincent*

A month later (23rd June 1941) the view looking west from the overbridge at the east end of the new yard at Hookagate shows that the connections to the main line had been laid in, though they were not connected to the signal box, which had yet to be built. The excavations for its foundations had just been commenced (to the right of the points in the Up main line). The signal box was not completed until January 1942. *Graham Vincent*

THE SHROPSHIRE & MONTGOMERYSHIRE LIGHT RAILWAY UNDER MILITARY CONTROL 1940-1960

A view from the west end of Hookagate Yard on 29th June 1941 gave an idea of the size of the yard, with only one siding still to be laid in. For a yard that was intended to be only an exchange point (marshalling was to be undertaken at Ford Yard) there was a considerable element of over-capacity, but it did give the WD the ability to hold incoming wagons here if the sidings onwards became clogged with traffic.
Graham Vincent

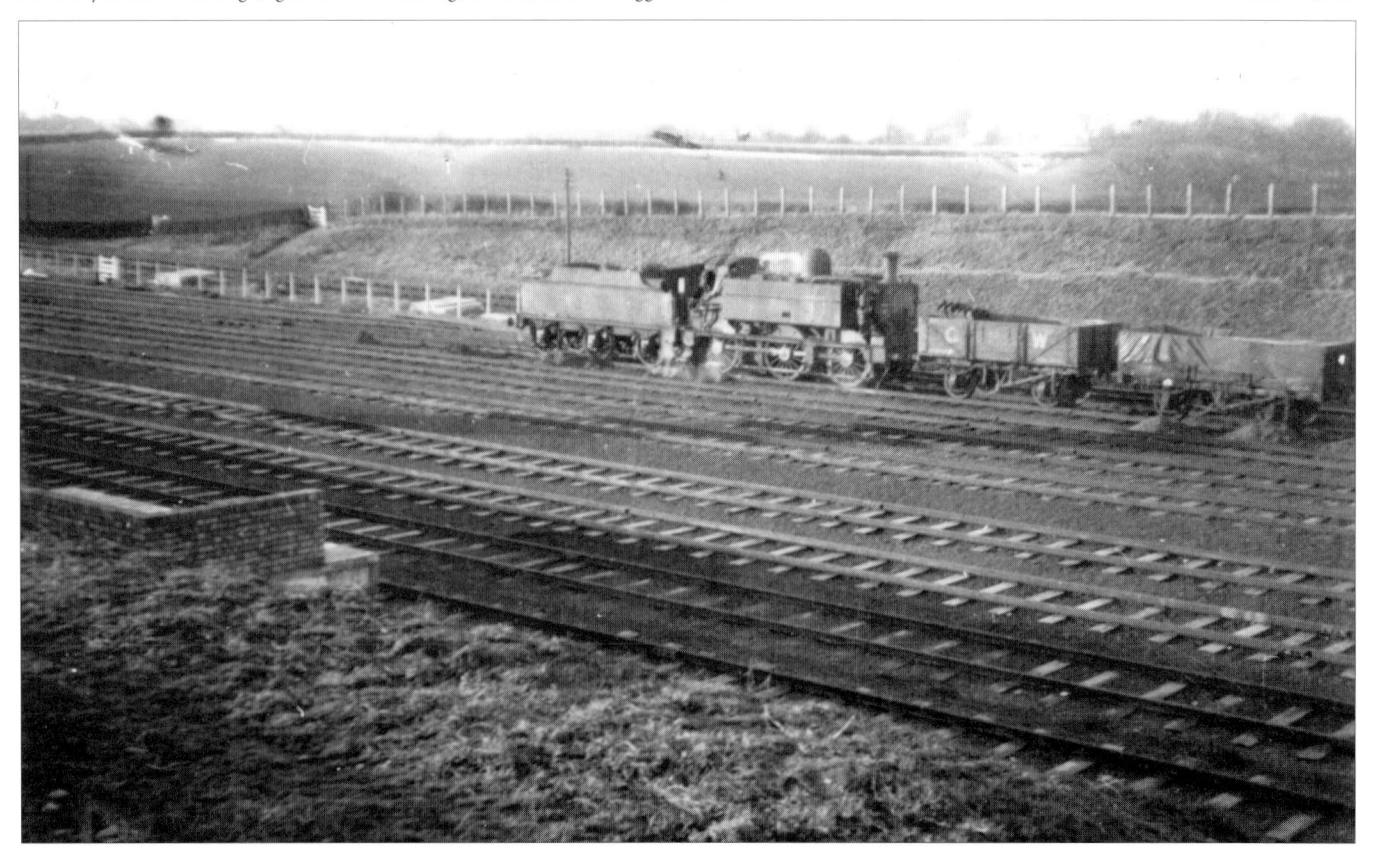

24th January 1942, and the railway was almost ready to receive incoming ammunition traffic in volume. WD 200 (GWR 2552) shunted at the west end of Hookagate Yard. This Dean Goods class locomotive was notable for the fact that it arrived on the S&M still fitted with the pannier tanks that the WD had provided on some of its Dean Goods engines to give extra water carrying capacity. The stage for locomotive coal had been completed (left foreground) and the footpath that crossed the site had been stopped up (left background).
Graham Vincent

THE CONSTRUCTION PHASE

Problems of locomotive supply to the construction sites

Complaints by McAlpines about the non-availability of locomotive power came to a head when the contractors wrote directly to the WD HQ on 9th December 1941 about two specific instances. A locomotive requested for Shrawardine for 08.30 on Sunday 30th November 1941 had not – it was asserted – arrived until 12.00. Captain A. H. Curtis, the Officer Commanding the Transportation Detachment, S&M Light Railway, was incensed at this complaint. He responded that the engine had been delayed because Mr Murphy (the McAlpine foreman) had asked for a Macaw wagon to be left in the section from Kinnerley to Edgerley for loading. After this delay the engine arrived at Shrawardine, only for Murphy to send it to Hookagate to work a ballast train to distribute building materials. The engine had not arrived back at Shrawardine until 12.00. The outcome of all this was that it was agreed that the engine would report to Murphy on arrival at site and then shunt to his orders.

The other incident concerned a crane. McAlpine had requested a crane to work on a Friday and Saturday, to unload transformers. The WD had replied that the crane was, at that time, at Ford and could only be moved at 5 miles per hour – and it would be needed by 161 Railway Construction Company for bridge work on the Sunday. The crane was placed by the railway at 16.00 on Friday and left all day Saturday. On the Sunday it was used by 161 RCC between Meole Brace and Abbey, and it was left at Hookagate at the end of work. On Monday at 09.15 Murphy asked for the crane, and was told that it would be available at 14.00. It was placed at 14.15.

On 15th December there was a further complaint about congestion of wagons. The WD papers noted that Tn 3b had arranged for two Dean Goods and one diesel to be sent to the S&M. One of the Dean Goods had arrived from Longmoor and was being made fit for service 'at the earliest possible moment'.

Sir A. McAlpine personally attended a progress meeting on 30th January 1942. He made it clear that for a project of this nature he would have wanted roads to give him ready access to the many shed (and other) construction sites for materials and men. Denied the use of roads (new roads are highly visible from the air and draw attention to the location of newly constructed targets), he considered that the contract required at least eight locomotives, six of them working at any one time. There were 525 PoWs working on construction, but some of the bricklayers had been idle for lack of a rail service. The WD responded that it had been asked for one extra locomotive, making a total of four. The WD had acquired additional locomotives, but both **Yeovil** and **Victory** needed major repairs. McAlpine stated their current need to be three locomotives daily at Shrawardine, and two at Kinnerley, with one more in a month's time for work at 'Kinnerley West'. To deal with the growing conflict for railway resources between arriving ammunition (which began from 12th January 1942) and the contractor's work, it was agreed to try to place the ammunition traffic each day before the contractors started work.

The meeting was not entirely one-sided. The railway operators managed to get agreement to high priority being given to the completion of work essential to the more efficient running of the line. Work on restoring the roof of the locomotive shed would be given high priority, so that men could work on locomotive repairs after the blackout. An engine pit outside the shed, which had been commenced eight weeks before but which was far from completed, would be finished immediately. Although most of the block posts were now 'fairly well on', they lacked doors and windows. This work would be completed within one week. The water supply at Hookagate would be completed 'soon', and the provision of full water facilities at Kinnerley and Ford would receive high priority.

The conflicts were not only with the civilian contractors – the WD Construction Companies were complaining as well. The small amount of correspondence that has survived illustrates the problems that the Operating Company faced at this early stage in the development of the Depot.

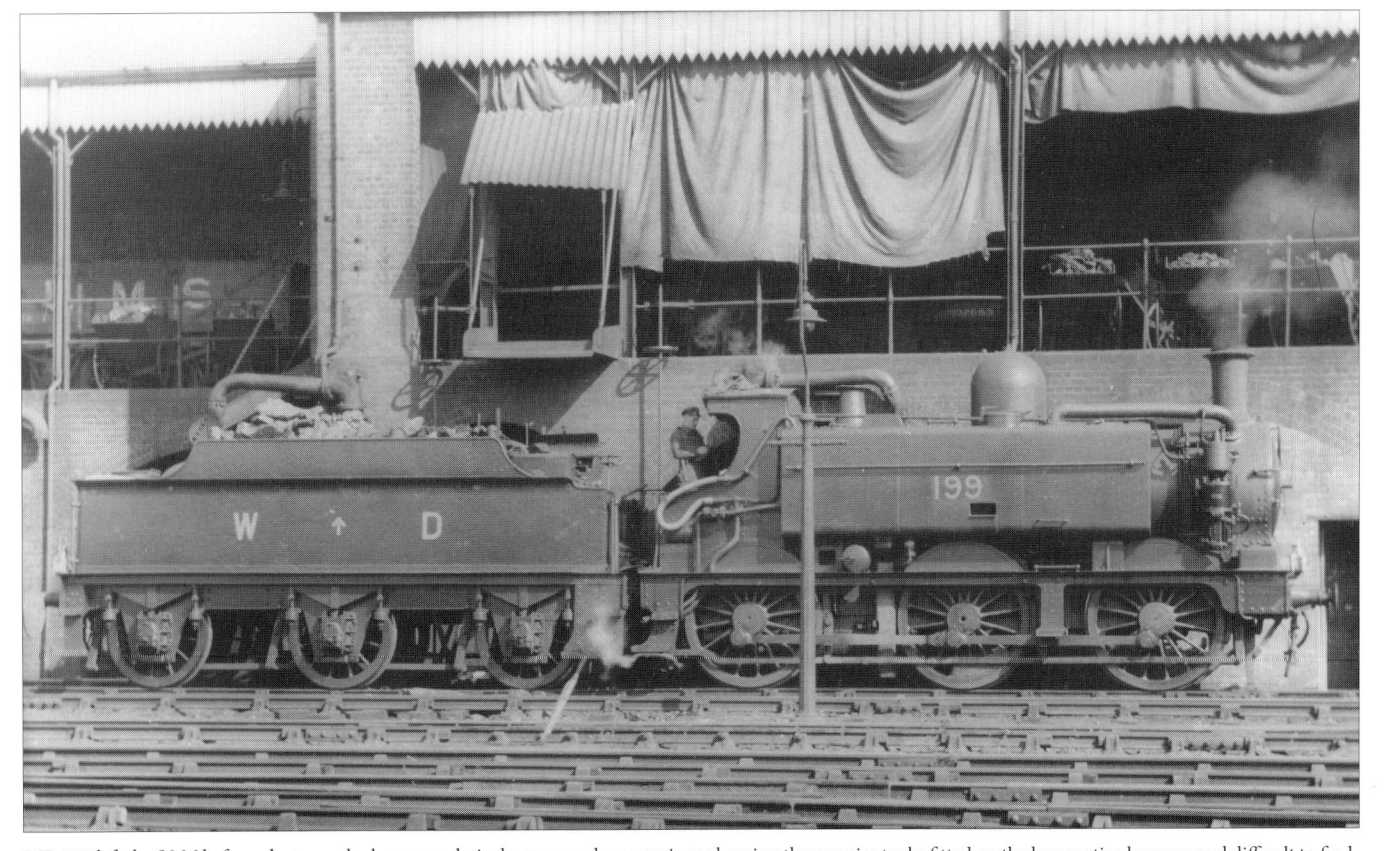

WD 200 left the S&M before photography became relatively easy, so close-up views showing the pannier tanks fitted on the locomotive have proved difficult to find. To illustrate the fittings added by the WD to some of the Dean Goods locomotives – air brake pump and side/pannier tanks for added water – we have included this view of sister engine WD 199, photographed at Hull.

R. K. Blencowe Negative Archive

THE SHROPSHIRE & MONTGOMERYSHIRE LIGHT RAILWAY UNDER MILITARY CONTROL 1940-1960

A typical passenger train of the early WD days in the S&M. 'Collier' locomotive 8182 heads a train of three coaches and a Southern Railway's pattern goods brake van towards Shrewsbury, passing the suburb of Meole Brace. The GWR/LMS double track line was on the right.
Millbrook House Ltd, courtesy Roger Carpenter

The passenger trip returned with WD 8182 running tender first. The empty coaches are seen here standing on the siding adjacent to the S&M running line, having just entered Hookagate Yard.
Millbrook House Ltd, courtesy Roger Carpenter

At a meeting on 11th February 1942, Lt Wisby said that two engines were standing for forty minutes waiting for the line to be free. He commented that the block post at Quarry should be completed forthwith to relieve congestion, and that a good NCO Foreman was required at Shrawadine Yard. Two days later, Wisby made a formal report which captures the state of the locomotive situation. 'The engine – the **Yeovil** – did not arrive until 08.55 hrs. On arrival it required water. It moved into the yard at 09.05 hrs to await the passing of the Civilian Goods train which was cleared at 09.18. The engine then commenced to draw out the first rake of ten trucks which took until 09.26 hrs – there being insufficient power. It was running round the wagons until 09.30 and at 09.32 hrs commenced to take the leading ten trucks to the site. First rake in position at 09.42hrs. Second rake of wagons in position at 10.00 hrs. Estimated loss of labour 108 man hours'. When challenged on the last point, Wisby admitted that alternative work had been found for the men until the wagons were placed. The simple fact was that McAlpines had all the bigger engines, and to allocate a smaller engine to them would increase the time wasted in coaling the engine. So the WD's Railway Construction Company had to make do with a locomotive that could not move twenty wagons on level track. As one officer ruefully noted about **Yeovil** – 'Anything over ten wagons makes for slow working with this engine'.

Not that McAlpine's men were satisfied with the locomotive power available to them. Curtis noted in a minute at the end of February, in response to a letter from the Ministry of Works of 25th February, that all requests from McAlpine for locomotives had been met. There were now thirteen locomotives on the S&M and nine were at work each day. Each day McAlpine had three engines at Shrawardine, one at Ford and one at Kinnerley. There had been occasions when advice of the receipt of ammunition had been late (or not received at all) which had meant that one of these five engines had been used for the occasional shunt of ammunition traffic – about which Murphy had complained.

Curtis attached his best Traffic Operator (a Corporal) to Murphy to ensure close liaison and that the engines did what Murphy wanted. This did not resolve matters, and a meeting was held on 10th March 1942 between the civil engineers and officers of the Director of Transportation (D Tn). The Resident Engineer for the Ministry of Works and Buildings (Mr Richmond) said that after a marked improvement in the supply of engines following the meeting at which McAlpine had been present, this had recently fallen off. The contractors said that their requirements for locomotive working at Shrawardine amounted to forty-four hours per day. They stated that on 4th March all that had been available was three locomotives for 22½ hours, and the average number of locomotives per day was three not five. The number of shunts missed had in consequence risen from about ten per day in early February to thirty-six on 18th February and thirty-eight on 4th March.

This time Curtis (now Major Curtis – this task had ensured his promotion) was ready and he supplied detailed figures:

Feb 9th	4 engines	38 hours
Feb 15th	3 engines	15 hours
Feb 16th	5 engines	41 hours
Feb 25th	5 engines	48 hours
Feb 26th	5 engines	48 hours
Feb 27th	5 engines	48 hours
Mar 1st	2 asked for and supplied	15 hours
Mar 2nd	5 asked for and supplied	58½ hours
Mar 3rd	5 asked for and supplied	57¼ hours
Mar 4th	5 asked for and supplied	43¾ hours
Mar 5th	5 asked for and supplied	45½ hours
Mar 6th	5 asked for and supplied	47 hours
Mar 7th	4 (asked for 5)	33¼ hours

THE CONSTRUCTION PHASE

That the War Department managed to run trains at all was a tribute to the men who, whatever the weather, undertook maintenance on locomotives under the most primitive conditions. Here 8236 is seen under repair at Kinnerley on a sunny day – 24th May 1942. The work was not lightweight – the buffer beam had been separated from the front end of the frames and stood resting on packing while the front cylinder covers had been removed. 0-4-0 Diesel No. 40 had the partial cover of the corrugated iron shed behind. Notably, the W↑D lettering on the tender had been painted out, and the locomotive carried no markings except its old LMS numberplate on the smokebox door. Graham Vincent noted in his diary that for reasons that he could not discover, all the WD ownership markings were painted out in the few days between 17th and 24th May 1942, except on the two diesels (which were owned by the War Department). *Graham Vincent*

Curtis said that at recent daily meetings, Murphy had expressed himself as being entirely satisfied with the engine arrangements.

The conflicts of 'evidence' did not go down well with W. E. Blakey, the Assistant Director of Transportation Tn3. He got Richmond to confirm that his need was for:

Shrawardine	Three engines full time – 44 loco hours per day (it might be necessary to work one night shift to obtain this)
Ford	Two engines – 18 loco hours per day
Kinnerley West	One engine – 10 loco hours per day
Total	Six engines – 72 loco hours

He then told Curtis that each day he was to agree with Richmond the number of engines and locomotive hours needed, to check that what was needed had been supplied and to try to reconcile the different facts as presented to the meeting.

By 1st April 1942 matters had improved, but only by a little. Of the twelve engines on the S&M, four were out of action. Of the eight working, four were working for the contractor (three at Shrawardine and one at Kinnerley). Ford was being shunted daily by one of the train engines. It was hoped to strengthen the engine power, as follows:

- A new diesel engine left Kilmarnock the previous day
- Diesel engine No. 47 from Branston was expected to be available in about a week
- A GWR steam engine 'will be available from Long Marston in about a weeks time when the new Hunslet engine is run in'.

A view of the line-up of locomotives that were serviceable at Kinnerley on 24th May 1942. From the front they were 'Collier' 8018, Dean Goods WD176 locally known as **Starflyer** and the 65 year old Manning, Wardle WD 654 (the official number for which was later changed to WD 92). The hand-operated crane on the left was of little use in locomotive repair work, but saw use on bridge reconstruction and construction tasks such as unloading transformers. *Graham Vincent*

Of the smaller engines on shed when Graham Vincent called on 24th May 1942 were 0-4-0ST 202 **Tartar** (43 years old) and the relatively new 0-6-0ST **Ashford**, built in 1920.
Graham Vincent

0-4-0 Diesel WD No. 40 standing half in, half out of a shed (if it can be called that), with another diesel locomotive behind. *Graham Vincent*

A different view of WD 40, showing the outdoor workbench on which the men had to undertake their work. It is little wonder that the diesel locomotives could not be maintained in a reliable state under these conditions. *Graham Vincent*

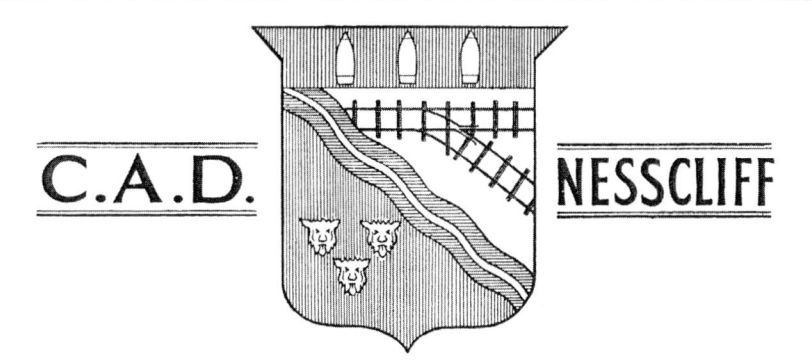

Chapter Three
THE WAR DEPARTMENT RUNS THE RAILWAY

Ammunition traffic began to arrive from 12th January 1942. On Sunday 15th February 1942, thirty wagons of Red traffic were noted in the sidings at Hookagate – with a considerable presence of Military Police.

A memo of 11th February reported that there was traffic congestion because the block post at Quarry was not yet ready for use. The line was being worked throughout by telephone and paper tickets. Many of the in-section point levers were not locked in any way, and it was recommended that interlocked frames be provided at Meole Brace Exchange Sidings (both ends), Meole Brace Station, Edgebold, Block Road (McAlpine's siding), Nesscliff Station (both ends) and Wern Las.

An idea of the traffic can be gauged by observations made over two hours at Ford on the afternoon of Monday 2nd March 1942:

3.40pm	8182 standing in down platform
3.55	8236 with one SR brake van passed in the direction of Hookagate
4.05	8182 departed for Kinnerley
5.15	WD 97 and one Italian van passed in the direction of Hookagate
5.20	Down passenger train passed, consisting of 8236, LT&S coaches 4784, 3070, 3069, 3068 and one SR brake van (this must have passed WD 97 at the new passing loop at Cruckton)
5.40	Up passenger passed consisting of 8182, two LT&S coaches and one Italian van.

A typical wartime scene at Kinnerley. The youthful fireman of a Dean Goods working 'B' duty waited for the photographer. The locomotive had not been cleaned for a long time, but despite the dirt it is clear that it carried no sign of its number apart from on the front buffer beam, nor any W↑D markings. The brake van in the Civilian Yard was one of the Southern Railway pattern vans extensively used by the WD.
Graham Vincent

THE SHROPSHIRE & MONTGOMERYSHIRE LIGHT RAILWAY UNDER MILITARY CONTROL 1940-1960

A rather poor quality photo (as many from the WW2 era are) showing one of the 'Collier' locomotives, 8182, taking water at the tank on the south side of the yard at Hookagate. Main line engines taking a block load train non-stop through Shrewsbury would fill up at this tank if necessary.
Millbrook House Ltd, courtesy Roger Carpenter

A meeting at the War Office on 5th March 1942 considered a recent survey of the line. The progress on constructing the sheds was as follows. At Pentre, Sheds 31-44 and 65-76 were complete or would be complete by 1st April, and those completed were receiving ammunition traffic. Shrawardine was under construction. Work was just starting at Ford and would not be completed before August. Nesscliff would not be ready before the end of the year and Kinnerley would not be available until 1943. The receipt for ammunition for the east end of Pentre at the same time as construction was proceeding was causing some problems, but this was expected to end in April.

As to the state of the mechanical signalling on the line, a report of 7th February 1942 from Captain Price (Officer Commanding No. 4 Railway Telegraph Company) commented that the existing signal apparatus was beyond reconditioning and re-instatement. To provide full signalling at all the block posts would be very expensive, and it would be difficult to obtain materials. There were only two signal fitters on the line with the experience necessary to do the work, and no NCO to supervise them. The report recommended that all the fixed signalling on the line be abolished, except that at Hookagate East (which had signals installed by the GWR). The other signals in place were not working properly (or at all) and it was a greater danger to have them than to dispose of them. On the WD line, hand signalling and hand-operated points would suffice. Intermediate points should be provided with two-lever ground frames locked by Annetts keys. The WD was working the railway throughout by telephone and paper ticket from block post to block post, with flagboard signalling (see pages 85 and 86) at block posts. Operating the line by telephone and ticket was unsafe despite the issue of clear instructions, and some form of Electric Train Tablet, Electric Train Staff or Electric Key Token working should be introduced.

The meeting on 5th March 1942 – attended by Lt Col Yorath (Officer Commanding No. 3 Railway Operating Company), Major Marson from Tn 3, Major Jackson from Tn 2, Major Curtis (Officer Commanding, Tn Detachment, Nesscliff) and Captain Price of Railway Telegraphs – considered these questions. The use of some form of electric token working was considered desirable to give greater safety in working than relying on a system of verbal messages (which indeed was to be the cause of a head-on accident on the single line). However, it was essential that the block posts could be 'closed' when not required for traffic purposes in order to save manpower, and suitable switching-out apparatus for electric instruments was simply not available at that time. So working by telephone and paper tickets would remain, against the report's clear recommendations.

On the question of full semaphore signalling with conventional lever frames, the meeting decided (again, contrary to the recommendations that had been received) that full signalling should be erected at the busiest locations. The proposals provide a list of the signalled locations at that date, and the new requirements:

Shrewsbury (Abbey)	nothing required
Meole Brace Exchange Sidings	two new 2-lever Ground Frames (GFs) with Annetts Key lock
Meole Brace Station	one new 2-lever GF with Annetts Key (AK) lock, key to be kept at Hookagate No. 1
Hookagate No. 1	nothing required
Hookagate No. 2	nothing required
Edgebold	new 2-lever GF with AK lock
Cruckton	nothing required
Ford	new 14-lever frame for points and signals
Quarry	nothing required
Shrawardine	new frame for 12 (approx) levers for points and signals
Nesscliff No. 1	new frame for 14 (approx) levers for points and signals
Nesscliff Station	two new 2-lever GFs, locked by AK to be held at Nesscliff No. 2
Nesscliff No. 2	nothing required
Edgerley	nothing required
Kinnerley	new frame for 24 (approx) levers for points and signals
Wern Las	new 2-lever GF, locked by AK to be held at Kinnerley when not in use
Maesbrook	three new 2-lever GFs, locked by AK normally kept at Kinnerley, to allow for a new loop here.

The meeting on 5th March also considered improvements that would assist in the handling of the traffic. That meeting agreed that it was not necessary to double the main running line, but proposed the following additions to existing plans:

A. A loop for 30/40 wagons at the east end of Pentre depot connecting to the Goods Line – otherwise known as the 'Dead Road' – (this was installed but on the Gathering Line).
B. A loop at the west end of Pentre Depot inside the triangle (done).
C. A loop at the west end of Shrawardine Depot (but it was doubted that this could be done, and it was not).
D. At Edgerley, a loop to hold 40/50 wagons connected to the Goods Line towards Kinnerley (not done).
E. At Kinnerley, a continuation of the Goods Line (later called the 'Dead Road') to form the third side of the triangle. This was done – prior to this there was a gap of a few hundred yards in the double line between Edgerley and Kinnerley. This shortcoming had been noted during the visit of the Director at Transportation in early November 1941.

Following the meeting, work was to be done on surveying the sites for signalling at Ford, Shrawardine, Nesscliff No. 1 and Kinnerley. Out of this developed a proposal to double the line from Ford to Shrawardine. The whole line from Shrewsbury to Llanymynech had originally been laid as double track but one line had been lifted, as early as 1867. Subsequent work on the single track had encroached on the alignment of the second track. On the basis that it was too expensive to alter the existing running line (and impossible to do so without unacceptable interference with the traffic that was already testing line capacity) the plan was to leave the existing line and lay new track at 12ft 2in. centres from the existing. This would require 3,000 cubic yards of cut and 10,000 cubic yards of fill (the amount of fill could be reduced to 7,000 cubic yards if the telephone pole route was moved). Getting line occupation for the muck trains would be problematic, so completion would take some two to three months. The scheme was not adopted.

On signalling, the meeting's decision was watered down in the light of what could practically be achieved. Full signalling was eventually provided at Kinnerley, where a frame of twenty levers was provided in a block post 16ft x 10ft. Elsewhere on the WD line there were block posts with flagboard signalling at Hookagate West (originally called No. 2), Cruckton, Ford, Quarry, Shrawardine, Nesscliff East (originally called Nesscliff No. 1), Nesscliff West (No. 2), Edgerley, Maesbrook and Llanymynech. The block posts were all built to internal dimensions of 8ft square, except that at Edgerley, which was 25ft x 17ft with a 3ft verandah (unfortunately no photograph has been found of this building).

Further locomotive requirements.
Further Dean Goods locomotives duly arrived during 1942. WD 98 (GWR 2415), WD 175 (GWR 2511) and WD 96 (GWR 2425, on the S&M by 21st February 1942) were transferred in together with WD 176 (GWR 2558) which was on the S&M by 22nd April 1942, but WD 200 was transferred away on 10th April. GW 2462 was on loan from the GWR for part of the year – from April until it was returned to its owning company on 6th July, when it was seen in transit together with LMS 28308 which could also be released back to its owners as a result of the arrival of the extra Dean Goods engines. Others of the class were moved to the S&M in the following couple of years, including two from Melbourne in 1943 and 1944, three from Bicester and two from Kineton. One was scrapped (WD 176) after collision damage. By the end of 1946 there were no less than twelve of this class of locomotive on the S&M, though many were close to worn out and indeed half of them were formally 'out of traffic'.

A number of locomotives acquired unofficial names, painted on locally. Collier 8108 was named **Kinnerley Flyer**, and names were given to four Dean Goods – WD 96 **Kinnerley Castle**, WD 98 **Kinnerley Spitfire**, WD 176 **Starflyer** and WD197 **Pretty Polly**. WD 70094 already had the name **Monty** when it arrived from Bicester in December 1946.

The WD acquired two other 0-6-0 tender locomotives of useful weight and power. These were LNER class J15 engines, which had been sold by the LNER to a film company, for the making of the film *Knights without Armour*. The locomotives were acquired by the War Office from London Film Productions Ltd of Denham in September 1942, WD 211 painted in black and WD 212 painted grey. In the event, they served only for a short time on the S&M. Both suffered accident damage, and after appraisal at the LNER works at Stratford (East London) they were written off in 1944. They were replaced on the S&M by two very different ex-LNER locomotives, 0-6-0 tank locomotives of Class J69 from a batch that the War Office had acquired in 1939. WD 91 (70091) was transferred from the No. 2 Military Port at Cairnryan in 1944, and WD 84 (70084) from the depot at Old Dalby in 1945. Both remained on the S&M until after the war, being sold on to John Lysaght Ltd of Scunthorpe in May 1948.

*Some of the Dean Goods locomotives acquired unofficial names while on the S&M, but this one arrived already carrying a name. WD 70094 was photographed – the notes with the photo say at Longmoor – with the name **Monty** added to the middle splasher, in addition to the extended cab roof. It arrived on the S&M in 1946.*
Photograph from the Geoffrey Bannister thesis, courtesy Andrew Bannister

THE SHROPSHIRE & MONTGOMERYSHIRE LIGHT RAILWAY UNDER MILITARY CONTROL 1940-1960

The scene, typical of Kinnerley at this time, which so annoyed the Director of Transportation during his visit in November 1941. Remains of half-dismantled S&M wagons, which had to be cut up on site because they could not even be moved out of the way, lay across the area where men were trying to maintain the barely serviceable locomotives in running order. The locomotives were 8236 and WD 176 **Starflyer**. *Graham Vincent*

Useful additions to the S&M motive power late in the war were two J69 Class tank engines that the WD had acquired from the LNER. 70091 came from Cairnryan in 1944, and is seen here at Kinnerley on 21st June 1947 still fitted with the Westinghouse brake. *R. K. Blencowe Negative Archive, number 37374*

A different view of WD 70091 on the same day. These engines had been designed for medium distance work, and had a coal bunker adequate for the trip working required on the S&M.
H. C. Casserley, reference 49041

For a short period in 1944 there were three 'USA' tanks on the S&M, but at 15½ tons axle loading they were not well suited to the weak bridges on the S&M and they were restricted as to which parts of the line they could work. Soon after the invasion of Europe at least two of these USA tank locomotives were shipped over the English Channel. 1427 ended up acquiring a SNCF (French) number.

In late 1944 and early 1945 the WD's three Coal engines (built in the years 1874, 1879 and 1881, so all were great veterans) went to Crewe Works for light repairs, but they were pretty much worn out. 8236 went to Crewe again in 1946 but an appraisal reported on 16th September that the boiler was not worth repair. The same month 8182 was stopped with a leaking firebox foundation ring. On 15th November 1946, 8108 was failed in traffic when a crack in the firebox was discovered. This engine had always been regarded as 'a terror' – WD crews dreaded being given 8108 and so far as possible it was left to the civilian driver who knew its quirks. All three were added to the row of locomotives stored out of use at Hookagate, where they remained for some years. As engines on lease they became the property of the Western Region of British Railways, were returned to BR in 1949 and scrapped at Swindon in October 1950.

The tiny locomotive **Gazelle** was really fit only to pull the lightest of vehicles. Under the auspices of the old S&M company a lightweight coach had been assembled that was within its haulage capacity, but in WD days this vehicle was in use as a Time Office, off the track but still on its wheels. **Gazelle** was only used as a personnel transport for a small number of people, and performed a useful function in this role prior to the arrival of the internal combustion rail cars. It was especially useful in the role of an inspection vehicle when the outload began prior to the battle at El Alamein. One group of men engaged on construction work were from the Non-Combatant Corps (the 'conscientious objectors'). Many NCC men felt that they should not be engaged on any work that furthered the war effort, and that constructing an ammunition depot was contrary to the terms on which they accepted assignment to an NCC unit. When the outload began, there were a number of instances of interference (at night time) with the facing points on the main line, especially in the Ford area. So each day **Gazelle** was sent to inspect the line, Sergeants Thorne and Dickenson (the other Sergeant on the line, who mostly did indoor work) taking turns each day to go out on early morning inspections. This was not at all to the liking of the L/Corporal driver of the locomotive (an LNER man from the Doncaster

THE SHROPSHIRE & MONTGOMERYSHIRE LIGHT RAILWAY UNDER MILITARY CONTROL 1940-1960

The tiny 0-4-2 locomotive **Gazelle**, S&M locomotive No. 1 – seen at Kinnerley on 27th July 1940, a few months before the commencement of the lease of all the locomotives and rolling stock by the War Department. It was still fitted with the cab on the tender, and looking smart after extensive overhaul in 1937. *Graham Vincent*

Gazelle was used by the WD (mainly as an inspection vehicle) for a few years, but by the end of the war these duties had been taken over by the rail cars. On 1st April 1947 the locomotive (now painted in the pale grey-green livery of the early war years) was out of use in a siding near Kinnerley. The rear cab had been removed. In the background can be seen two of the Explosive Store Houses (ESHs), commonly known as 'Sheds'. The poles at each corner of the sheds, linked by a wire, had lightning conductors to carry electric discharges. *Graham Vincent*

area), who was fond of his beer of an evening and did not appreciate having to turn out early in the mornings. Dickenson was a tall man, and during the journey had to look over the cab roof. The rear cab on the locomotive was removed by the WD. The Police were soon satisfied that the sabotage was the work of NCC men, an opinion strengthened by the fact that incidents ceased when the NCC were swiftly transferred away.

The other regular service performed by **Gazelle** was for unofficial journeys to Llanymynech or Criggion for a trip to the pub by the NCOs and 'office staff' at Kinnerley. The pub in Kinnerley was often very overcrowded, and was notable for having no lights at all inside.

Passenger rolling stock

Arguably the most distinctive vehicles acquired by the War Office were the coaches built for the London, Tilbury & Southend Railway. They were robust vehicles, and most of those on the S&M lasted until the line closed. The coaches, as two sets, had been built for use on a through service from Ealing Broadway to Southend, a service that was withdrawn when the Emergency Timetable (prepared in May 1939) was brought into use from 11th September 1939. The LMS moved them off the Southend line – one was seen at Dronfield (near Sheffield) – and re-designated them as 'Excursion Sets', though their practical use was limited by the fact that they were fitted with the Westinghouse air brake.

THE WAR DEPARTMENT RUNS THE RAILWAY

During the war years, the WD coaches were painted in a colour described as 'darkish grey-green' – a lighter colour than the dark green more generally adopted later. Seen here in sidings near Kinnerley were an ex-GWR clerestory roofed coach and WD 6400, one of the former London, Tilbury & Southend Railway Brake/Third coaches. Initially the War Department adopted the LMS numbers for these coaches, simply adding WD to the numbers. The sliding door arrangement on the LT&S coaches (used because their original service included journeys on the London sub-surface Underground line to Ealing) is apparent here. Photographed on 1st April 1947. *Graham Vincent*

From 19th November 1939 the War Office entered on to the Melbourne Branch of the former Midland Railway – near Derby – to develop it as a military training railway. Special attention would be given to training troops to work in France and experience with the air brake was essential. Most British railways used vehicles with automatic vacuum brakes. So when in November 1939 the War Office asked for some coaches for the Melbourne Military Railway, the use of the Ealing stock was an obvious choice. Eight of those stored by the LMS were formally loaned to the War Office on 4th January 1940. These were the coaches of No. 66 Excursion set, then stabled at Burton on Trent – Third Class coaches 3067, 3068, 3069, 3070 and 3073, Composite 4784, and Brake/Thirds 6399 and 6400.

A different set of WD coaches, consisting of two ex-GWR and two from the LT&S, standing on the running line at Hookagate West. The train engine, Dean Goods 70169, was running round via one of the sidings in the yard on 1st April 1947. *Graham Vincent*

By mid 1941 the demands within the War Office had changed. The fall of France made training for operating trains using the air brake less significant. However, the requirement to provide coaches to the increasing number of military depots in Britain was growing rapidly. So from 5th July 1941, four of the Ealing coaches were transferred to the S&M. Coaches 3067, 3068, 3069 and 6399 duly arrived painted in LMS red (the 'last painted' date was 1939), and still lettered 'M M R'. The remainder of the LT&S coaches on loan to the WD came to the S&M later in the year – 3070, 3073, 4784 and 6400. 3067, 3070 and 6399 were later written off after collision damage.

On 10th February 1942 the Director of Transportation at the War Office asked the Railway Executive Committee (as the organisation having oversight of the 'Big Four' main line companies) to find twenty coaches and four passenger brake vans to meet the needs of the various military railways then being developed. Non-corridor coaches with old upholstery 'will do'. By the 16th February forty-five vehicles had been offered:

GWR	Six coaches including two Brake Thirds, seating for 300 men
LMS	Eleven coaches including two Brake Thirds, seats for 580
LNER	Up to 20 but with no brake compartment vehicles
SR	Eight vehicles

On 16th March 1942 allocation was made of the coaches offered. The S&M was assigned (on hire) four vehicles – GWR Third Class bogies 2929, 2266 and 3190, with Third-Brake No. 2323 – all of which arrived on the 09.15 trip from Coleham (Shrewsbury) on Wednesday 1st April. They had been through Swindon works, which had done some repainting (painted dark brown with no lettering) and made the roofs watertight. By the end of the war one of these vehicles, painted brown, was noted as having compartment doors lettered 'Officers', 'WOs and Sgts' and 'Ladies'. Bicester was allocated five LMS coaches including one Brake Third, and the Cairnryan line at Military Port No. 2 (Stranraer) got six LMS coaches (again, including one Brake Third).

This was not the end of the War Office requirements, and on 17th August 1942 the WD asked the REC to find more coaches, including four (including one brake) for the S&M. On 21st October the following were allocated from the GWR – Third Class bogies 333, 720 and 2230, with Third-Brake No. 945. Yet more coaches for the S&M and Bicester lines were requested on 1st July 1943 and the LMS offered seven, of which Lavatory Composites 19406 and 19463 went to the S&M, though not before the LMS had removed all the light fittings and sealed up the lavatories – at the request of the WD.

Coaches were sometimes exchanged for replacements. For example, on 12th August 1943 GWR Brake Third No. 945 went back to the GWR to be replaced by Third 2790 and on 16th February 1944 No. 333 was replaced by Third No. 1244.

Problems with civilian traffic

Working the civilian traffic and incidents of petty pilfering from it was always a problem for the military. This was highlighted by the loss on 19th May 1943 of a carton of 2,000 cigarettes which had been consigned to Nesscliff. Cigarettes were a most important commodity at the time – almost a second currency – and the carton was valued at £16 19s 7d. It had been signed for by the S&M checker at Shrewsbury (Abbey) when brought down by road from the main station, and he in turn obtained a signature for it from Sapper J. Mellor, the WD guard on the 'civilian goods'. Unfortunately, Mellor did not obtain a signature for its disposal and the WD had to pay out on the resultant loss claim. The military were not pleased and decided that as an ex-S&M civilian guard was on the payroll, he should henceforth work all civilian goods trains so that any loss would be a purely S&M matter. Indeed, it was minuted on 19th May 1943 that the S&M should provide all the staff dealing with the receiving, delivery and levying of charges on civilian traffic, since the Company took all the receipts from this business and the WD had only undertaken to work the train free of charge.

When the LT&S and GWR coaches arrived, any of the original S&M coaches that were still in a fit state to run were used largely for engineering department purposes. This former North Staffordshire three compartment Brake/Third (No. 12) had been repaired and was noted as being repainted inside and out on 1st December 1940, just days after the WD survey party had been around the railway. When seen early in 1941 it was painted in green, with the 'Breakdown Van' lettering in red, colours it still carried when photographed on the 25th May 1942.

M. N. Clay

THE WAR DEPARTMENT RUNS THE RAILWAY

Under the terms of its leasing agreement, the WD was required to work all civilian traffic on the line – though this could be done mixed with military traffic if circumstances allowed. Working tender first, WD 70196 passed Edgebold on 1st April 1947 with a freight headed for Hookagate. *Graham Vincent*

Also on 1st April 1947, Dean Goods WD 70180 (GWR 2514) was pictured at Nesscliff & Pentre Station working a short freight train with one of the WD (SR pattern) brake vans at the rear. Not all workings included a brake van. Although four of the new 0-6-0ST Austerity locomotives had been delivered they could not yet be used, pending bridge strengthening work to allow for their higher axle loading, so the aged Dean Goods locomotives remained in use. *Graham Vincent*

THE SHROPSHIRE & MONTGOMERYSHIRE LIGHT RAILWAY UNDER MILITARY CONTROL 1940-1960

Transfer of traffic from Hookagate to the main line marshalling yards at Shrewsbury was often undertaken by LMS locomotives from Coleham shed in Shrewsbury. Here LMS 0-6-2 tank 7746 is seen shunting in Hookagate Yard on 31st March 1947.
Geoffrey Bannister, courtesy Andrew Bannister

Traffic for the Civilian Yard at Kinnerley was considerable, as this photograph of 16th April 1949 reveals. The view is towards Llanymynech. In the middle distance is the block post put up by the Army, still in unpainted corrugated iron at this time (it was later painted black). Beyond that, the connecting line into Maesbrook and Argoed Sub-depot can be discerned, diverging to the right of the main line. The poles visible behind the block post are the lightning protection poles of Sheds 154 and 155.
R. K. Cope (RKC/B313) from the 'Detachment Photograph Album'

Below: The view from the brake van along a train composed mainly of empty open wagons, between Edgebold and Cruckton. Notable is the new pole route, put in by the WD along the line to carry the extra telephone circuits. Renewing the pole route along the whole line had itself been a considerable task. 14th February 1959. *Photographer unknown*

THE WAR DEPARTMENT RUNS THE RAILWAY

More problems with S&M management

Relations between the military and the S&M – usually in the person of James Ramsay, its Managing Director – became strained at times. On 1st June 1942, one year after the commencement of operations by the WD, Ramsay wrote claiming that he must have access to all military lines so that he could check 'on behalf of the main line companies' the use and retention of their wagons. The WD was not at all happy about this idea, but it was pointed out that Ramsay could not be denied access to land owned by the S&M that the WD was only leasing. Ramsay strained relationships too far when he claimed the use of a Wickham Rail Car – or the locomotive **Gazelle** – for his inspection trips. The WD reply was that he could not expect this to be supplied free of charge. In October 1942 Ramsay's request for a Wickham Rail Car to transport his platelayers on the Criggion Branch (where laying of newly-acquired rail was in progress) was refused.

Ramsay also tried to get the WD to pay, through the provision of manpower, for maintenance work on the Criggion Branch. On 5th June 1942 he telephoned the Ministry of War Transport to say that the S&M company had purchased a mile of rail and a supply of sleepers in order to relay part of the Criggion Branch but did not have sufficient labour to lay them (the S&M had just one ganger and two platelayers). Ramsay tried to imply that the relaying could bring to an end the arrangement (which had been in operation for some six months) under which the War Office was working traffic up to one side of the bridge at Melverley and pushing the wagons over to the other side from whence they were taken by the quarry engine. Wearily, H. W. W. Fisher at the Ministry of War Transport (MoWT) – no doubt with memories of a meeting he had chaired in May 1941 to discuss the reconstruction of Melverley Bridge and the track on the Criggion Branch – wrote to the War Office asking that it help out.

The Wickham Rail Cars (smaller than the Drewry cars) were the most common type on the S&M. Here two are seen standing on the siding outside the rail car shed at Kinnerley, in the company of two of the rail car trailers. Both the cars and the trailers had bench seating longitudinally down the centre of the vehicle – the trailers also had handrails to reduce the chances of passengers being thrown off. The tiny (and barely adequate) brake blocks operating on the wheels of both axles of the rail car are visible. Handles were provided on the end of the vehicle to assist manhandling the rail car on and off the line. Four Wickham Rail Cars were delivered to the S&M in March 1942. These may not have been the first. *Graham Vincent*

The WD did not work the quarry traffic (to and from Criggion) south of Kinnerley. This was handled by the Sentinel steam locomotive owned by the quarry company, which would come into the WD station at Kinnerley to collect its train. Here the Sentinel is seen leaving the junction with its train of empties. Two Wickham Rail Cars (of two different types, note the design of the roofs) were waiting to leave after this shunt move was completed. One was standing at the Stop board at the exit from the rail car siding to the Criggion Branch line, and the other car was still on one of the storage spurs. This view demonstrates that the rail cars, especially the low roof version, were barely visible above a low sided wagon – or a bank of earth. For this reason it was the practice for rail cars out on the line to display a prominent flag, to try to increase their visibility to other traffic (especially in the Sub-depots). *David Petterson, from the 'Detachment Photograph Album'*

THE SHROPSHIRE & MONTGOMERYSHIRE LIGHT RAILWAY UNDER MILITARY CONTROL 1940-1960

The Permanent Way gang attending to the packing of a length within Kinnerley Station. Whereas much of the line, and the pointwork at Kinnerley, had been relaid with the WD standard of 75lb per yard flat-bottom rail, some of the old S&M bullhead rail was still in use in the station and sidings – this view shows the joint between the two types (in the foreground). Jacks and packing shovels were the traditional way of keeping the top of the rail level. One of the smaller Wickham Rail Cars had just dropped off a passenger at the far end of the Down platform. Two vans of the breakdown train were in the bay platform – the nearest lettered 'S M R No. 1 WD Breakdown Train' – together with the L&SWR Saloon and a WD standard brake van. *David Petterson, from the 'Detachment Photograph Album'*

Looking eastwards through Kinnerley Station, from just in front of the block post, towards Shrewsbury. Standing on the bay platform line, on the right, were two vans from the breakdown train, the nearest lettered 'SMR WD Breakdown Train No. 2'. In front of the vans were two lightweight trolleys of a type that could be towed by rail cars if necessary. The points in the foreground (lever 4 in the block post) had already been taken out of use – note the fishplate screwed to the sleeper to prevent the switch rails from accidentally moving. *R. K. Cope (RKC/B309) from the 'Detachment Photograph Album'*

THE WAR DEPARTMENT RUNS THE RAILWAY

On a railway run by men who were young and often inexperienced, derailments were a fact of life. Some might say 'accidents will happen' but the Sergeant Instructor would probably reply 'accidents never happen, they are always caused'. Here in an incident in the 1950s one of the LT&S coaches had split the points and each bogie had gone down a different side of the passing loop until both derailed. Another job for the jacks. The coach, now owned by the War Department, had been renumbered WD 9200 in the post-war number series.
Photographer unknown, from the 'Detachment Photograph Album'

Sometimes Ramsay's intervention was soundly based, his experience of the line being greater than that of the military. In 1942 the WD, prompted by complaints from the civilian police in Shrewsbury, recognised the urgent need for toilets at Abbey Station for use by soldiers awaiting recreational trains back to Camp after a night out in the town. The Army quickly erected a small suitable structure just inside the entrance gates. When Ramsay found out about this he objected to the location chosen, while acknowledging that it was too late to make any change because the building had been completed. The toilet had been placed just beyond the buffer stops at the end of the main line, and Ramsay knew that on more than one occasion trains approaching Abbey Station down the steep gradient had got out of control and crashed through these buffer stops.

Accidents

On 5th November 1941, the tender of WD 8236 derailed on the points at the west end of the station at Nesscliff, blocking the line and partly blocking the public road. WD 8108 attended with a breakdown train, consisting of the horsebox, now lettered 'Engineering Dept. Kinnerley'.

Friday 13th March 1942 saw a 'heavy shunt' at Abbey, in which two vans (one was NE 150107 and one belonging to the GWR), were pushed over the buffer stops at the end of the platform line and into the centre of the public road beyond, coming to rest on their sides. Two locomotives were in attendance by 12.50. The Royal Engineers placed lengths of rail on their sides in the roadway, levered the vans on to them, and pulled the vehicles clear. Graham Vincent's diary recorded 'No-one hurt – all was cleared up in a few hours'.

Whilst derailments were to be expected on a line operated by inexperienced (and often young) soldiers, they seldom did serious damage – though they did add to the burden for the maintenance men. There were also some more serious accidents. In December 1941, WD 97 (which had only arrived on the S&M on 15th December) was involved in a collision with the new diesel WD 44. The diesel had to be returned to its makers, and a new tender found for WD 97.

Most serious of all was a head-on collision between Quarry and Shrawardine block posts in good weather early on the morning of 26th July 1943. Discipline in the working of the train by telephone had become slack. An unauthorised man took a phone call and gave a 'line clear' permission. As the result of this irregular working, both drivers were in possession of 'line clear' tickets. Dean Goods WD 176 hauling six coaches collided with WD 212 (one of the J15 Class, ex-LNER) hauling two brake vans as a passenger train. Eighteen soldiers were injured, but only one was hospitalised – fortunately there were few men in the coaches that telescoped. Both locomotives suffered severe damage at the front end, and the tender of WD 212 was so heavily damaged that it was broken up on site. Dean Goods WD 176 was scrapped in January 1944 because the damage resulting from the collision was beyond economic repair. There was some telescoping of the coaches, and ex-LT&S vehicles 3070, 3067 and 6399 were judged to be 'not worth repair' – indeed, they were stripped down at the site of the collision.

Safety at level crossings

One consequence of the much greater use of the line was that the local authority became concerned about the increased danger at the three locations where the railway crossed a public road. On Tuesday 13th October 1942 a lorry travelling towards Kinnerley was crossing the line at Pentre (Nesscliff) when it was struck by a train travelling tender first. The

WD 212, stabled on a back siding in the yard at Ford (Quarry) after sustaining damage in a head-on collision on 26th July 1943. Its tender is absent – it had been so much damaged during the collision that it had been cut up on site. Behind WD 212 stood the tender of the Dean Goods locomotive that had been hauling the Down direction train. The dent in the tender shows where the buffers of the following coach had ridden up over the buffers of the tender on impact. On the extreme right of this picture can be seen the end of one of the French Ferry vans which had been trapped in Britain at the fall of France and which were taken by the Army for its use.

S. H. Pearce Higgins, reference 44/2

lorry was pushed some distance up the line. The lorry driver was pinned between the wreckage of his vehicle and the wheels of the locomotive tender and died at the scene. His assistant on the lorry received serious head injuries. The inquest opened the following day to take evidence of identification only, and was adjourned until 13th November. At the resumed hearing, the WD engine driver, aged 23, gave evidence that he blew the engine whistle continuously for a considerable distance before the level crossing, and was travelling at a speed of between 8 and 10 miles per hour when he reached the crossing. He was unable to see the lorry until he was about 200 yards from it, and he thought that the lorry was going to turn off the road before reaching the level crossing. His engine was about seven yards from the crossing when the lorry moved on to the railway. He immediately applied the brake and reversed the locomotive, but the lorry was pushed some distance into Nesscliff Station. A foreman for the General Post Office, who was travelling in a van nearby, confirmed the driver's evidence, and that the speed of the train was not more than 10 mph. The Coroner returned a verdict of 'Accidental Death', with the rider that since it was clear that the lorry driver was not aware of the approach of the train, more prominent notices warning road users should be placed.

By 16th February 1943, when the issue came to a head, there had been three accidents and one fatality. It was agreed that at Maesbrook, on the line from Kinnerley to Llanymynech, the increase in rail traffic was insufficient to be a danger, but at Nesscliff (600 yards west of Nesscliff East block post) and at Shoot Hill (500 yards east of Ford & Crossgates), on the main line to Hookagate exchange sidings, it clearly was. The Army decided to erect pole barriers (in those days still called 'continental crossings') at these two stations. They were the standard WD design and cheap to build. Local authority approval was readily obtained, but the S&M objected. The Light Railway Order stipulated that if any level crossing gates were provided they should normally be closed against the railway. The S&M was concerned that after the War the local authorities would insist on the pole barriers being replaced by full level-crossing gates. Nonetheless, the installation of the barriers was authorised by the WD on 4th February 1944 at a cost of £103, and on 13th April the contract was let for the provision of the pole barriers and Type 'C' huts for the crossing keepers. The barriers had red targets fitted and hooks on which red lights could be hung at night. The crossing-keepers' huts were apparently not equipped with telephones at first, for an order for two sets of 'F' Mark II phones to put the keepers on the omnibus telephone circuit was placed on 21st September 1944. Photographs show that pole barriers were later installed at both Maesbrook and Wern Las.

Old and new platforms – and other new works

The WD retained in use the platforms of the old S&M stations, except at Shoot Hill, Cruckton, Edgerley, Shrawardine (where the running line was on a different alignment from the old S&M line) and Hookagate, where the old platform had been removed during the construction of the exchange sidings. New platforms were built on the main line at:

- Ford Yard (180 feet long plus the ramps, adjacent to the Traffic Offices in the main yard and thus several hundred yards north of Ford & Crossgates S&M Station)
- Shrawardine, on the opposite side of the level crossing from the old platform
- Pentre, east of the old Nesscliff & Pentre Station
- Nesscliff, west of the old Nesscliff & Pentre Station
- Kinnerley, about a half-mile east of the main Station.

These platforms were located relatively close to the depots to which men had to travel, and although termed 'halts' they were substantially built of concrete and were much longer than many of the old S&M platforms. Further platforms were constructed away from the main lines, on the lines in Sub-depots. These were also substantially built, the three authorised on 10th November 1943 costing £1,340.

The WD also built a four-platform station on the short spur into the main camp, sometimes known as Lonsdale (after the Colonel of that

THE WAR DEPARTMENT RUNS THE RAILWAY

name), but referred to in the Working Instructions as Nesscliff Camp. No shelter was provided on the platforms, though there was a building on Platform No. 1.

The authorisation of 10th November 1943 also included two Area Foremen's Huts (£170), three observation shelters for the police (£100) and a Yard Foreman's office, telephone huts, water supplies and a water tower (location not specified) at a cost of £2,135.

Additional lighting was found necessary for Road/Rail Transit (RRT) work, and authority was given on 4th February 1944 for Category 'C' lighting in Ford Yard plus lighting in Nesscliff RRT, at a cost of £235.

Traffic

The munitions traffic built quickly after the Depot was ready for 'receipts' as from 12th January 1942. Details of the ordnance traffic are hard to discover, but papers note that during the first three weeks of February 1942 346 wagons were received and 73 dispatched. Daily observations recorded that on 14th April 1942, 9.30am, 40 wagons outwards were worked by LMS 0-8-0 No. 9273, and on Friday 17th April 57 wagons hauled by LMS 0-8-0 9205 passed Meole Brace on the GWR line at 8.15. A census for one week in October 1944 recorded 2,974 wagon movements and 9,002 passenger journeys.

Sergeant Thorne recalled that in the run up to the Second Battle of El Alamein (23rd October to 5th November 1942), the Depot was working night and day to get ammunition out. The Depot was so busy that the operators had to get special permission to allow loose shunting (propelling wagons sharply and then stopping the engine so that the wagons ran on down the siding on their own until stopping by collision – at very low speed if the shunters judged the use of the hand brake properly – with the stationary wagons). Most of the loaded outwards wagons went via the docks in South Wales. To ease congestion the empty wagons came back on to the S&M via Llanymynech.

The WD was required to work the civilian traffic offering, of which the stone traffic was the most significant element – as this table prepared by Geoffrey Bannister shows.

Year	Tons
Jan to Dec 1940	Nil (Melverley bridge out of use)
Jan to Dec 1941	Nil
Nov 1942 to Oct 1943	22,540
Nov 1943 to Oct 1944	24,920
Nov 1944 to Oct 1945	22,856
Nov 1945 to Oct 1946	20,246
Nov 1946 to Oct 1947	20,536
Nov 1947 to Oct 1948	21,169

The other civilian traffic outwards was primarily agricultural produce, though traffic in livestock had all but ceased by 1938 (when only 106 animals were carried, 66 of them being pigs). Foremost in this was the seasonal traffic in sugar beet.

Year	Wagons	Total beet traffic (tons)
1936	159	1,398
1937	68	549
1938	58	468
1939	330	2,753
1940	158	1,342
1941	181	1,434
1942	183	1,498
1943	218	1,932
1944	226	1,854
1945	370	3,384
1946	396	3,611
1947	348	3,207

The loading of this traffic fell disproportionately on a few stations, as these figures for 1947 show:

Edgebold	140 tons
Ford	1,098 tons
Shrawardine	448 tons
Nesscliff	293 tons
Kinnerley	972 tons
Maesbrook	256 tons

There were times when the Depot was very busy with ordnance traffic and some of the beet traffic had to go away by road.

Apart from the 'hub' of the system at Kinnerley, Ford and Crossgates was the principal intermediate station. In the year from March 1946 to February 1947, the tonnage of civilian traffic handled (in addition to 1,099 tons of sugar beet during the 1946-47 'campaign') amounted to:

Month	Outwards (barley, wheat, potatoes)	Inwards goods	Inwards basic slag and lime	Inwards coal	Inwards total tonnage
1946					
March	193	94	114	46	254
April	345	160	35	46	241
May	259	25	56	46	127
June	10	30	–	40	70
July	1	30	42	57	129
August	14	38	38	24	100
Sept.	79	27	32	41	100
Oct.	76 (a)	44	34	52	130
Nov.	156	51	26	56	133
Dec.	130	45	30	37	112
1947					
Jan.	264 (b)	39	14	40	93
Feb.	22	17	24	44	85

Notes: (a) Mainly fruit (damsons) (b) All potatoes

One train daily usually shunted the intermediate civilian goods yards, although if necessary the traffic could be worked by any trip. One working that was exclusively for civilian traffic was the trip working from Hookagate to Shrewsbury Abbey, over which section of line there was no military goods traffic. The level of traffic is shown by the number of wagons inwards to Abbey in the year 1949:

January	115	July	92	Total for the year	1,367
February	111	August	98	Average per week	26
March	115	September	132		
April	93	October	160		
May	115	November	113		
June	103	December	120		

Even if the civilian traffic remained at a low level, it was anticipated that the military traffic would be considerable. A meeting was held on 29th January 1942 in Shrewsbury – attended by representatives of the WD, the S&M company, the LMS and the GWR – to consider how to avoid the expense of keeping duplicate records of all the traffic. By this date the new exchange sidings at Hookagate were in use for military and contractor's traffic, but it was envisaged that Meole Brace sidings would continue to be used for civilian traffic. WD and contractor's traffic would henceforth be labelled 'Shrewsbury (via GW or LMS) for Hookagate'. The WD made up its daily return of rolling stock on hand (the 'daily state return') at 17.00 each day. The main line companies had for many years undertaken this task at 10.00. It was agreed to take the WD report at 17.00 as the 10.00 report for the following day – not much would have changed in between. Demurrage (the charge for retaining wagons beyond the allotted time for unloading them) came into sharp focus. The WD wanted an extra day (that is, demurrage time only to run from when the wagon was placed on the destination siding for the customer on the S&M). The main line companies (under very heavy pressure from the Government and customers in the use of rolling stock of all kinds) had to insist that the demurrage time begin from the date the wagons were handed over at the exchange sidings – and won their point.

The WD provided a small shed at Hookagate for GWR staff involved on invoice work, and a grease store for the GWR wagon examiners. Numbertaking work would be done by WD men. The GWR would send a man across daily to extract such details as the GWR needed. For the civilian traffic exchanged at Meole Brace, the signalman there would act as numbertaker. Wagon labels would be the responsibility of the WD, the GWR providing a copy of the Merchandise Route Book to allow this to be done. Movement Control of the WD dealt with the labelling and routing. The WD was told that its wagon labels were too flimsy to survive wet weather on any length of journey, so Standard Wagon Labels were to be used. The WD undertook to collect wagon sheets (tarpaulins) and ropes – including those from wagons unloaded by the contractors – and return them to the GWR.

The GWR was concerned that so far as possible, military traffic should be made up in train-loads through to its destination. What was not wanted was for wagons to be sent out by the WD 'rough' and thus requiring sorting in the main line marshalling yards at Shrewsbury (though this was unavoidable for the civilian goods traffic). The marshalling yards at Shrewsbury were already under intense pressure as a result of coastwise shipping being diverted from the east coast to west coast ports – from which the GWR then had to handle traffic for the eastern side of England in addition to traditional traffic flows. The expansion of the GWR yard at Coton Hill was expected to provide enough capacity for that company to handle additional traffic, but the LMS envisaged that any extra sorting might have to be done as far away as Crewe.

In order to allow military traffic to work through Shrewsbury non-stop, it was agreed that the Shrewsbury to Welshpool line, (at that time classed as a GWR 'Blue route' [LMS route category 3]) would be upgraded on the section from Shrewsbury to Hookagate to GWR 'Red' allowing the use of larger and heavier locomotives (including LMS Class 5 Mixed Traffic and Class 6 Freight). The WD for its part agreed that main line engines could take water in the WD yard at Hookagate, to reduce the need to come to a stand on the main lines in the Shrewsbury area. There was adequate water capacity at Hookagate – the tank there was 5,000 gallons capacity fed at 1,000 gallons per hour. The WD also undertook to keep one reception line at Hookagate free at all times, so that any incoming train could immediately be shunted clear of the main line.

Traffic receipts on the Joint line were pooled. Either the GWR or the LMS would provide locomotive power for full load trains. Mixed traffic would be worked by the LMS. The timetable for the exchange workings for civilian goods traffic was:

09.15 Coleham Yard (Shrewsbury) to Meole Brace (arrive 09.20)
09.55 Meole Brace to Coleham (arrive 10.00)
12.45 SX Coleham to Cruckmeole Junction (call at Meole Brace at 12.50). Saturdays Excepted.
13.45 SX Cruckmeole Junction to Coleham (call at Meole Brace 14.20). Saturdays Excepted.
12.51 SO Coleham to Meole Brace (12.56). Saturdays Only.
13.20 SO Meole Brace to Coleham (13.25). Saturdays Only.

Civilian traffic, made up and awaiting a locomotive. A view westwards through Kinnerley Station on 21st June 1947. *H. C. Casserley, reference 49038*

Chapter 4
LOCAL RAILWAY WORKING INSTRUCTIONS (LRWI)

In common with most railways operated by the British Army, the S&M Light Railway was run in accordance with the Military Railway Rule Book of 1938 (and any amendments thereto) supplemented by Working Instructions specific to the S&M. These rules applied to the whole of the S&M system except the Criggion Branch beyond the 'Limit of WD Operating and Maintenance' board at the south end of the locomotive roads at Kinnerley. This continued up to the closure of the line, although from 1947 the railway was 'WD Civilian' and operated by civilian personnel of 1 Railway Group Royal Engineers. The content of this chapter is based on the LRWI issued in 1958. By then the block posts at Llanymynech, Maesbrook, Edgerley, Nesscliff West, Shrawardine and Cruckton had been taken out of use, but the basic operating principles remained unchanged.

The Central Ammunition Depot (CAD) was divided into four Sub-depots, each with two Districts:

No. 1 comprising Maesbrook and Argoed Districts
No. 2 comprising Kinnerley and Nesscliff Districts
No. 3 comprising Shrawardine and Pentre Districts
No. 4 Alberbury comprising Ford and Loton Park.

The UP direction of working was Llanymynech to Shrewsbury (Abbey).

Station codes were used to abbreviate communications. The codes set out in the 1958 LWRI were:

Llanymynech	LNK	Shrawardine	SDN
Maesbrook	MBK	Ford Quarry	QRY
Wern Las	WLS	Ford and Crossgates	FRD
Argoed	AGD	Criggion	CGN
Kinnerley	KNY	Shoot Hill Level Crossing	SHL.X
Edgerley	EGY	Melverley	MLY
Nesscliff Level Crossing	NCF.X	Hookagate West	HGT.W
Nesscliff East	NCF.E	Hookagate East	HGT.E
Pentre	PNT	Meole Brace Station	MBE
Abbey Station	ABY		

Some maps, and some Army documents, spell the place name of Nesscliff as 'Nesscliffe'. The LRWI use the spelling Nesscliff, and this has been adopted in this book.

Train working on the single line

The railway was single track throughout, and most of the single line sections were worked by Telephone and Ticket. The exceptions were:
a) the sections from Llanymynech to Kinnerley and from Hookagate East to Abbey (both of which were worked by 'One Engine in Steam').
b) the section from Kinnerley to Nesscliff East, which was worked by electric token instruments – but if Nesscliff East Block Post was not open, Kinnerley worked to whichever block post was open using Telephone and Ticket. This method of working would be required if the blockman for Nesscliff East travelled out from Kinnerley on the first train.

There were three standard Army forms in regular use:

Army Form A3127. Line Clear Ticket. This was a white ticket that served the same function as a train staff – it was the driver's authority to travel on the single line.

Army Form A3128. This orange coloured form could be used either as a Caution Ticket or a Caution Order (the wording not required being crossed out). It was used as a Ticket as an authority to enter a section of line at Caution (the reason of caution being required to be added to the form). It was used as a Caution Order where there was some other form of authority to enter on to the single line (such as a train staff) or where no such authority was required (such as on a siding or Gathering Line).

Army Form A3129. This red coloured form – the Special Caution Ticket or Order – was used whenever it was necessary to warn a driver of an obstruction or possible obstruction. It could be used either as a Ticket (authorising the driver to enter a single line section) or as an Order where there was some other form of authority to enter on to the single line (such as a train staff) or where no such authority was required (such as on a siding or Gathering Line).

Under Telephone and Ticket working, the blockman first obtained acceptance of the train into the single line section by exchange of messages by telephone. In normal working, the blockman at the end of the section at which the train was to enter then wrote out a paper

A form for a 'Line Clear' ticket, printed in black on off-white paper.

Top: A form for a Caution Order or Caution 'Line Clear' ticket, printed in black on orange paper. *Bottom*: A form for a Special Caution Order or Special Caution 'Line Clear' ticket, printed in black on red paper.

'Line Clear' ticket, which was handed to the driver. The tickets were kept in a book, but there was no counterfoil to be retained in the book by the issuing blockman. When a train had passed through the single line section, the driver surrendered the paper ticket to the blockman, who wrote the word 'Cancelled' across the face of the ticket. Used tickets were kept on a spike at the receiving block post for one month from the date of issue, and were then burned. The Orange and Red ticket books did have counterfoils for the tickets/orders issued – these counterfoils were kept for one month, and then sent to the Line Inspector for disposal.

Telephone and Ticket working allowed block posts to be opened by men travelling by train. The first train in effect 'opened the line'. The Controller authorised the opening of block posts, and no block post would be allowed to open with a train in section. Kinnerley normally opened first. For the working of the train that opened the line, special arrangements were made, since there was no blockman at the far end of the section to confirm that the line was clear and to accept the train. In these circumstances the driver was given a red Special Caution Ticket, endorsed 'Opening and Examination of Line' and made out to the furthest block post to be opened. A Special Caution Ticket was used because it was possible that the line was obstructed – there was no blockman at the other end to accept the train at 'Line Clear'. The driver then proceeded with appropriate caution. The train stopped to set down the blockmen to open the block posts as required by Control. The driver gave up the Red Caution Ticket when he reached the furthest block post named on it. If for any reason his train needed to proceed beyond that block post, it would be worked by 'One Engine in Steam' on instructions from Control.

If a block post was already open and it was necessary to open an intermediate block post, the driver was issued with an Orange Caution Ticket, endorsed 'Opening of Intermediate Block Posts' made out to the furthest block post already open. The blockman would be set down at the intermediate block post, but the block post was not opened until after the train had reached the further block post already open (since a block post could not be opened with a train in section).

The door keys for all block posts, level crossing huts and yard foreman's offices were kept in a key case in the Control Office at Kinnerley, from which they had to be drawn by early turn men at the start of each day – and to which they had to be returned daily by the late turn men.

When closing a block post and travelling by train, the blockman obtained a 'Line Clear' acceptance from the block post ahead. When his train arrived, he sent 'Train out of Section' and 'Closing block post' to the block post in rear and 'Train entering section' and 'Closing block post' to the block post ahead. He then boarded the train. The blockman in rear then awaited to hear from the blockman at the block post in advance of the one closing down that the train had left the section there, and that the extended block section was clear.

Points at intermediate sidings worked by single hand levers were to be set and clipped for the main line when not in use. At some locations, ground frames were provided, released by keys:

Llanymynech and Maesbrook – released by a key on the 'One Engine in Steam' staff.
Nesscliff & Pentre (frames at each end of the loop siding in the Civilian Yard) – Annetts Keys, normally kept in the Nesscliff Level Crossing hut. If the crossing was unmanned, Control had to ensure that the key to the hut was carried by the Guard of the train.
Nesscliff East – released by Annetts Key held at the block post.
Shrawardine, Civilian Yard and the entrance to the North Balloon Gathering Line – Annetts Key, kept at Control and carried by the Guard on the Civilian Goods.
Meole Brace – released by Annetts Key normally kept at Hookagate East, and carried by the Guard on the Civilian Goods.

Working the traffic

Standard maximum loads were set out in the LRWI:

Llanymynech to Ford	Up (towards Shrewsbury) and down directions, 33 Loaded or 55 in total.
Ford to Hookagate West	Up direction, 33 Loaded or 55 in total. Down direction 25 loaded or 45 in total.
Hookagate West to Abbey	Up direction 15 loaded or 25 in total. Down direction 10 loaded or 20 in total.

All (oil) tank wagons hauled between Hookagate and Abbey had to be separated from the engine by one wagon either empty or containing non-flammables.

Loose shunting of Red Stores (ammunition) was strictly prohibited. Loose shunting towards sheds was also prohibited, and the brakes of the three leading wagons were to be pinned down before any rakes of wagons were placed on shed spurs. Following accidents in the early days of the Depot in which vehicles were shunted into shed doors, sabots (removable wheel stops) were provided on all shed spurs at the 50 feet mark (a white mark on the nearest sleeper) and were to be in position at all times except when a movement in to or out of the shed was taking place. The person responsible for the shed was responsible for the correct position of the sabot (not the train crew). It was forbidden for engines or rail cars to enter the sheds. The wagons had to be pushed by hand out as far as the fifty feet marker, and thus outside the sabot. The earlier decision to lower the rails inside some of the sheds to reduce the height (and cost of construction) of the walls resulted in some gradients up out of the sheds that made the task of manhandling the wagons out of these sheds significantly harder.

The number of wagons propelled into any shed spur was limited to twelve wagons. When approaching any wagons to be moved, the shunter was required to:

Check that the wagon nearest the shed was more than fifty feet from it and that the sabot was in place.
Check that the brakes on each standing wagon were applied and that the wagons were coupled together.

Internal user stock was not to be allowed to leave the S&M on to the GWR/LMS (later BR) main line without first being examined by a Railways representative. This applied to all coaches and vans owned or hired by the WD, all brake vans, all internal user wagons, all flat wagons owned by the WD – and all Criggion wagons bearing a plate 'N.P. 2'.

Rail cars could be used to carry small loads. Wickham Cars could carry 10 cwts (half a ton) and Drewry Cars 30 cwts. A Wickham Trailer was allowed 10 cwts, and a Drewry Car Trailer 30 cwts. The use of two trailers at the same time, whether loaded or not, was prohibited, as was the use of trailers between two rail cars. Rail cars were not to be used during the hours of darkness or in bad visibility (fog) expect by special permission.

Speed restrictions applied throughout the Depot:

On the Main Line, 25 mph (15 mph for rail cars) reduced to 10 mph at Paper Mill and Shrawardine level crossings
In the Sub-depots, 15 mph on Gathering Lines, 5 mph over all facing points and all level crossings

Water supply columns existed only at Abbey, Hookagate, Ford Marshalling Yard, Kinnerley locomotive shed and Argoed. Inspection pits were provided at Hookagate, Ford Yard and Kinnerley locomotive shed. Drivers were not permitted to clean or draw fires on the main line, in stations, yards (except over the pits) or on shed spurs.

The centre of the operation of the railway. Kinnerley locomotive shed and yard, looking towards Criggion on 21st September 1958. The water tower dominated the scene, with the shed for Wickham Rail Cars to the left, and the turnouts leading to the Drewry Rail Car shed in the right foreground. This view shows two types of Stop board in use. That for movements from the Drewry Rail Car shed has no provision for the use of lamps at night, because rail cars were not to be used during the hours of darkness without special permission. The Stop board leading from the Criggion Branch and the locomotive shed, from where movements after dark would be more common, was fitted with a ledge on which a lamp was placed during hours of darkness, to make the location of the Stop board clear. H. C. Casserley, reference 94270

THE SHROPSHIRE & MONTGOMERYSHIRE LIGHT RAILWAY UNDER MILITARY CONTROL 1940-1960

The entrance from the road to the S&M station was hardly welcoming, even when the railway was still open for passenger traffic – this photo was taken on 9th October 1931. The entrance for passengers is to the left, the roadway into the goods yard on the right. *R. K. Cope (RKC/BB45) from the 'Detachment Photograph Album'*

Abbey (Shrewsbury)

The points to the sidings were normally set for the platform line, and were operated from a two lever ground frame released by the 'One Engine in Steam' staff. Incoming trains were required to halt at a Stop board 74 yards in the approach side of the facing points, to allow the fireman to go forward, check that the points were correctly set, and hand signal the driver forward. There were also Stop boards applying for movements from the sidings onto the main line. Drivers had to obtain authority before passing them. Shunting operations were in the charge of the brakesman/shunter who travelled with the train. The brakesman/shunter (the driver in the case of a rail car) was required to telephone Control (using a telephone on the platform, code ring 3 long 1 short) to advise that any returning train was ready to depart, and to be given any additional messages that might have become necessary.

The recreational train (6d return fare), which ran every Saturday night during the war years, was an operational headache. The return trip was timed to leave Abbey at 23.00, but the drunken passengers seldom all arrived on time. With three coaches packed and passengers standing it was a difficult climb out of Abbey up the 1 in 50 gradient from a standing start – often made more difficult by men pulling the communication cord (which made a partial brake application). Military Police were assigned to the train to try to prevent the problem and generally keep order, but the train crew sometimes had to disconnect the continuous brake between the locomotive and the coaches simply to make any progress at all.

Beyond the uninviting entrance was a ramshackle covered walkway from the gap in the roadside wall (to the left) through to the platform ramp, seen here on 22nd May 1955. There was no shelter for the passengers on the platform, so when the 'recreational' train was running on a wet night, this limited accommodation could be rather crowded. Evident is the proximity of the buffer stops to the latrines (on the left) that the War Office constructed to accommodate the soldiery after their night out in the town – a matter complained about by Ramsay. *Brian Hilton, reference 53/9*

'Collier' locomotive 8236 shunting the Civilian Goods traffic at Abbey, with the Sapper brakesman/shunter checking the whereabouts of the photographer. Note that the tender is lettered W D without any arrow in between.
S. H. Pearce Higgins, reference 44/5

Above: The rear of the goods warehouse at Abbey Station was typical of the state of disrepair that the S&M Railway had reached before the WD leased the railway. The WD did very little by way of repairs at Shrewsbury, where the traffic was purely for 'civilian goods'. *Lens of Sutton Association*

Right: Shrewsbury Abbey Station was well named. The Abbey of Saint Peter and Saint Paul, commonly known as Shrewsbury Abbey, was a Benedictine monastery founded in 1083 by the Norman Earl Roger de Montgomery. Much of the structure was dismantled following the Dissolution of the Monasteries, and Telford constructed his road to North Wales through part of the site. The Abbey church, which survived and has seen considerable restoration work, is across the road from the site of the station entrance. The Pulpit of the refectory of the former Abbey was at the end of one of the sidings in the goods yard. In this photograph, posed for *Soldier* magazine, one of the men gives scale to just how close the Pulpit was to the buffer stops. *Photo by courtesy of* Soldier *magazine*

THE SHROPSHIRE & MONTGOMERYSHIRE LIGHT RAILWAY UNDER MILITARY CONTROL 1940-1960

In August 1946 one of the Dean Goods engines – WD 70094 – in the platform at Abbey with a recreational train made up of four of the LT&S coaches. For once the locomotive had been lightly cleaned, revealing the W↑D lettering on the tender. The locomotive carried headlamps with the code of 'express passenger'. Across the platform, on the bay line, can be seen part of one of the former North London Railway vehicles in use as a store. *Millbrook House Ltd, courtesy Roger Carpenter*

Looking outwards from beside the buffer stops at Abbey Station in 1947, the bleak aspect of the platform was reinforced by the rather unhappy sight of so many vans and old coaches finishing their days in use as warehouses, slowly rotting away under wagon sheets. Even part of the slope up to the platform from the entrance passageway had broken down. There was one gesture towards safety – four wooden poles with the most basic lighting for when recreational trains returned in the hours of darkness. *Graham Vincent*

LOCAL RAILWAY WORKING INSTRUCTIONS (LRWI)

The Abbey church of Saint Peter and Saint Paul dominates this view of the S&M station in April 1947. The lack of shelter for passengers on the platform is notable, as is the number of old wagons still in use as warehouses with wagon sheets draped over them in an attempt to keep the water out. Only the main running line had been relaid in WD 75lb flat bottomed rail.
Millbrook House Ltd, courtesy Roger Carpenter

A view of the yard at Abbey Station, taken on 21st September 1958, showing the hand-operated crane in the yard as well as the substantial water tank which in times past had fed the 'parachute' water column at the end of the platform. By this date all the old vehicles used as warehouses had been cleared away by the Army, making the yard look quite empty. WD 188 stood waiting to return with empty coaches after hauling an enthusiasts' special.
Bluebell Railway Museum Archive – J. J. Smith Collection, reference 6-86-6

THE SHROPSHIRE & MONTGOMERYSHIRE LIGHT RAILWAY UNDER MILITARY CONTROL 1940-1960

A busy time at Abbey Station, with 8236 in the goods yard – its brakesman/shunter striding purposefully towards the engine – and a passenger train in the platform. The Dean Goods on the passenger train still carried its GWR number plates – 2425 – with the lettering WD 96 rather crudely stencilled on the cabside above. WD 96 had been one of the first Dean Goods to arrive on the S&M and was later given the unofficial name of **Kinnerley Castle.**
S. H. Pearce Higgins, reference S&M 2

The approach to Shrewsbury Abbey terminus was down the steepest gradient on the line. This view shows that the WD had removed the signals here, so driving an evening recreation train down into Abbey Station in the blackout was not an easy task.
A. E. Bennett, Transport Treasury B4267

On 26th July 1948, WD 75131 was photographed with a substantial train climbing the bank out of Abbey Station. *Geoffrey Bannister, courtesy Andrew Bannister*

THE SHROPSHIRE & MONTGOMERYSHIRE LIGHT RAILWAY UNDER MILITARY CONTROL 1940-1960

EXCHANGE SIDINGS BETWEEN WD LINE AND THE LMS & GWR JOINT LINE

MEOLE BRACE

[Track diagram showing lines from Hanwood and Hookagate, with Down Main / Up Main, 372 feet clear sidings, W.D. Running Line, Footbridge, Coal Stack, Shrewsbury West Platform, to Shrewsbury (Abbey)]

HOOKAGATE
From a Tn 4 plan dated 20 November 1941

[Track diagram showing Footpath (now closed), GWR Signal Box, Down Main / Up Main, Station Limit board for West Block Post, W.D. Running Line, signals W, V, X, Y, Z, sidings of 1380 feet clear, 1486 feet, 797 feet, 700 feet, 598 feet, 485 feet, From Ford, Hookagate West Block Post, Water Tower, Coal stage, Shunting Neck 678 feet, to Meole Brace and Shrewsbury]

Hookagate East Block Post

Ground frame of four levers, working
Up WD stop signal (W)
Trap points in WD Sidings (X)
Release on GWR/LMS signal box for crossover Y (lever 3 in GF)
Down WD Stop signal (Z)

Crossover Y is operated from the GWR signal box, after release from Hookagate East.
The GWR signal box operates ground disc signal (V).

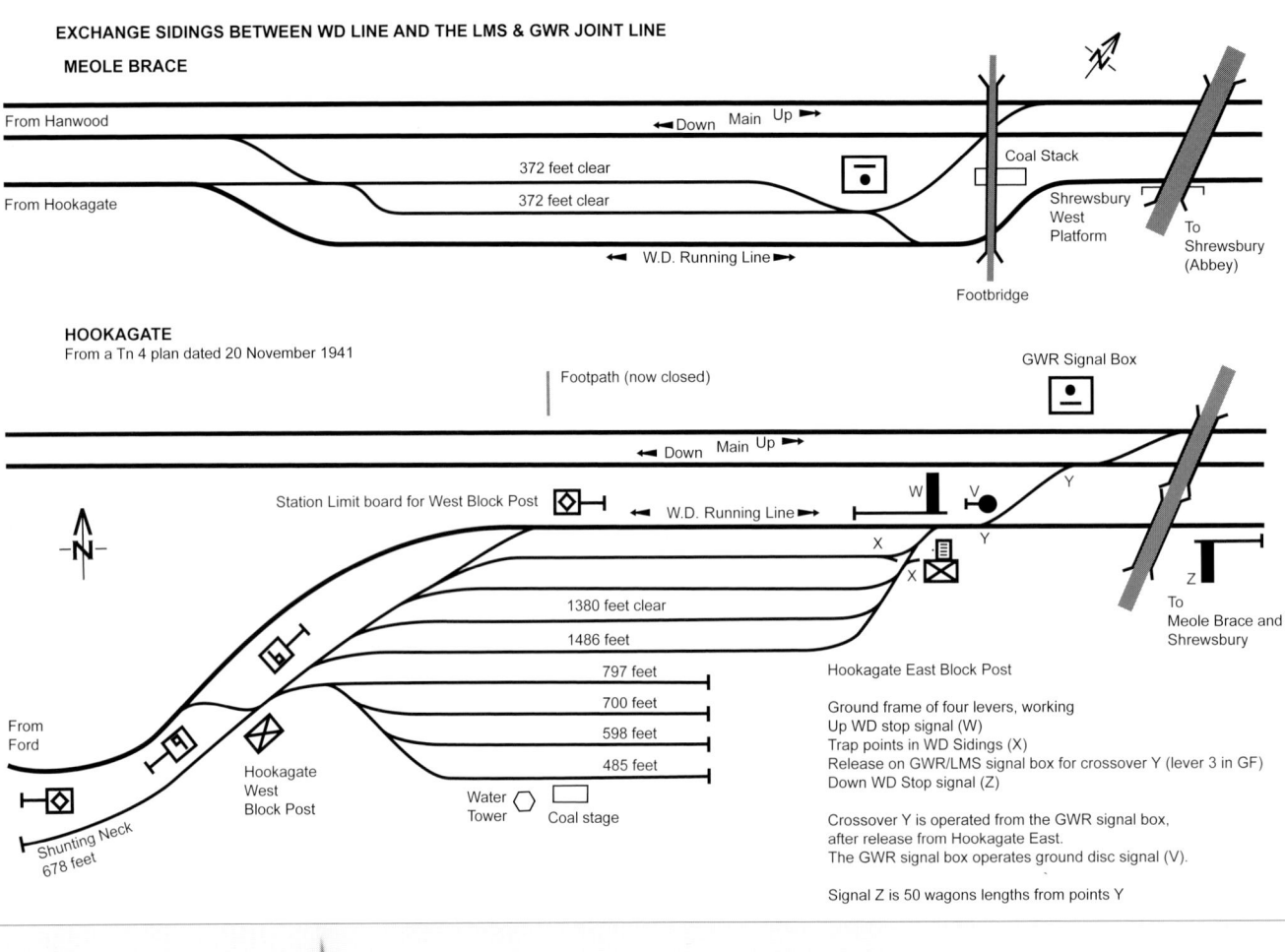

Signal Z is 50 wagons lengths from points Y

A view of the east end of Hookagate Yard, with the GWR/LMS Joint line on the left, and the WD running line in the centre foreground. The WD signal applying to this line had been supplied by the GWR, which had provided all the signalling for this installation. The brick-built hut was Hookagate East Block Post. Photo taken 16th April 1948.

R. K. Cope (RKC/B321) courtesy Roger Carpenter

A closer view of the junction, looking towards Shrewsbury on 12th October 1957, from a position just in front of East Block Post. The pointwork on the WD line was in WD standard 75lb rail, that of the GWR line in the then usual bull head pattern rail. Both ends of the crossover were worked from the GWR signal box (released by rod from a lever in the WD ground frame), as was the disc signal leading from the WD line on to the main line. *M. N. Bland*

Hookagate

Hookagate West Block Post was regarded as a crossing place, but the East Block Post was not. The Yard Foreman, situated at the West Block Post, was responsible for the working of the whole yard. The Hookagate East blockman had to obtain the Foreman's permission before allowing any train to enter or leave the yard – the Foreman authorised acceptance and decided the road on which the train was to be received.

Down direction trains were not to be stopped outside East Block Post unless absolutely unavoidable, thus leaving the access from the GWR (later British Railways) line free at all times. The line nearest to the GWR line was worked as the S&M running line (as a single line) and thus used only for the passage of trains between the East and West block posts. One other road had to be kept free at all times for the reception of incoming traffic from the main line, and the shunting neck at the west end of the yard was also to be kept free of stabled traffic.

A view through the junction, as seen by the driver of a main line train proceeding towards Welshpool, albeit after the closure of the S&M line. The crossover from the main line to the WD running line is clear, but the WD East Block Post is almost obscured behind the lamp post behind the signalman. The line from Hookagate towards Hanwood was singled in 1965, and thereafter Hookagate Signal Box had to be manned whenever trains were running (when it had been a block post on double line, it could be switched out when not required for traffic). The signal box was abolished on 18th November 1973 (five months after this photograph was taken), when the line was singled through to Shrewsbury Sutton Bridge Junction. *Photographer unknown*

THE SHROPSHIRE & MONTGOMERYSHIRE LIGHT RAILWAY UNDER MILITARY CONTROL 1940-1960

Hookagate East Block Post, photographed during an enthusiasts' visit (for which a Drewry Rail Car had been provided) on 12th October 1957. The ground frame levers were covered by the small lean-to extension to the block hut visible behind the member of the tour party. By this date the brick-built block post hut had – in common with many other structures on the WD railway – been painted with bitumen black paint. The inside of the open window shutter had been painted white, to give a clear background when it was necessary to give hand signals by flag.

M. N. Bland

The Yard Foreman decided the precedence of traffic. No train from Ford was to be allowed to enter the yard if a train had been accepted from the GWR, and once a movement on one of the reception roads had been agreed, no fouling movement was to be permitted. Before giving the release lever to the signalman in the main line signal box (lever number 3) the blockman at Hookagate East, in addition to obtaining the Yard Foreman's authorisation, had to ensure that any Up direction train accepted from West Block Post was either at a stand or had passed clear. The movement from the GWR on to the WD running line was protected from unauthorised movements out of the WD sidings by two trap points – very necessary in view of the gradient in this part of the yard. Adjacent to these trap points were Stop boards – drivers were not to pass these boards until handsignalled to do so by the blockman.

Down direction trains from Abbey, if going into the yard, were to do so at the West Block Post. An Up train was only to be accepted from West by the blockman at East if the 'One Engine in Steam' staff for the section from Hookagate East to Abbey was at the East Block Post. Hookagate East Block Post was not to close whilst the main line signal box was open, nor while a train was in the section Hookagate East to Abbey.

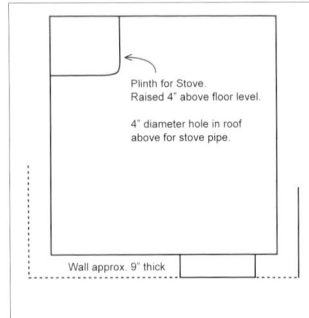

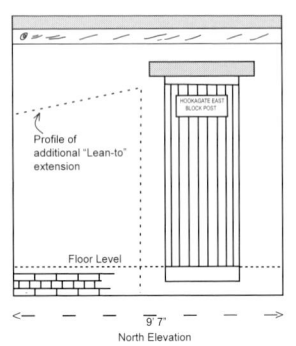

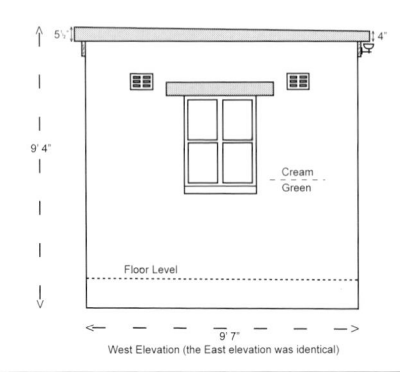

HOOKAGATE EAST BLOCK POST

Standard Hut, 8 feet square internal.
Walls of brick, English Bond.
Floor, roof and lintels of concrete.
Windows fitted with external shutters hinged to open towards rear of hut.
Painting - exterior, bituminous black
  - exterior wood, green
  - interior, green to 40in. above floor, cream above

LOCAL RAILWAY WORKING INSTRUCTIONS (LRWI)

The west end of Hookagate Yard on 6th February 1949, by which time some of the sidings were given over to the storage (and breaking up) of locomotives no longer required now that the Austerity 0-6-0ST locomotives had taken over the traffic. The water tank and coal stage on the back siding line can be seen, though access to coal was no longer necessary and was partly blocked by the line of dead engines. The GWR/LMS Joint line curved away north-westwards from the WD line, the location of the stopped-up footpath still clearly marked by the white painted gates. Just visible above the farthest tender in the dead engine line was the white-painted flagboard for the West Block Post (the block post was out of sight round the corner). The dead engines, from left to right, were WD 70169, 70196, 8182, 8108. The pale green paintwork on the 'Colliers' shows as markedly different from the black on the Dean Goods. *Norman Glover (No. 2640) courtesy F. A. Wycherley*

Hookagate Yard, looking over the sidings to the GWR/LMS Joint line. The GWR Down starting signal was at 'clear'. In front of the GWR signal, adjacent to the WD running line, was the Station Limit board for Hookagate West Block Post. The two Dean Goods engines were 70169 and 70196. 70169 had received the extended cab roof that the WD fitted to some engines of this class that worked in more exposed locations, such as on the Cairnryan Military Railway at No. 2 Military Port near Stranraer. *Norman Glover (No. 2644) courtesy F. A. Wycherley*

Beyond Hookagate towards Kinnerley, the WD line curved to the north-west and crossed over the GWR/LMS Joint line. This view shows the curve, looking towards Hookagate, on 16th April 1949. The end of the headshunt line for Hookagate Yard is visible on the right, as is the 'black diamond on white' Station Limit board applying to Up direction trains approaching Hookagate West.
R. K. Cope (RKC/B317) courtesy Roger Carpenter

Bridge No. 15 carried the S&M over the GWR/LMS Joint line. The abutments had been built to carry double track, but the girders were now for only a single line. The handrail was on one side of the bridge only, extended across the empty second abutment to reduce the risk of accidents. This view eastwards towards Hookagate shows standard WD 75lb flat bottom rail spiked to timber sleepers, using baseplates.
Photographer unknown

A view of the abutments built for double track, showing the handrail fitted on one side only of the S&M bridge – looking towards Cruckton.
R. M. Casserley, reference 18163K

LOCAL RAILWAY WORKING INSTRUCTIONS (LRWI)

Above: Looking uphill across Bridge No. 15 towards Cruckton, with the empty abutments on the left. This part of the main line had been relaid using 75lb rail bolted to WD pattern concrete sleepers. The WD concrete sleepers had slots cast in the centre, to reduce weight and materials required for manufacture. This meant that if the sleepers were packed more firmly under the centre of the sleeper than under the rails – and it was easier to do shovel packing this way – the load of passing trains could break the sleeper at the slotted portion. For this reason, it was standard practice where concrete sleepers were used to have a central V in the ballast – with stone (or ash) ballast used only under the rails and for the boxing in of the ends of the sleepers.
R. K. Cope (RKC/B314)

Above: On 21st September 1958 the SLS (Birmingham Area) special, hauled by WD 188, climbed the gradient away from Bridge 15 towards Cruckton – a view from one of the LT&S coaches. Note the very basic pole route on this section of line. *Photographer unknown*

Edgebold Station, by now showing the effects of years of disuse, looking towards Kinnerley. As on most of the S&M main line, the WD had provided ash as ballast when relaying in 1941. *Photographer unknown*

Cruckton

The loop north of the station was noted as out of use and had already been removed by 1st April 1947. No layout plan has been found.

Cruckton Station looking towards Kinnerley c1949, with the new flat bottomed rail laid beside the line in preparation for re-laying.
Geoffrey Bannister, courtesy Andrew Bannister

The station building at Cruckton was half covered by vegetation by the early 1950s, when a Drewry Rail Car paused briefly for visitors to take photographs. The WD track here was 75lb flat bottom rail fixed to 'pots', the gauge being maintained by steel tie bars between the 'pots'. *Brian Connell (Photos/Fifties Ref B63/10)*

LOCAL RAILWAY WORKING INSTRUCTIONS (LRWI)

Shoot Hill level crossing, looking towards Hookagate on 1st April 1947. The once tidy platform showed signs of decay, with the wooden railings all but collapsed although the S&M company's water tank was still standing, out of use. The track was still the original S&M bull head rail, though now on a neatly maintained bed of ash ballast. The original constructors of the railway line – the Potteries, Shrewsbury and North Wales Railway (PS&NWR) – had purchased land for a double track railway. This gave the additional width of the formation to the right of the running line on which the occupants of the Station House had established a lineside chicken coop. To the left was the Rule 103 Board, on which a fixed white light was displayed during the hours of darkness. If no crossing keeper was on duty to display a 'Proceed' hand signal, the driver had to stop his train at the board so that a member of the train crew could check that the crossing was clear, stop road traffic, and then handsignal the train over the crossing.
Graham Vincent

Shoot Hill Public Road Level Crossing

Pole barriers were installed at this crossing. They were normally kept in the raised position, and were lowered for the passing of each train. The barriers were fitted with red targets, and at night red lights were also to be fitted. The barriers were operated by a crossing keeper, for whom a hut was provided. There was a telephone in the hut. The crossing keeper was to listen to all calls and conversations passing between the block posts on either side, but he was not to initiate a call except in an emergency. The keeper was to lower the barriers immediately on hearing the 'Train Entering Section' (TES) message from Ford for an Up direction train, and keep them lowered until the train had passed. If Ford Block Post was closed, on hearing the TES message from Quarry, the keeper was to 'maintain a constant look-out in the direction of Ford', and to lower the barriers when the train passed through Ford Station. Similarly, on hearing the TES message from Hookagate (West or East) Block Post, he was to keep a constant look-out towards the overbridge to the east of the crossing, and to lower the barriers on first observing the train.

The approaching train was signalled over the crossing by the crossing keeper giving the 'move towards' hand signal (either arm moved across the body at shoulder level). During the hours of darkness, the signal was a white light waved slowly from side to side. The signals were to be given in such a way that they could not be seen from the road. If the driver of the train did not see any hand signal, he was to stop his train at the Rule 103 Board, and carry out that rule.

Rule 103 was not in the Military Railway Rule Book (MRRB) of 1938, but was added in the No. 2 amendment to the MRRB, dated 1st August 1942. It set out that where no one was on duty at a level crossing, the guard or fireman was to go ahead on to the road and after ascertaining that the crossing was clear and that approaching road traffic (if any) was at a stand, he was to handsignal the train over the crossing. Rail cars usually had a driver only. In these circumstances, the driver was to stop dead at the edge of the level crossing, alight from the rail car and look both ways along the road. If no road traffic was approaching, or any road traffic had either stopped before the crossing or passed clear of the crossing, the driver was to rejoin the rail car and proceed over the level crossing at walking pace. Normally, trains were restricted to 10 mph over this crossing.

The Rule 103 Boards were serviced by the early turn crossing keeper. Only signal oil (not paraffin) was to be used in the lamps, which were to be exhibited at all times during darkness or bad visibility. If a train from Ford to Hookagate exceeded twenty loaded wagons on a Saturday, a level crossing keeper had to be on duty at Shoothill.

THE SHROPSHIRE & MONTGOMERYSHIRE LIGHT RAILWAY UNDER MILITARY CONTROL 1940-1960

Shoot Hill level crossing on a later occasion (21st September 1958), looking along the straight towards Ford & Crossgates Station. The hut provided by the WD for the crossing keeper here was at the end of the platform. The original bull head rail had by this date been replaced with flat bottom rail on pressed steel ('tin') sleepers.
R. M. Casserley, reference 18160K

Ford Station, looking towards Shoot Hill and Hookagate, on 12th October 1957. The buildings in this photo are those that the WD inherited – the block post hut was just out of view to the photographer's left. The raised portions of the platforms, to create loading ramps for heavy loads, are apparent. The rear of the Down direction flagboard can be seen on the platform on the left – the Station Limit board is little more than a dot in the far distance. On the back of the flagboard were the two small shelves on which hand lamps could be placed (the light shining through the holes in the front of the flagboard) to give indications to the driver at night.
M. N. Bland

LOCAL RAILWAY WORKING INSTRUCTIONS (LRWI)

FORD SORTING SIDINGS AND FORD DISTRICT

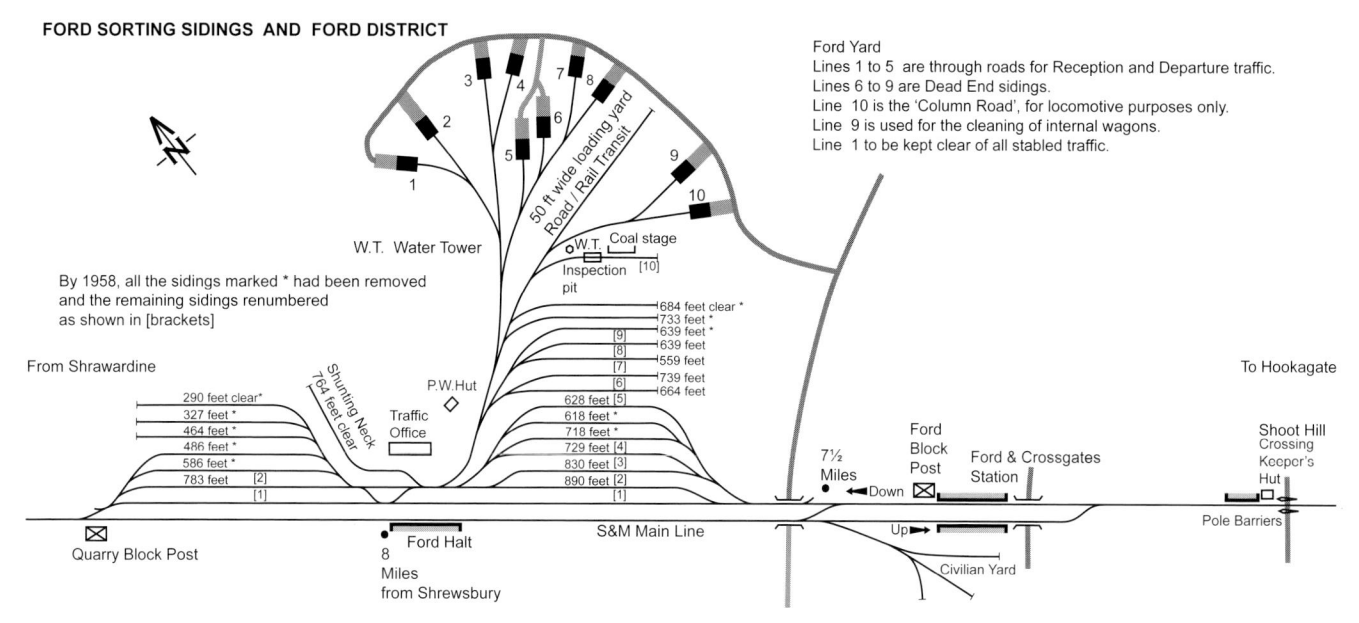

Ford Yard
Lines 1 to 5 are through roads for Reception and Departure traffic.
Lines 6 to 9 are Dead End sidings.
Line 10 is the 'Column Road', for locomotive purposes only.
Line 9 is used for the cleaning of internal wagons.
Line 1 to be kept clear of all stabled traffic.

By 1958, all the sidings marked * had been removed and the remaining sidings renumbered as shown in [brackets]

Ford and Crossgates

The block post here – the name of which was usually abbreviated to simply 'Ford' – worked single lines by Telephone and Ticket (T&T) to Quarry and Hookagate (West or East). There was also a single track line leading to Ford Marshalling Yard. This was not worked by T&T, but before the Yard Foreman dispatched a train towards the block post he had to obtain the permission of the blockman. Similarly the blockman had to obtain the Foreman's permission before allowing a train to enter the Yard. Because Down direction trains entering the Yard had to travel along the northern side line through the station and passing loop, the usual direction of running through the loop was reversed to give right-hand running. The northernmost line was the Down Main, and the southernmost was the Up main. Where practicable, trains proceeding from the Yard in the direction of Hookagate were not to be accepted from the Yard Foreman until the train had been accepted by Hookagate and so have a clear run through Ford Station. If, unusually, an Up direction (eastbound) train had to pass through the passing loop on the left-hand side, no train could be allowed to approach the block post from the Yard until the Up train had passed clear through the Down line.

Any train proceeding out of the Civilian Yard had to halt at the Stop board until authorised by the blockman to pass the board.

Looking through Ford Station towards Kinnerley, with the S&M station buildings (supplemented by a grounded van body) on the right hand platform. In S&M days this was the Up direction platform (see page 15) but the WD had reversed the direction of running through this station so this was now the Down platform, with the line continuing straight on beyond the station into Ford Yard. The single running line to Quarry Block Post was a continuation of the line in the left hand platform. 21st September 1958.
R. M. Casserley, reference 18159K

THE SHROPSHIRE & MONTGOMERYSHIRE LIGHT RAILWAY UNDER MILITARY CONTROL 1940-1960

An air photograph of the Ford District, taken by the RAF on 11th March 1948. The S&M line from Cruckton enters the frame at the top left and the line towards Shrawardine is at the foot of the photograph – so northwards is at the bottom. The sheds making up Ford District can be seen at the end of the shed spurs, with the wagons in the marshalling sidings to the right. This photograph shows why – to the considerable annoyance of McAlpine – most of the sheds were not served by rail. The roads were some six years old when this photograph was taken, yet the roadways clearly stand out as white lines when viewed from altitude – a telltale pointer for enemy aircraft. The broad roadway down the centre of the site was the road/rail transit facility which allowed the loading of road lorries directly from rail vehicles. These sheds at Ford wrere to a different layout from the others in the Depot. Designed for handling the transfer to road vehicles, not for long term storage, each had two end doors opening on to the roadways, against which lorries could back up to load.

National Monuments Record of English Heritage and reproduced by courtesy of the Ministry of Defence reference number CPE/UK/2492 frame 4320

LOCAL RAILWAY WORKING INSTRUCTIONS (LRWI)

Ford & Crossgates Block Post, seen on the 12th October 1957, like the others on the line did not house the lever frame. That was outside, and consisted of two Tyer & Co. two-lever frames side-by-side, one frame to work the points and Facing Point Locks at each end of the loop. Prominent was the flagboard applying to Up direction trains leaving Ford Yard. The holes permitted the display of indications by lamp at night time. During the day, flags (in the form of square sheets of metal, or failing that cloth flags) were hung on nails on the front of the flagboard. A simple step made of old sleepers assisted men of short stature in reaching the topmost flag. *M. N. Bland*

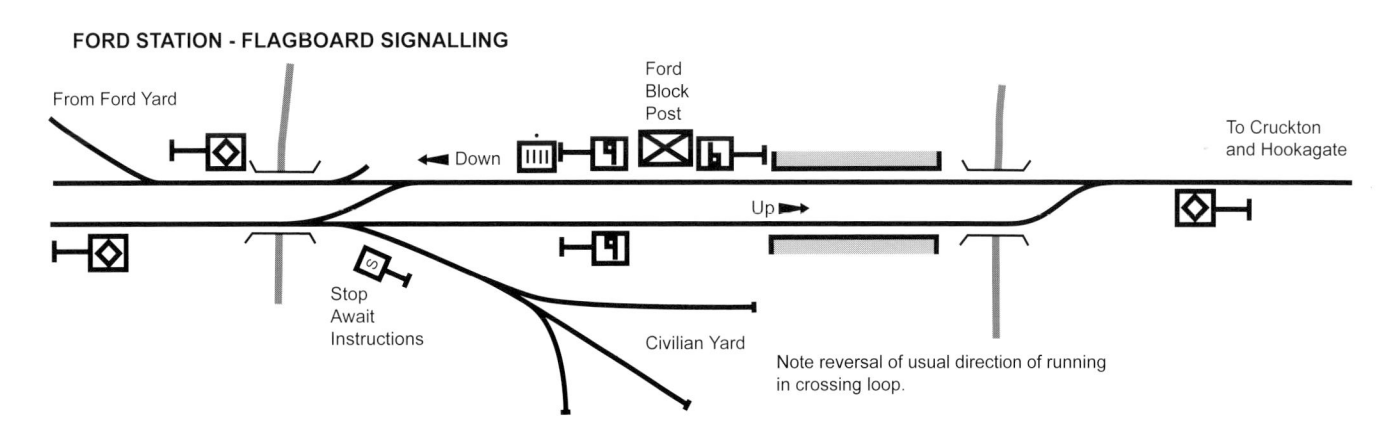

FORD STATION - FLAGBOARD SIGNALLING

From Ford Yard

Ford Block Post

← Down

To Cruckton and Hookagate

Up →

Stop Await Instructions

Civilian Yard

Note reversal of usual direction of running in crossing loop.

85

FLAGBOARD SIGNALLING
Military Railway Rule Book, Rules 8 and 11
STATION LIMIT BOARD

Side facing Section (Approaching train)

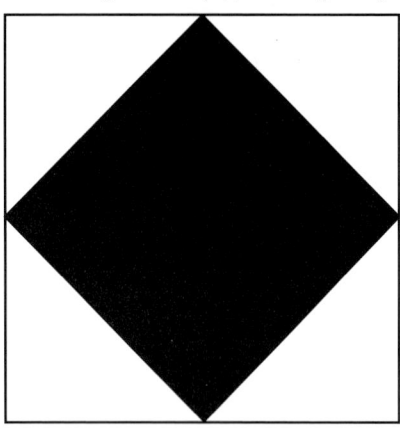

Side facing station (and Departing train)

Approx 3ft square.
Black diamond on a White background.

Black lettering on a White Ground

FLAGBOARD
(Modified design as used on the S&M)

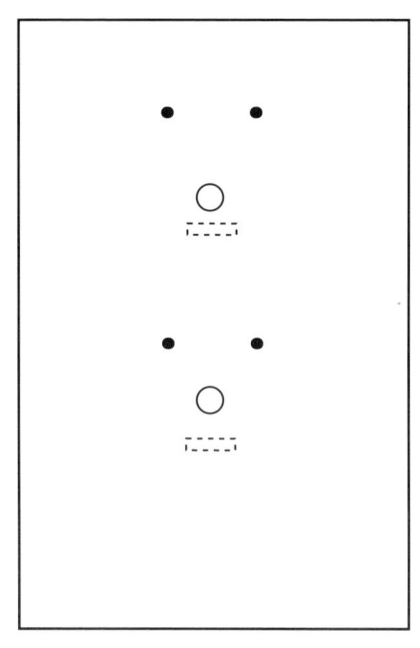

FLAGS
Approx 1 foot 6 inches square.

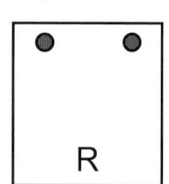

Front - Painted red

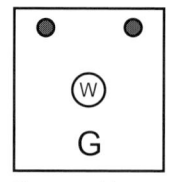

Reverse side - Painted green with white 4 inch circle in the centre.

Approx 3ft wide and 4ft 6 inches deep.
Painted white.
Screws for metal flags.
Holes for handlamps, with small brackets on rear for lamps to be placed upon.

The Station Limit board acts as an Outer Home signal. The Flagboard acts as a Home signal, controlling the entrance to the section of line to the next Block Post.

Flags will be displayed as necessary on the Flagboard (lamps during the hours of darkness), one above the other. Flags may be of metal sheet with holes to fit hanging screws, or cloth flags if no metal flags are available.

Red in top position (acting as the Home signal), above
Red in lower position (acting as the Station Limit Board)
    Indicates – Stop.

Red above Green   Indicates – that an approaching train may pass the Station Limit board and draw up to the Flagboard where it must stop.

Green above Green   Indicates – that an approaching train may proceed through into the next single line section.

Green above Red   Indicates – that a train at the Flagboard may proceed, but that any train approaching the Station Limit board must stop there.

LOCAL RAILWAY WORKING INSTRUCTIONS (LRWI)

The crew of the Drewry Rail Car await the approach of a train in the opposite direction, as their progress with an enthusiasts' special is halted at Ford on 12th October 1957. Looking towards Hookagate, three flagboards are visible. The one on the left applied to trains coming out of Ford Yard. That on the right applied to movements on the main line from the direction of Quarry Block Post. The flagboard in the background, behind the train crew, applied to movements from Hookagate (this is the board seen in the photograph at the bottom of page 82). *M. N. Bland*

On a different occasion, the tour rail car was halted whilst one of the Austerity 0-6-0 saddle tank locomotives came past, working hard on lifting its load out of Ford Yard (which was some feet below the level of the main line). The flagboard applying to Down direction trains is prominent, with two red flags hung on the nails provided. The Station Limit board for trains from the yard can be seen just beyond the rear of the train. The crew of the rail car have taken the opportunity to brew up – what else was the stove in the block post hut for?
Hugh Davies (Photos/Fifties reference 12B)

The blockman at Ford was having a busy time on 16th August 1955, and had all his red flags out (green flagboards are distinguishable in black and white photographs, because they had a white circle in the centre of the metal flag). Vehicles stood on the Up platform line, and the Drewry Car on an enthusiasts' trip stood by the block post on the Down line. Although the two tracks here were nominally the Down and Up loop lines, the Up line (on the right) was often used as a siding for goods wagons in transit, with all other traffic in both directions using the line nearest the block post. Photographs from the early 1950s show that only the down line had been relaid in flat-bottom rail with S&M bull head rail still on the Up line, though it had been replaced by the date of this photograph.
Brian Connell (Photos/Fifties reference B63/11)

THE SHROPSHIRE & MONTGOMERYSHIRE LIGHT RAILWAY UNDER MILITARY CONTROL 1940-1960

The difference in levels between the main line and the yard at Ford is apparent in this view, taken from a viewpoint on the main line looking towards Kinnerley. The photographer's conveyance – one of the Drewry Rail Cars – stood on the main line. The return afternoon workmen's train, consisting of two of the LT&S coaches and a standard brake van, stood on No. 4 siding in the yard. The brick building in the middle distance was the Traffic Office building. This still stands, now isolated in the middle of a field.
Photographer unknown

Ford Sub-depot

Ford Sub-depot consisted of ten sheds adjacent to the sorting/marshalling sidings, and one Road/Rail Transit (RRT) siding. Wagons left on the RRT siding were to be placed as near the buffer stops as possible. Unlike the other sheds in the Depot, those at Ford were not used for long term storage, but only for transfer storage. All were accessible by road, and formed part of the facility that allowed for the transfer of 'sensitive' munitions to the open air storage in Loton Deer Park, to where the munitions were taken the short distance by road. Loton Deer Park was used by American Forces as a depot for chemical weapons. The 'Protocol for the Prohibition of the Use in War of Asphyxiating, Poisonous or other Gases, and of Bacteriological Methods of Warfare', usually called the Geneva Protocol, prohibited the first use of chemical and biological weapons. Signed in Geneva on 17th June 1925, the protocol banned the use of chemical and biological weapons but did not prohibit the development, production, stockpiling, or transfer of them. Moreover, many of the signatory states reserved the right to retaliate in kind if another state used chemical weapons first. Loton Park was evacuated by the US Army in November 1945 and was then incorporated into CAD Nesscliff for the 'peacetime storage of CW [chemical weapons] ammunition C.S. reserves'. As an indication of the volume of traffic, in the quarter to September 1946, 17,000 tons of CW ammunition was received.

Ford Halt was located on the main running line. This view, looking towards Ford & Crossgates (the Station Limit boards for Ford Block Post are just visible in the distance) shows the method of construction of the WD halts – precast concrete slabs resting on a series of brick-built piers. The ash ballast only came half-way up the sides of the sleepers – with concrete sleepers on straight track this was considered sufficient.
Lens of Sutton Association

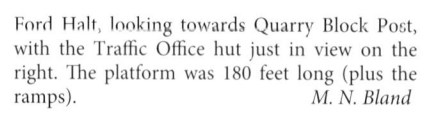

Ford Halt, looking towards Quarry Block Post, with the Traffic Office hut just in view on the right. The platform was 180 feet long (plus the ramps).
M. N. Bland

LOCAL RAILWAY WORKING INSTRUCTIONS (LRWI)

A view of the marshalling sidings in Ford Yard, looking south-east towards Ford Station. The coaches of an enthusiasts' train had been left on No. 2 Siding, while the locomotive detached and went to the water column. The Austerity 0-6-0STs had a limited water capacity and would have to go to a water column in the middle of any long trip. By the time this photograph was taken on 22nd May 1955, several of the sidings in Ford Yard had already been lifted (see the plan on page 83). The line leading off to the left served Sheds 1 to 8. Ford Halt is visible on the right – it would not have been acceptable to block the running line for as long as it took to take on water, so the special train had to run via the yard.
Brian Hilton, reference 53/13

Quarry

Quarry Block Post controlled access to the sorting sidings at Ford Yard from the northern end, where there was a small additional group of sidings known as Quarry Yard. Parallel to the single line to Ford Block Post, but at a slightly lower level, was No. 1 siding, which ran through both Quarry Yard and Ford Yard and which was to be kept clear of stabled traffic except in an emergency, to allow its use as a second running line. Quarry was not a crossing place for ordinary purposes, but if necessary trains could be shunted into Quarry Yard. Trains proceeding from Quarry Yard on to the main line were required to halt at a Stop board, until they received the blockman's authority to proceed.

The hours of the blockman at Ford and of the Yard Foreman normally coincided. When these men were not on duty, reception and dispatch of trains to and from the main line was under the control of the blockman at Quarry. Only one train was then allowed into the Yard and District at any one time.

This is the only photograph found that shows Quarry Block Post, and then it is only half visible at the extreme left. The view, taken on 11th January 1942, shows the ends of the four loop sidings at the Quarry end of Ford Yard, and also the three dead-end sidings. It was to the latter that the WD brought the rolling stock that was beyond use, to wait until it could be broken up.
Graham Vincent

THE SHROPSHIRE & MONTGOMERYSHIRE LIGHT RAILWAY UNDER MILITARY CONTROL 1940-1960

The one part of the Central Ammunition Depot that was not rail served was the chemical weapons storage area in the remote location of Loton Deer Park at Alberbury. Here, small sheds were laid out amongst the trees in the park. The whole area was served by road from Ford Yard – which is why the sheds at Ford had to have lorry access.
The Welsh Office (now the Office of the Welsh Assembly Government) and reproduced by courtesy of the Ministry of Defence reference number CPE/UK/2492 frame 4315

LOCAL RAILWAY WORKING INSTRUCTIONS (LRWI)

Shrawardine Bridge (Bridge No. 28), seen from the upstream side. An enthusiasts' train heading for Kinnerley was posed for photographs. The girders of the original bridge still stood on the upstream side – the new WD bridge was built within the piers of the downstream side. The acute angle of one of the downstream piers can be seen under the rear of the locomotive.
S. Edginton

Bridge No. 28 viewed from the downstream side. The angle to which one of the original piers had moved is evident, as is the fracture of the bracing that was supposed to retain the integrity of the structure. It was understandable that WD engineers were worried that this pier might fail completely in a serious flood, and that in collapsing it would damage the girders of the replacement bridge (which rested on the new built-up cribs such as the one immediately below the locomotive).
Photographer unknown

Immediately on the Shrawardine side of Bridge No. 28, a set of hand points gave access to the Dead Road, which extended from here to Nesscliff East Block Post. Looking towards Kinnerley, the WD running line was on the right and the Dead Road (which had been the S&M running line until the WD took over) was on the left. To the left side can be seen the end of Shed 31. *Photographer unknown, from the 'Detachment Photograph Album'*

A view from a few yards further north than the preceding photo showing the points leading to the (by now lifted) Gathering Line of the South Balloon and the back view of the Stop board applying to movements from the South Balloon on to the Dead Road. Shrawardine Halt was just beyond the second board on the running line on the right. *Photographer unknown, from the 'Detachment Photograph Album'*

LOCAL RAILWAY WORKING INSTRUCTIONS (LRWI)

SHRAWARDINE AND PENTRE SUB-DEPOT

Shrawardine District (also known as the North Balloon) consists of Sheds 11 to 30, Shrawardine Civilian Yard and Camp Station
Pentre District (also known as the South Balloon) consists of Sheds 31 to 76

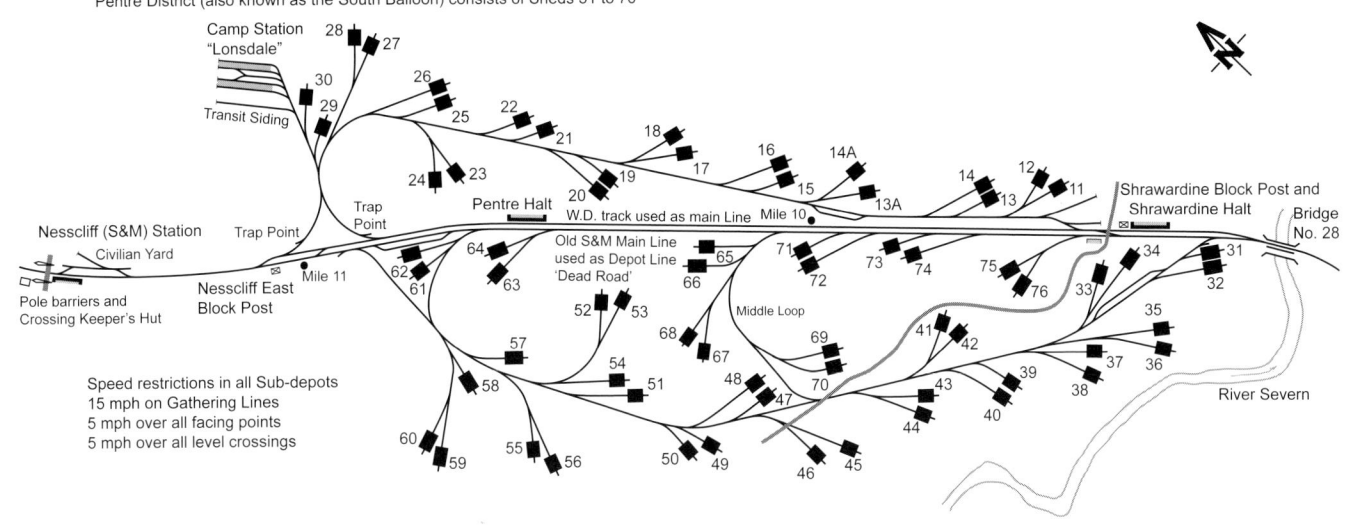

Speed restrictions in all Sub-depots
15 mph on Gathering Lines
5 mph over all facing points
5 mph over all level crossings

Shrawardine and Pentre

This Sub-depot consisted of two Districts. The North Balloon Area included Camp Station, sheds 11 to 30 inclusive, and the Civilian Yard at Shrawardine. This District could be accessed in three places, at Nesscliff East Block Post via the west leg of the triangle or via the east leg, and also at Shrawardine Station yard. It was permissible for more than one train to operate in the District, except in darkness when 'One Engine in Steam' only was allowed. When a second train entered the District, the blockman at Nesscliff East gave the driver a Red Special Caution Order (because there was a known obstruction – the other train) and a verbal warning stating the number of trains already in the District and the description of those trains. If the additional train entered the District at Shrawardine, this Red Special Caution Order was issued by the blockman at Quarry. All crews were required to keep a 'sharp look-out' at all times for other trains operating in a District, especially since the crew of the first train in could not be advised when any second train entered the District.

All points within the District were operated locally by hand levers. It was required in all Districts that the points to shed spurs, sidings and loops be left set for movements along the Gathering Line and away from the dead end line.

In addition to the normal traffic to sheds, the North Balloon handled the daily Works Passenger trains to and from Camp Station. The blockman at Nesscliff East was not to allow a second passenger train to proceed towards Camp Station until he had received information by telephone from the person in charge of the first train that it had arrived inside clear on one of the platform roads, and that this person had set the points for the reception of the second passenger train. Departures from the Camp Station could be made when the train was ready, but any second train was to allow an interval of at least two minutes after the departure of the first train, and its crew were then to keep a sharp look-out. The blockman at Nesscliff East was not to allow any train to enter the District when passenger trains were due to enter or leave. Any train

Shrawardine Halt, viewed from a workmen's train on 14th September 1958. The one-time block post hut was at the far end of the platform.
Photographer unknown

THE SHROPSHIRE & MONTGOMERYSHIRE LIGHT RAILWAY UNDER MILITARY CONTROL 1940-1960

In WD ownership, the former S&M station at Shrawardine was situated on the Dead Road, (sometimes referred to in papers as the 'Goods Line') – hence the need to build the new Shrawardine Halt platform. In any event, the S&M platform was typically short and unfit for military traffic. The road over the level crossing became part of the Depot and was closed off to the public. The connection into the Civilian goods yard and thence access to the North Balloon was controlled by a Tyer & Co. ground frame locked by key, but the points in the running line for the crossover to the Dead Road were on a simple hand lever. A view looking north-west towards Kinnerley.
R. M. Casserley, reference 18157K

already operating in the area between sheds 27/28 and Shrawardine was not to obstruct the passenger train route within five minutes of the times when those trains were booked to enter or leave Camp Station.

The South Balloon was worked as a single yard, with access normally via the Dead Road from Nesscliff East (although there was access at Shrawardine in an emergency). Only one train was allowed into the District during the hours of darkness. During daylight the driver of any second train was warned of the circumstances by the issue of a Red Special Caution Order and verbal advice of the circumstances. As was conventional, the shed sidings were all laid out facing in the same direction around the Gathering Line. Entry via Nesscliff East, however, meant that it was sometimes quicker to propel the movement. Propelling on the Gathering Lines was permitted in this District where there were no facilities for running round, but the first opportunity was to be taken to run round the train and pull it. Propelling movements were limited to 5 mph. There were level crossings in this District at Shrawardine Station and on the Gathering Line between Middle Loop points and spur 44 points – drivers were required to sound the whistle or horn on approaching these crossings and to be ready to stop short of any obstruction. Rail traffic had precedence over road traffic. Movements out of the District were controlled by a Stop board at the west exit (permission to proceed being given by the blockman) and a Stop board at the east exit at Shrawardine, where there was a set of trap points that had to be held over for a movement on to the main line (when this had been authorised).

A level crossing existed on the main line at Shrawardine Station. This was treated as a Sub-depot level crossing (not a public road) so rail traffic had precedence over road. Rail drivers were required only to sound the whistle, reduce speed to 10 mph, and be prepared to stop short of any obstruction.

Although there was no crossing loop here, Nesscliff East Block Post was a crossing place. Trains were shunted into the Dead Road as necessary to allow other traffic to pass. The busy single line section to Kinnerley was controlled by electric token (miniature staff), the only single line section to have this facility. There were Stop boards at:

The exit from the Dead Road in the South Balloon
The exit from the North Balloon via the West Leg of the Triangle
The exit from the North Balloon via the East Leg of the Triangle.

Beside each Stop board were trap points, normally set for the 'derail' position, which had to be held over for the passage of each train.

The blockman at Nesscliff East was responsible for ensuring (by telephone) that after any shunting had been done into the Civilian sidings at Nesscliff Station, the Annetts Keys to the ground frames there had been returned to the possession of the crossing keeper.

LOCAL RAILWAY WORKING INSTRUCTIONS (LRWI)

Shrawardine level crossing, looking south-east towards Bridge No. 28 and thence to Ford, showing the disused block post hut and Shrawardine Halt beyond. An undated photograph, but taken shortly before closure and certainly after September 1958 – one end of the by now disused crossover between the running line and the Dead Road had already been removed.
Photographer unknown, from the 'Detachment Photograph Album'

A more distant view of Shrawardine level crossing, showing the disused S&M platform and also the station house, restored by the WD after the fire that had gutted it while it was in use by the construction troops who were refurbishing the line. The house still stands, in use as a private residence.
Photographer unknown, from the 'Detachment Photograph Album'

The view north-west from the disused S&M platform at Shrawardine, showing the tiny water tank that was available to locomotives on the Dead Road. This water tank does not appear in any of the lists of watering facilities. On the right, the Gathering Line into the North Balloon can be seen, with the sidings that fed back from the Gathering Line to the Civilian Yard at Shrawardine. Unlike many of the points in the running line, which were operated from simple hand levers, the connection to the North Balloon was operated from a two lever Tyer & Co. ground frame (just visible in front of the nearer of the two vans).

Photographer unknown, from the 'Detachment Photograph Album'.

A view along the running line towards Kinnerley, just south of Pentre Halt. To the left of the van standing on the Dead Road, the points leading to Shed 64 (visible on the left) had already been lifted. The running line at this location had been relaid using pots under each rail, connected by metal tie bars to retain the gauge.

Photographer unknown, from the 'Detachment Photograph Album'

LOCAL RAILWAY WORKING INSTRUCTIONS (LRWI)

Pentre Halt, looking towards Kinnerley on 21st September 1958, with the Dead Road on the left. The different methods of construction of the WD track is again evident, as is the fact that despite the run-down to closure having been announced, the track was remarkably free of any weeds. *R. M. Casserley, reference 18156K*

Looking towards Kinnerley from the north end of Pentre Halt. The spur from the Dead Road towards Sheds 61/62 and the triangle line diverged to the left. In the distance can be seen the Station Limit board (black diamond on a white background) for Down trains approaching Nesscliff East Block Post.
Photographer unknown, from the 'Detachment Photograph Album'

THE SHROPSHIRE & MONTGOMERYSHIRE LIGHT RAILWAY UNDER MILITARY CONTROL 1940-1960

LOCAL RAILWAY WORKING INSTRUCTIONS (LRWI)

Above: There was no Mechanical Handling Equipment (MHE) in the sheds, though roller ramps were provided to ease the manual tasks.

Below: The handling of larger calibre shell required different techniques, involving rolling the shell up a wooden ramp. Sometimes a rope was placed loosely round the shell and held by a man at the top of the stack, so that if anyone slipped at least the shell would not roll backwards.
Imperial War Museum, references H 28920 and H 28899

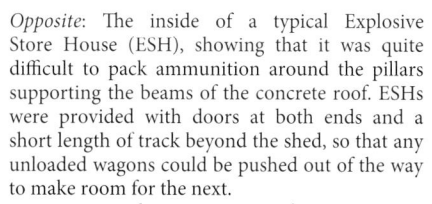

Opposite: The inside of a typical Explosive Store House (ESH), showing that it was quite difficult to pack ammunition around the pillars supporting the beams of the concrete roof. ESHs were provided with doors at both ends and a short length of track beyond the shed, so that any unloaded wagons could be pushed out of the way to make room for the next.
Imperial War Museum, references H 28919

THE SHROPSHIRE & MONTGOMERYSHIRE LIGHT RAILWAY UNDER MILITARY CONTROL 1940-1960

An air photograph taken by the RAF on 8th December 1948. In the centre is Wilcot Camp, the principal army camp at Nesscliff CAD. Across the road from the camp can be seen the four-platform station serving the camp, officially known as 'Lonsdale' but universally called simply 'Camp'. To the right of the station was the single siding for Transit, providing a facility for loading and unloading rail wagons to road vehicles. Transit siding joined the line from Camp Station beside sheds 30/29, and a few yards beyond that it joined the Gathering Line for the North Balloon. Sheds 28/27, 26/25 and 24 are all visible. The Gathering Line then divided to form two sides of a triangle. One side curved south-east (towards the top of this photo) to join the main running line beside sheds 62/61. The other side of the triangle joined the running line at Nesscliff East Block Post, which can just be discerned as a small white square (again showing that concrete shows up a very clear white in air photos – many of the concrete buildings were painted black for this reason). From here the line passed through Nesscliff & Pentre Station (centre right) and thence towards Kinnerley. At the end of the straight track from Nesscliff & Pentre Station was the junction into Nesscliff District at Nesscliff West Block Post. A few of the sheds in this District are visible – 107/108 near to the three repair shops buildings, and 105/106 in the bottom right hand corner of the photo. The shadows of the shed spur lines for sheds 105/106 show that the track to these sheds had been lowered some three feet below the level of the land – which saved brickwork in building up the shed walls.

National Monuments Record of English Heritage and reproduced by courtesy of the Ministry of Defence reference number 541/214 frame 3036

LOCAL RAILWAY WORKING INSTRUCTIONS (LRWI)

Nesscliff East

None of the enthusiasts' trains went into the Camp Station, so this view of one of its platforms and the centre locomotive escape line is something of a rarity. It was taken in 1947 by Geoffrey Bannister, using his special freedom to explore the railway. The extremely run-down nature of the coaches provided for one of the workmen's trains is evident. Many of the windows on these ex-LMS coaches were broken. The platforms were devoid of any buildings, but the rows of poles carrying basic light fittings can be seen.

Geoffrey Bannister, courtesy Andrew Bannister

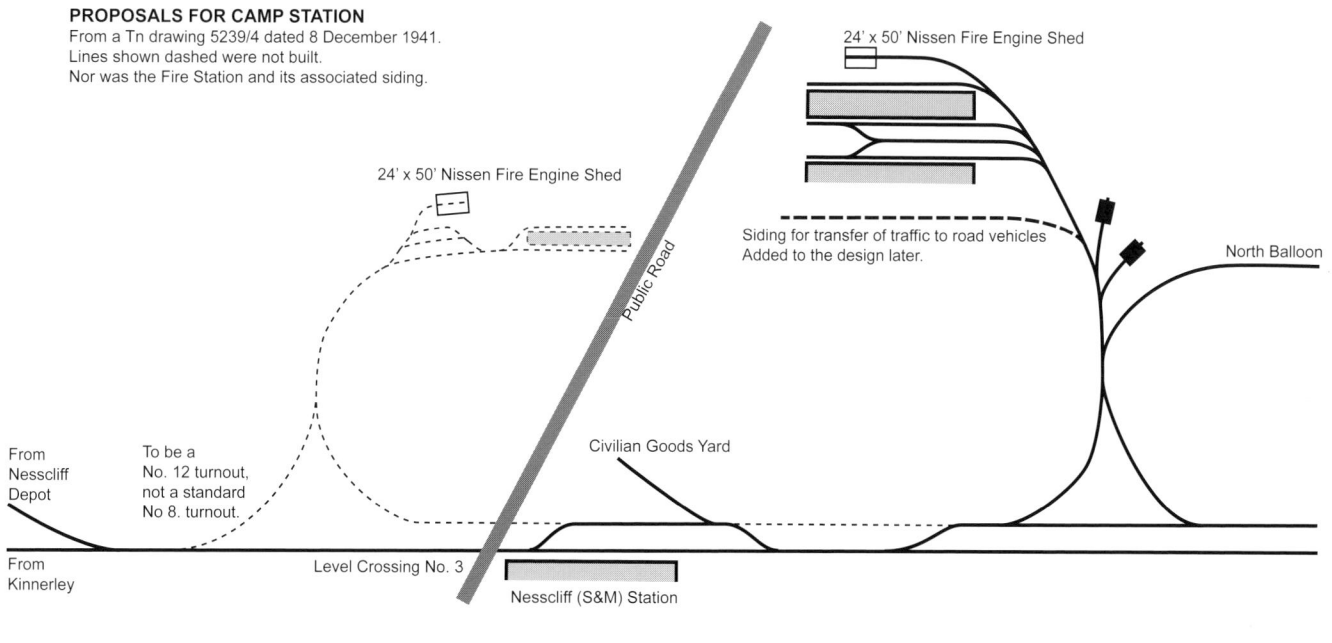

PROPOSALS FOR CAMP STATION
From a Tn drawing 5239/4 dated 8 December 1941.
Lines shown dashed were not built.
Nor was the Fire Station and its associated siding.

24' x 50' Nissen Fire Engine Shed

24' x 50' Nissen Fire Engine Shed

Siding for transfer of traffic to road vehicles
Added to the design later.

North Balloon

From Nesscliff Depot

To be a No. 12 turnout, not a standard No 8. turnout.

Civilian Goods Yard

From Kinnerley

Level Crossing No. 3

Nesscliff (S&M) Station

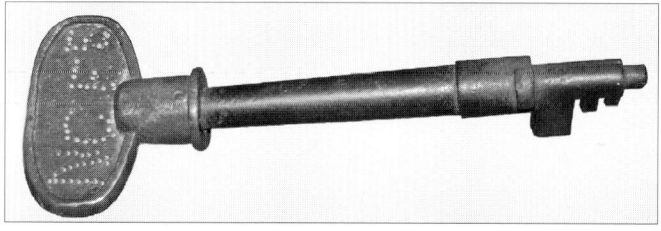

Public Road

The key for the Tyer's lever frame at Nesscliff East, similar to that for Shrawardine and the other frames of this design. A small nib on the side of each key (differently located on each) meant that each key would only fit the frame for which it was intended. Each of the keys was lettered to show the location to which it applied, using the WD's standard abbreviation. The key for NCF E had the letters rather crudely drilled into the brass head of the key as well as being stamped (the usual method) into the steel shaft of the key.

Author

101

Approaching Nesscliff & Pentre Station from the south-east on 21st September 1958, showing the very short platform. The main line had been relaid in flat bottom rail, but the original S&M rails remained in the siding. The Rule 103 Board, with its fixed lamp, was on the left. In the far distance, down the straight towards Kinnerley, can be seen Nesscliff West Block Post.
R. M. Casserley, reference 18155

Nesscliff Public Road Level Crossing

This was worked under similar instructions to those for the level crossing at Shoot Hill. On hearing the telephone message 'Train Entering Section' (TES) from Kinnerley, the crossing keeper was to keep a constant lookout in that direction and to lower the barriers when the train came into view around the curve at Nesscliff Halt. When he heard TES from Nesscliff East he was immediately to lower the barriers.

Nesscliff & Pentre (S&M) Station, looking towards Kinnerley. The pole barriers protecting the level crossing had been raised after the train passed.
Stations (UK) reference number 11027

LOCAL RAILWAY WORKING INSTRUCTIONS (LRWI)

The WD relaid the points leading into the siding at Nesscliff with flat bottom rail on re-used sleepers. The trap point had a single switch rail, worked from the ground frame visible beside the level crossing.
Brian Connell (Photos/Fifties Ref. B62/4)

A view from Nesscliff & Pentre Station along the straight towards Nesscliff West Block Post. The keeper's hut beside the road crossing carried a board 'Nesscliff Level Crossing', though this had disappeared by the late 1950s.
R. M. Casserley, reference 18109K

Access to the station sidings at Nesscliff was controlled by a two lever ground frame of Tyer & Co. design at each end of the loop line. Here Chris Ainsworth is seen – in a photograph posed for a newspaper – operating the frame at the north-west end, beside the level crossing. He had already reversed lever No. 2, which operated the point lock and released the lever for the points in the running line and the trap. At the base of lever 2 can be seen the Annetts key that had been used to release the lock lever. This key was normally kept in the crossing keeper's hut. During the years of the Great Depression when work was hard to come by in the UK, Col Stephens had used his influence to obtain work for Chris Ainsworth in India. Having worked for 21 years on the Madras & Maharatta Southern Railway as a driver and later Locomotive Foreman, Chris returned to the UK around the time of Indian Independence and found work on the S&M.
Photographer unknown, from the 'Detachment Photograph Album'

THE SHROPSHIRE & MONTGOMERYSHIRE LIGHT RAILWAY UNDER MILITARY CONTROL 1940-1960

Nesscliff & Pentre (S&M) Station, looking towards Ford on 5th September 1947. One of the Dean Goods locomotives paused with a westbound train of empty wagons. The construction of the pole barriers is evident – two concrete uprights supporting a simple pivot pin, with a wooden pole counterbalanced so that it would remain in the raised or lowered position. They were simply pushed into the required position, the weights being an adequate counterbalance to the weight of the pole. Note the pin on the rear of the barrier pole, behind the circular red 'target', on to which a red lamp could be hung during the hours of darkness.

R. K. Blencowe Negative Archive, number 6392

LOCAL RAILWAY WORKING INSTRUCTIONS (LRWI)

This photograph, not quite of the quality of others, shows the crossing keeper watching a freight train bound for Kinnerley at Nesscliff level crossing. Of note is the chain between the outer end of the pole barrier and a nearby post, that acted to prevent the pole – which was quite finely balanced on its pivot – from accidentally rising while a train was approaching the crossing.
*Geoffrey Bannister,
courtesy Andrew Bannister*

Between Nesscliff S&M Station and Kinnerley the WD put up two halts to serve the Kinnerley and Nesscliff Sub-depot. A few hundred yards north-west of Nesscliff West Block Post was Nesscliff Halt, seen here from an enthusiasts' special train.
Stations (UK) reference number 11010

Almost within sight of Kinnerley Station, which was about half a mile ahead, was Kinnerley Halt. By the time that this view was taken on one of the 'final' railtours, the Dead Road beside the running line had already been lifted.
Stations (UK) reference number 11011

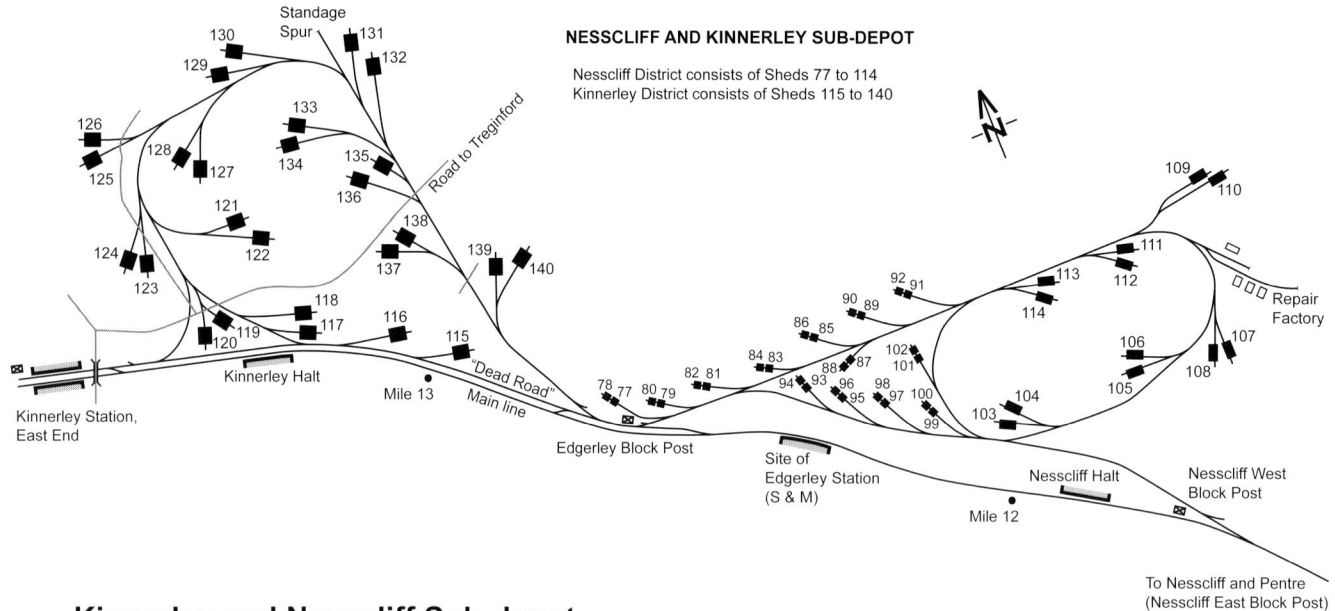

THE SHROPSHIRE & MONTGOMERYSHIRE LIGHT RAILWAY UNDER MILITARY CONTROL 1940-1960

NESSCLIFF AND KINNERLEY SUB-DEPOT

Nesscliff District consists of Sheds 77 to 114
Kinnerley District consists of Sheds 115 to 140

Kinnerley and Nesscliff Sub-depot

This Sub-depot consisted of sheds 77 to 114 in Nesscliff District and 115 to 140 in Kinnerley District. The whole was worked as a single yard, with entrance and exit at Kinnerley (in an emergency also at Edgerley). Only one train was allowed to operate during darkness. During daylight subsequent trains could be allowed to enter, given verbal warning and Red Special Caution Orders. Propelling was allowed, subject to a speed restriction of 5 mph and the requirement to run round at the first opportunity and then pull the train. There were level crossings at:

The west leg of the Kinnerley District Triangle
The lead from the Gathering Line to 119/120 spurs
The east leg of the Kinnerley District Triangle
Shed 136 spur
The Gathering Line between 135 and 136 spurs.

As usual drivers were to sound the whistle and be prepared to stop short of any obstruction.

LOCAL RAILWAY WORKING INSTRUCTIONS (LRWI)

An air photograph taken on 8th December 1948 – in this view north is towards the top of the photograph. Kinnerley Station is at the centre of the photograph, with the Criggion Branch curving away to the bottom left of the photo. The right hand half of the photo shows Kinnerley District as far east as sheds 115, 137/138, 136, 133/134 and at the top 129/130. To the left (west) of Kinnerley Station the photograph shows part of Argoed District from sheds 155/154 up to 163/162 and 156/157. It is not just new concrete that shows up shiny white in an air photograph – corrugated iron or asbestos does as well. The new roof on the locomotive shed is prominent beside the Criggion Branch, and the curved metal roofs of the three huts beside the Civilian goods yard at Kinnerley Station are equally stark. The circular feature just east of Kinnerley Station and south of shed 123 is a relic of an earlier time of warfare and defence – Belan Bank, an old 'Motte and Bailey'.
National Monuments Record of English Heritage and reproduced by courtesy of the Ministry of Defence reference number 541/214 frame 4141

Opposite: By March 1960, the War Department had lifted many of its tracks, leaving just the running lines that were the property of the Western Region of British Railways. This was the view eastward from the road bridge at Kinnerley on 5th March 1960, with the main line towards Nesscliff on the right and the Dead Road on the left. Of the tracks from the Dead Road leading to the Kinnerley District, only the turnout beyond the trap points remained. The signals were to the designs of the LMS. Note the former goods van, made redundant in the purge of old rolling stock in 1952 and now in use as a platelayer's cabin, just beyond the turnout into the Sub-depot (compare with the photograph on page 19).
Photographer unknown, from the 'Detachment Photograph Album'

THE SHROPSHIRE & MONTGOMERYSHIRE LIGHT RAILWAY UNDER MILITARY CONTROL 1940-1960

The view through Kinnerley Station, looking east on 21st September 1958, with the Civilian Yard on the left and the Criggion Bay platform on the right. The straight post signal on the left applied to movements from the Up platform towards Llanymynech. The two disc signals at the base of the post read to Maesbrook & Argoed Sub-depot (to the right as viewed by the driver) or to the Criggion Branch (to the left as viewed by the driver). Either signal was worked by lever 14 in the Block Post. Which signal cleared was selected by the lie of the points, by means of the apparatus connected to the signal wires just to the left of the switch rails of the points. Notable was the fact that the Up platform had a very pronounced raised section (adjacent to the store shed, allowing for the easier loading of goods) and that it was much shorter than the Down platform. For this reason passenger trains in both directions usually used the Down platform. Beyond the bridge, the line through the Up platform continued as the Dead Road to serve Kinnerley District. To the left was a short row of Nissen huts used as offices. On the right can be seen one of the bungalows put up by the S&M company (it is believed that this was done in 1924) for company staff. They were roomy buildings with three bedrooms and cedar interiors, but with a 'tin roof' they were cold. The bungalows were raised on brick pillars. It was not unknown for flood waters to reach as far as these dwellings.
Bluebell Railway Museum Archive – I. J. Smith Collection, reference 6-87-5

22nd May 1955, and an enthusiasts' special had arrived at Kinnerley behind WD 189. This view shows the arrangements for working traffic out of the Civilian Yard. A 'Stop' board on the left acted as the location at which all shunting movements had to stop until called forward by the blockman – there was no other signal. In the unlikely event that there was a shunting movement into the yard during the hours of darkness, a handlamp could be placed on the small shelf at the rear of the Stop board, to reinforce the message. The water tank beside the locomotive was never used by the WD. If the driver needed water, it was the practice to 'hook off' from the train and leave it standing in the platform while the locomotive went 'on shed' to take water.
Brian Hilton, reference 53/20

Kinnerley

This block post had the only fully signalled layout on the S&M system, operated from an enclosed lever frame of twenty levers. The station limits were:

- The Up and Down Home signals
- No. 10 signal leading from the Argoed District
- No. 18 signal leading from the Kinnerley District
- The Stop board fixed on the Drewry Rail Car shed road
- The Stop board situated on the Loco Shed Road of the Criggion Branch.

The single line section to Llanymynech was worked by 'One Engine in Steam', the staff being in the form of a key bearing the inscription 'KNY-LNK'. This key released the ground frames at Maesbrook Station sidings and the east end of Llanymynech Yard. The section to Nesscliff East was worked by electric token. The starting signal controlling the entrance to either section was not to be pulled off unless the driver was in possession of the appropriate single line authority.

A 'call attention' bell was provided on a post just in front of the Down home signal. The code to Kinnerley Block Post was:

1 Ring – Train standing on Main line
2 Rings – Train standing on Dead Road.

The Locomotive Foreman had full jurisdiction over all roads, including the Bay Road, south of the Stop board in rear of the Criggion Branch Home signal (signal 5a/b) as far as the board inscribed 'Limit of WD Operating and Maintenance'. Any brakesman/shunter operating in this area were under his immediate control. The blockman was required to obtain the Locomotive Foreman's permission before allowing any movement on to the Criggion Branch or the Locomotive Roads.

The Roads were designated as follows:

- Criggion Branch (commonly known as Melverley Branch)
- Criggion Loop (commonly known as the Melverley Loop)
- Carriage & Wagon Repair Road (commonly known as the Weighbridge Loop)
- Weighbridge Road
- No. 1 Loco Shed Road (the left hand road on entering the shed)
- No. 2 Loco Shed Road
- No. 1 Coal Road (the road serving the rear side of the Coal Stage)
- No. 2 Coal Road.

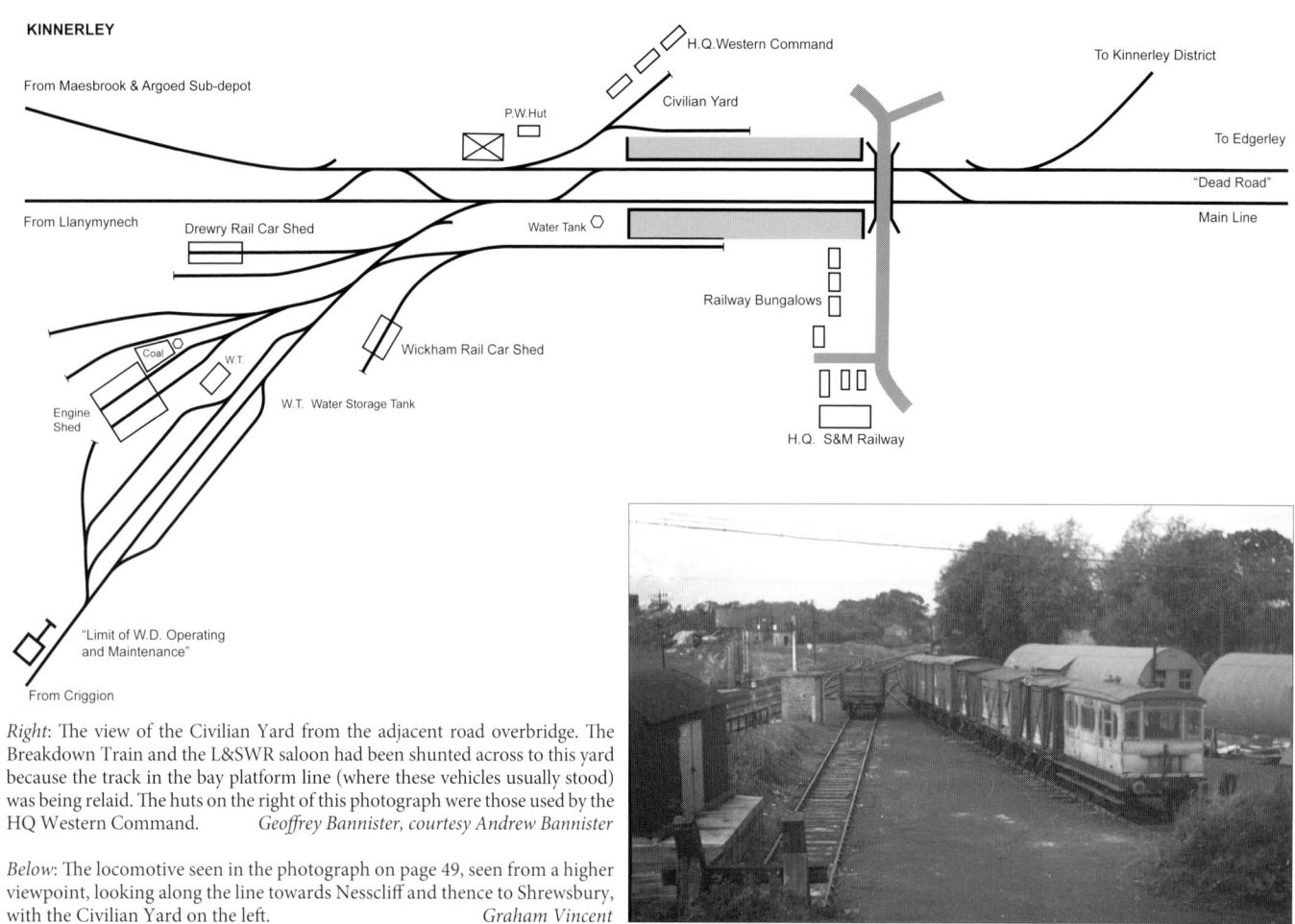

THE SHROPSHIRE & MONTGOMERYSHIRE LIGHT RAILWAY UNDER MILITARY CONTROL 1940-1960

KINNERLEY

Schematic track diagram of Kinnerley showing: From Maesbrook & Argoed Sub-depot, H.Q. Western Command, To Kinnerley District, P.W. Hut, Civilian Yard, To Edgerley, "Dead Road", Main Line, From Llanymynech, Drewry Rail Car Shed, Water Tank, Railway Bungalows, Coal, W.T., Wickham Rail Car Shed, Engine Shed, W.T. Water Storage Tank, H.Q. S&M Railway, "Limit of W.D. Operating and Maintenance", From Criggion.

Right: The view of the Civilian Yard from the adjacent road overbridge. The Breakdown Train and the L&SWR saloon had been shunted across to this yard because the track in the bay platform line (where these vehicles usually stood) was being relaid. The huts on the right of this photograph were those used by the HQ Western Command. *Geoffrey Bannister, courtesy Andrew Bannister*

Below: The locomotive seen in the photograph on page 49, seen from a higher viewpoint, looking along the line towards Nesscliff and thence to Shrewsbury, with the Civilian Yard on the left. *Graham Vincent*

110

LOCAL RAILWAY WORKING INSTRUCTIONS (LRWI)

A ground level view west through Kinnerley Station towards Llanymynech on 21st September 1958. The block post is on the Up side of the line, with the coaches of the enthusiasts' special temporarily stabled in front of it on the Down line. The manner in which the height of part of the Up platform had been raised can be seen – a mixture of brickwork and stone. The 'Black Shed' on the Up platform had traditionally been used to store basic slag (an agricultural fertiliser).
Bluebell Railway Museum Archive – J. J. Smith Collection, reference 6-87-3

A view westwards on 23rd July 1948 from the higher viewpoint of the road bridge showed the position of the locomotive shed, situated beside the Criggion Branch, in relation to the main line. The Down line, through the left hand platform, continued straight on as the single line to Llanymynech. The Up line extended beyond the block post, where it can be seen diverging to the right towards Maesbrook and Argoed. Some vehicles can just be seen standing in one of the sidings of Argoed Yard. The Civilian Yard is to the right, and the Criggion Bay platform to the left – the latter (as usual) used to stable the vehicles of the breakdown train.
Bluebell Railway Museum Archive – J. J. Smith Collection

A similar view to the previous photograph, but with two notable differences. The first is that a new shed had been constructed for the Drewry Rail Cars, on the site of a small clay pit. The curved roof of the new shed can be seen just to the left of the water tank on the Down platform. The home signal from the Criggion Branch was, as a consequence, now much nearer to the main line. The second change is that two of the S&M's worn out goods vans had (in 1952) been placed as 'grounded' storage sheds, just on the station side of the block post. In the far distance can be seen the outline of Llanymynech Hill. Some vans had been stabled on the line from Argoed Yard, just beyond the trap points, awaiting further shunting.
courtesy Roger Carpenter

A view southwards from the junction at Kinnerley, looking towards the locomotive shed. The rail car shed is on the siding to the left of the Criggion line, but it was by no means large enough to house all the cars. Many were therefore stabled outside overnight, on the short spurs laid in at 90 degrees to the rail car siding. They were simply lifted off the siding, turned and placed on the spurs. Handles had been built into the rail cars to assist the process. This photograph was taken on 1st April 1947, before the construction of the Drewry Rail Car shed, which necessitated that the signal controlling movements from the shed and Criggion Branch be moved closer to the block post.

Graham Vincent

The entrance to Kinnerley engine shed in 1947. The principal line here was the Criggion Branch, which curved to the left behind the Wickham Rail Car shed (on the left). Prominent in the centre was the substantial water storage tank (erected by the War Department) which fed the water tank visible to the right of the Dean Goods locomotive. One of the J69 tank engines can just be seen behind the base of the signal post.

Graham Vincent

LOCAL RAILWAY WORKING INSTRUCTIONS (LRWI)

Kinnerley shed on 22nd May 1955. The various lines (from the left) were the Criggion Branch, the Criggion Loop, the Carriage & Wagon Repair Road from which diverged the Weighbridge Road, then to the right of the water tower the No. 1 Loco Shed Road, the No. 2 Loco Shed Road, the No. 1 Coal Road and the No. 2 Coal Road. The overlapping switches and crossings in the foreground were unusually complicated for a military depot, in which such 'difficult to maintain' arrangements would normally be avoided. Here they had been dictated by the layout of the shed that the WD had inherited. The locomotives from left to right were WD 121, WD 185 and WD 141.

Brian Hilton, reference 53/24

The inside of the locomotive shed, whilst better than the set-up that the WD had inherited, was still fairly simple – primitive almost – considering the nature of the repairs that the fitters were expected to undertake during the war years to keep the traffic moving. *R. K. Blencowe Negative Archive, number 51744*

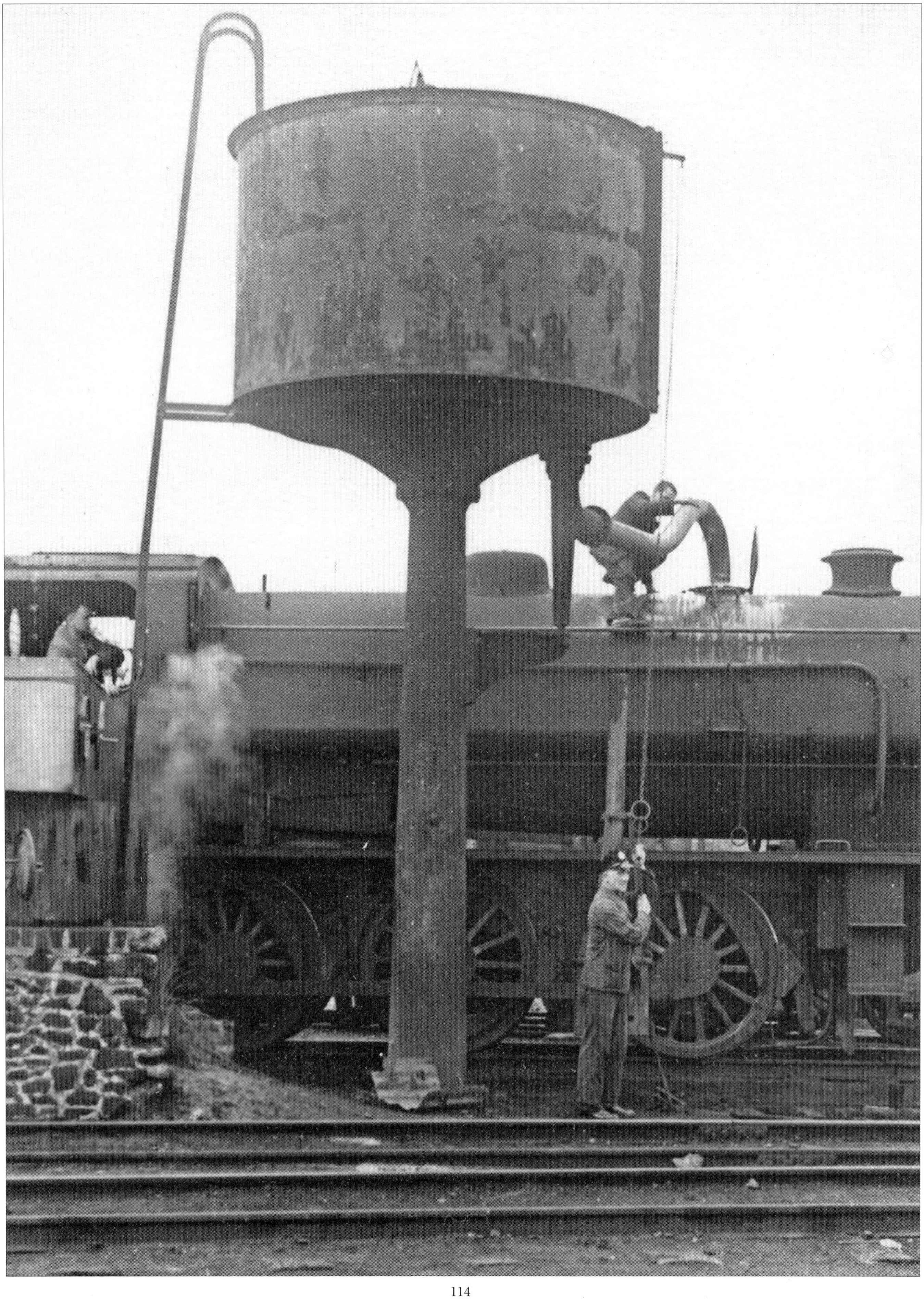

LOCAL RAILWAY WORKING INSTRUCTIONS (LRWI)

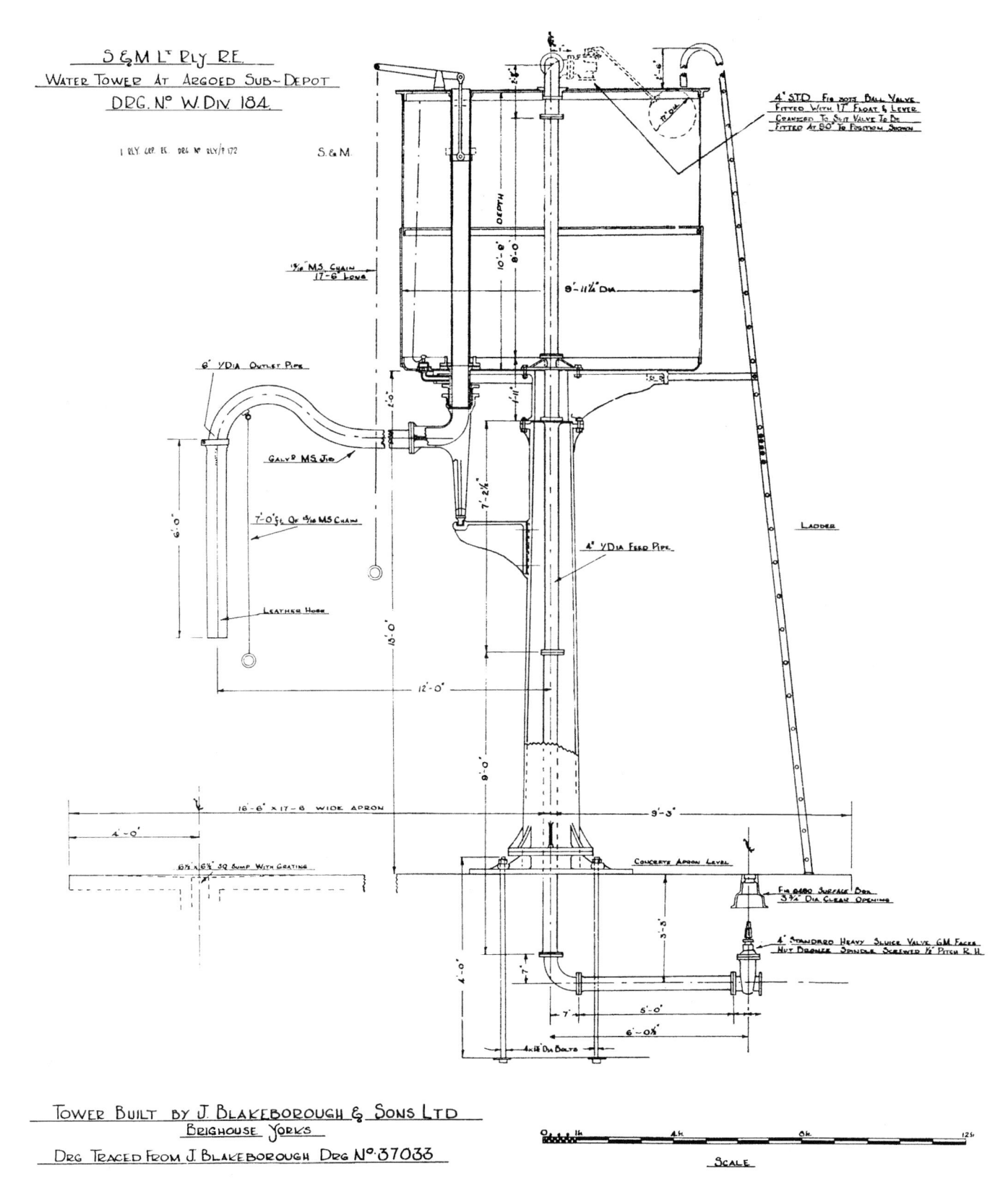

Opposite: A good close-up view of one of the water tanks that the WD installed at a number of locations on the S&M system – this one at the shed at Kinnerley.

David Petterson, from the 'Detachment Photograph Album'

THE SHROPSHIRE & MONTGOMERYSHIRE LIGHT RAILWAY UNDER MILITARY CONTROL 1940-1960

A view of Kinnerley from the direction of Criggion. From the right the lines were the Criggion Branch (which despite its name was usually used as a storage siding for granite traffic), the Criggion Loop (usually kept free as a running line), the Carriage & Wagon Repair Road and the Weighbridge Siding. From the latter there was a short siding on which much of the wagon repair work was done, hence the spare wheelsets beside the line. Once again, the L&SWR Saloon had been shunted to the end of the siding - anywhere to get it out of the way.
Lens of Sutton Association

The domain of the shed foreman extended as far as the Limit of Occupation and Maintenance board on the Criggion Branch, seen here looking towards Criggion. Note that close by the board the WD flat bottom rail ceased, and original S&M track lay beyond.
A. E. Bennett, Transport Treasury B4251

LOCAL RAILWAY WORKING INSTRUCTIONS (LRWI)

The Drewry Rail Car shed, constructed c1950 to house the four Drewry Rail Cars allocated (new from the builders) that year. This photo gives a useful comparison between the sizes of a Wickham Rail Car (on the left) and a Drewry Car. The Drewry Rail Cars could not readily be manhandled clear of the line. The Drewry Cars were 936 coupled to 937 with Wickham Car 915 to the left. Duty E was usually a Wickham Car turn – see page 170. *Brian Hilton, reference 53/23*

The view from the Civilian Yard across to the locomotive shed at Kinnerley on 21st September 1958, with the enthusiasts' special train temporarily stabled on the Down line beyond the block post. The pointwork giving access to the Drewry Car shed is visible in the mid distance, as are the two new Stop boards (one on the Criggion Branch and one on the Drewry Rail Car Shed Road). The substantial bogie wagon standing on the Criggion Bay line is one of the WW2 era 'Warflat' wagons, designed for carrying large loads and in particular to replace the 'Rectank' wagons for the carriage of AFVs (Armoured Fighting Vehicles, mainly 'tanks'). *Bluebell Railway Museum Archive – J. J. Smith Collection, reference 6-87-4*

THE SHROPSHIRE & MONTGOMERYSHIRE LIGHT RAILWAY UNDER MILITARY CONTROL 1940-1960

Kinnerley Block Post (BP) on 1st April 1947. This simple (the men would have called it 'basic') block post housed an LMS pattern lever frame of 20 levers, installed to face the back of the structure giving an unimpeded view through the front windows – though the fact that the structure was at ground level meant that any train stationary in front of the block post completely obscured the blockman's view anyway.

Graham Vincent

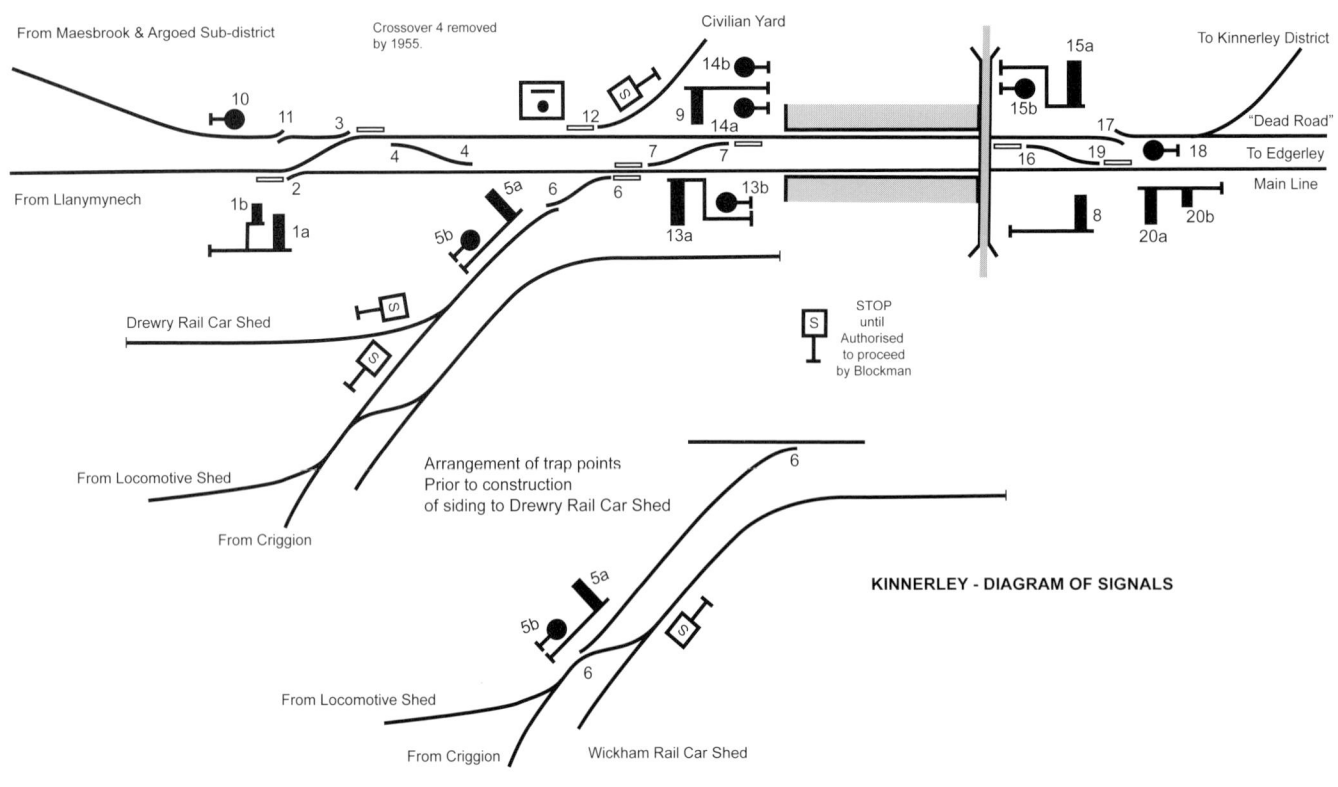

KINNERLEY - DIAGRAM OF SIGNALS

LOCAL RAILWAY WORKING INSTRUCTIONS (LRWI)

At times it could get quite busy at Kinnerley Block Post. In this view there was an engine on the Up/loop line, a Wickham Rail Car standing on the Down line outside the BP, another engine in Argoed District (the plume of steam in the distance) and an engine ready to leave the locomotive shed on the left. Added to this, the track repair gang were intermittently blocking the line in the Up platform by placing their packing jacks under the rail (though at this time they had taken their jacks out and were sitting on the rail instead). Note the parcels traffic waiting on both platforms. *David Petterson, from the 'Detachment Photograph Album'*

Kinnerley Station, viewed from the west end points, taken on 22nd May 1955 – by which time the crossover from the Down line (on the right) to the Up line and hence to Argoed (No. 4 points) had been removed. The block post is on the left, and the Criggion Branch converged from the right. The Stop board in the right foreground applied to the siding from the Drewry Rail Car shed. *Brian Hilton, reference 53/1*

THE SHROPSHIRE & MONTGOMERYSHIRE LIGHT RAILWAY UNDER MILITARY CONTROL 1940-1960

An interesting comparison between the size of a Wickham Rail Car and an ordinary locomotive (and showing the reason why the Wickham Cars carried flags) as a Wickham entered Kinnerley from the Llanymynech direction while one of the Austerity 0-6-0STs drew a train on to the Up line out of Argoed.
David Petterson, from the 'Detachment Photograph Album'

The west end at Kinnerley, looking towards Llanymynech on 22nd May 1955, with the line to Argoed Yard climbing away to the right. The bracket signal applied to the Up main line – the upper arm read along the straight route and thus to the Down platform, and the bracketed subsidiary signal through the crossover to the Up platform. Bi-directional running through the Down platform was the norm. All the signals were standard LMS designs. *Brian Hilton, reference 53/22*

LOCAL RAILWAY WORKING INSTRUCTIONS (LRWI)

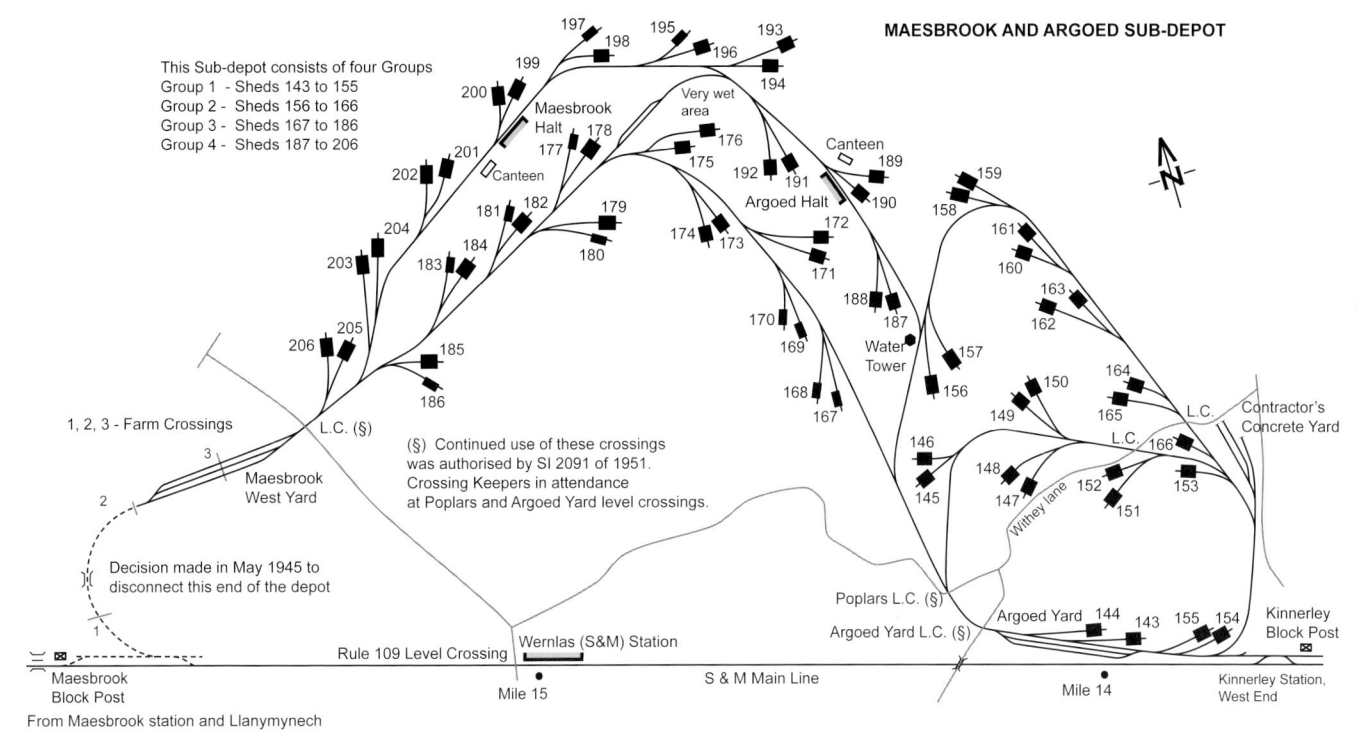

MAESBROOK AND ARGOED SUB-DEPOT

[Track diagram of Maesbrook and Argoed Sub-depot showing Sheds numbered 143 to 206 arranged in four Groups, with Maesbrook Halt, Argoed Halt, Canteens, Water Tower, Maesbrook West Yard, Argoed Yard, Kinnerley Block Post, Maesbrook Block Post, Wernlas (S&M) Station, Mile 14, Mile 15, S & M Main Line, and various level crossings including Rule 109 Level Crossing, Poplars L.C. (§), Argoed Yard L.C. (§), and Withey lane. Notes on diagram:

- This Sub-depot consists of four Groups
  - Group 1 - Sheds 143 to 155
  - Group 2 - Sheds 156 to 166
  - Group 3 - Sheds 167 to 186
  - Group 4 - Sheds 187 to 206
- Very wet area (near sheds 175/176)
- (§) Continued use of these crossings was authorised by SI 2091 of 1951. Crossing Keepers in attendance at Poplars and Argoed Yard level crossings.
- 1, 2, 3 - Farm Crossings
- Decision made in May 1945 to disconnect this end of the depot
- From Maesbrook station and Llanymynech
- Contractor's Concrete Yard
- Kinnerley Station, West End

Maesbrook and Argoed Sub-depot

Early papers called this Knockin Sub-depot. It consisted of four Groups:

Group 1 – Sheds 143 to 155
Group 2 – Sheds 156 to 166
Group 3 – Sheds 167 to 186
Group 4 – Sheds 187 to 206

Groups 1 and 2 comprised Argoed District, and Groups 3 and 4 were Maesbrook District.

The whole Sub-depot was worked as one yard. During the hours of darkness 'One Engine in Steam' only was allowed. In daylight, a subsequent train could be allowed to enter, with the usual Red Caution Order rules applying. Propelling was allowed, subject to the usual 5 mph speed limit and the requirement to run round in either Maesbrook West or Argoed Yard at the first opportunity.

There was a passenger platform at the western end of Maesbrook District, to which a daily workmen's train ran. The Controller was not to allow any other train to enter the Sub-depot within five minutes of the passenger train either being due to enter the Sub-depot at Kinnerley, or to depart from Maesbrook West Yard. Trains already in the Sub-depot were required to be clear of the route of the passenger train at least five minutes before the booked times of the passenger train from Kinnerley or Maesbrook West Yard.

There were level crossings in the Sub-depot at:

i) West end of Argoed Yard
ii) Junction of Groups 1 and 2 at the west end of Argoed Yard (Poplars level crossing)
iii) Gathering Line (Group 1) near shed 151 (Withey Lane)
iv) Gathering Line (Group 2) between spurs 166-165 (Withey Lane)
v) Maesbrook West Yard (Wern Las Public Road)

Crossing keepers were in attendance at (i) and (ii) to hand signal trains over the crossing. The crossing keepers were to show red signals against the road traffic (red flag by day, red light during darkness) and when road traffic had been brought to a stand, hand signal the train over the crossing. The Argoed crossing keeper was responsible for passing any messages to the crossing keeper at Poplars as necessary. In the absence of the crossing keepers, Rule 103 was to be applied at the Rule 103 boards provided (the same requirements as at Shoot Hill applied, see page 81).

Wern Las and Paper Mill Level Crossings

At Paper Mill level crossing, rail drivers were required only to sound the whistle, reduce speed to 10 mph, and be prepared to stop short of any obstruction. The level crossings with public roads at Maesbrook and Wern Las were more restrictive.

Wern Las level crossing, looking east towards Kinnerley c1949. On the right was the pole for closing off the road when rail traffic approached (there appears to have been only one pole at this crossing, not one either side of the railway). Waiting on the platform were some milk churns, a reminder that until 1st May 1949 Wern Las was open for civilian traffic, so the WD had to work a Civilian goods service between Llanymynech and Kinnerley, not just east of Kinnerley.

Geoffrey Bannister, courtesy of Andrew Bannister

THE SHROPSHIRE & MONTGOMERYSHIRE LIGHT RAILWAY UNDER MILITARY CONTROL 1940-1960

Wern Las, looking west towards Llanymynech shortly before closure. The crossing keeper's house dated from the original line built by the Potteries, Shrewsbury & North Wales Railway, which operated from 13th August 1866 until it was closed by the Board of Trade as from 22nd June 1880 because it had become unsafe. The short platform had been built for the re-opening of the line as a Light Railway in 1911. Few people lived in the vicinity, so the pole barriers at the road crossing had been removed. Rule 103 now applied here. The rear of the Rule 103 Board for Up trains can be seen in the distance.

Stations (UK) reference number 11026

At the road crossing at Maesbrook, as at Wern Las, pole barriers were installed during the war years. The 'WD Land. Entry Prohibited' signs were prominent along the S&M and deterred many photographers – so photographs taken inside the Sub-depots are very rare. On this day one wagon, probably delivering coal, was standing on the short siding at the Kinnerley end of the station. Coal was about the only civilian traffic that the WD had to work to this rather remote location. A photograph taken on 1st April 1947 – note that the pre-war bull head rail was still in use here, as it was generally west of Kinnerley at this time.

Graham Vincent

LOCAL RAILWAY WORKING INSTRUCTIONS (LRWI)

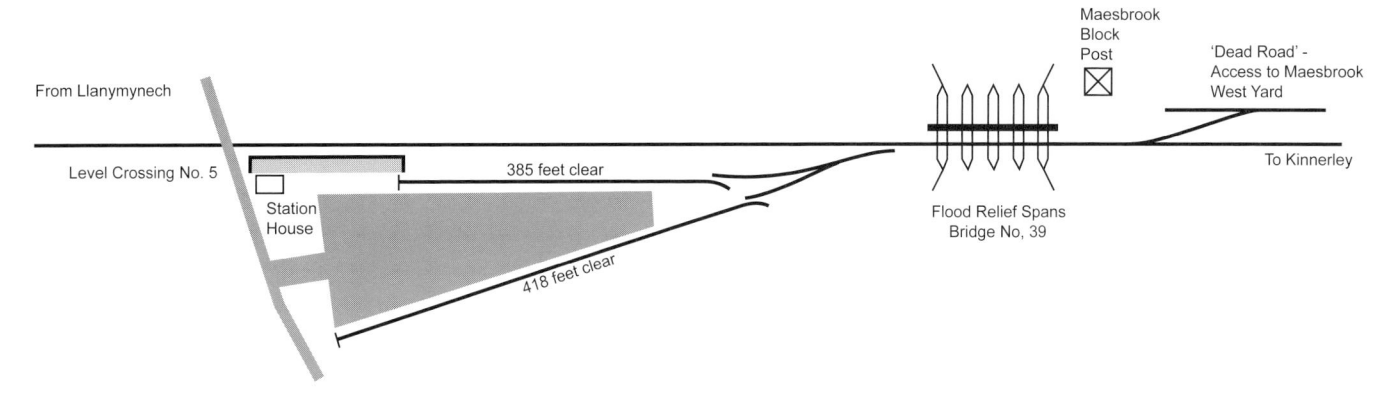

Maesbrook

The War Department laid in an additional siding here and moved the connection to the running line eastwards nearly to the abutments of underline Bridge No. 39 so as to extend the existing siding, giving sidings of 418 and 385 feet clear distance from the trap points, and made up level of the roadway in the yard between them. This produced an 'emergency RRT' – road/rail transfer point.

The emergency exit from the west end of Maesbrook and Argoed Sub-depot joined the route of the running line some distance east of Bridge 39. Here the line from Maesbrook West Yard connected to a 'Dead Road' siding constructed by the WD on the formation of the former double track, the Dead Road being accessed from the running line by connections at both the east end of Bridge No. 39 and at the Kinnerley end. Beside Bridge No. 39 the WD constructed Maesbrook Block Post, allowing this block post to control the access to both the sidings at Maesbrook Station yard/emergency RRT and the emergency access to the Sub-depot via the Dead Road.

The public road at Maesbrook was sufficiently busy to warrant the installation of pole barriers, but these were removed when the line was relaid in the 1950s and replaced by Rule 97 boards. A revised Military Railways Rule Book was issued on 8th November 1955, replacing the 1938 version. In the new rule book, the wording of what had been Rule 103 became part of Rule 97. Only Stop boards installed after this change were painted with the new Rule number – existing Stop boards were not changed.

Maesbrook, looking westwards on 14th February 1959 after the WD had relaid the track with 75lb rail on concrete sleepers. The pole barriers at the level crossing had been taken away and replaced by Stop boards. The board is lettered 'Stop Rule 97'. *Photographer unknown, from the 'Detachment Photograph Album'*

Looking eastwards through Maesbrook Station on 16th August 1955. Concrete sleepers and flat bottom rails had been laid out in readiness for track renewal, though someone might regret unloading the rails on to the platform rather than to ground level. The connection into the goods yard can be seen beyond the Drewry Rail Car, and Maesbrook Block Post can just be seen to the left of the head of the chap stepping over the pile of concrete sleepers. The old 'conditional stop' signal lasted until the closure of the line – always set at 'Stop'. Indeed, it appears to have been repainted between 1947 and 1955 – the white horizontal band had been painted over.

Brian Connell (Photos/Fifties Ref. B63/12)

Maesbrook Station in its final years. A general air of decay pervaded because although the WD had spent a lot of money on replacing the track, the line from Kinnerley to Llanymynech was only regarded as an 'emergency exit' from the CAD (Central Ammunition Depot) and it saw very little use.

Photographer unknown, from the 'Detachment Photograph Album'

LOCAL RAILWAY WORKING INSTRUCTIONS (LRWI)

West of Maesbrook on 22nd May 1955 with new rail and concrete sleepers unloaded ready for the wholesale renewal of the old S&M bull head rail and life-expired sleepers. A view looking towards Llanymynech, with the rear of the Stop board for Maesbrook road crossing on the left. *Brian Hilton, reference 53/25*

About a quarter of a mile west of Maesbrook was a low viaduct, Bridge No. 41. This was formed of a number of flood relief spans, creating a gap in the embankment to allow flood waters to pass through – the railway at this point was encroaching on the flood plain of the River Morda (which joins the River Vyrnwy about a mile away). It is not unknown for the land either side of the railway to be flooded to a depth of several feet – the reason why no Sheds were built on the south side of the line west of Kinnerley (north of the line the land is slightly higher as far west as Maesbrook). In the distance can be seen – just – the level crossing (Level Crossing No. 6) with the lane leading down to the Paper Mill beside the River Morda (the mill is out of view on the left). *R. M. Casserley, reference 18151K*

THE SHROPSHIRE & MONTGOMERYSHIRE LIGHT RAILWAY UNDER MILITARY CONTROL 1940-1960

Looking east across the WD sidings at Llanymynech on 22nd May 1955. The running line was to the left, dividing into two lines through the platforms, with the sidings on the south side (to the right in this view). An enthusiasts' special train had reversed into the sidings. The water tank existed before the WD lease, but was not reliable and was not used. The siding behind the platform, accessed through the gate visible behind the 'WD Land No Entry' sign, led to Mason's Timber Yard (maintained by the WD but by this date normally shunted by a main line engine). Note the 'concrete post and wire' fence put in on either side of the gateway to the timber siding, enclosing the additional land purchased by the WD to allow the construction of this group of sidings.
Brian Hilton, reference 53/31

The two WD platform lines at Llanymynech, looking towards the junction (beyond the road overbridge) with the BR lines. The main line platforms, and station buildings, are to the right. The WD had been compelled to relay the left hand track, but that on the right was still in original bull head rail.
Bluebell Railway Museum Archive – J. J. Smith Collection

LOCAL RAILWAY WORKING INSTRUCTIONS (LRWI)

The WD platform lines were continuously curved, which (coupled with restricted vision) led to an instruction that all shunting movements here had to be restricted to low numbers of vehicles. The pre-war S&M station building on the Down (left hand) platform still looked quite smart – the wall cabinet with black and white stripes was an addition to house a telephone. The WD lines converged beyond the platform ends, and beyond that was a disc signal controlling any movements through the trap points that protected the main line. In the distance, beside the junction stands the BR (ex-GWR) signal box, a main line train can be seen departing in the direction of Welshpool. 26th June 1954.
Bluebell Railway Museum Archive – J. J. Smith Collection

Llanymynech

Llanymynech Yard was the emergency exchange point with the national railway system. The initial WD layout constructed in 1941 provided four loop sidings, but this was later reduced to just two yard roads, numbered 1 and 2 respectively from the main line. After the block post was taken out of use, trains approaching from Kinnerley had to halt at a Stop board short of the points giving access to the sidings at the east end. The brakesman/shunter then checked that the line was clear, bearing in mind that wagons might have been placed from the GWR (later BR) end, before hand signalling the train forward. At the east end of the yard trap points were provided, worked from a ground frame.

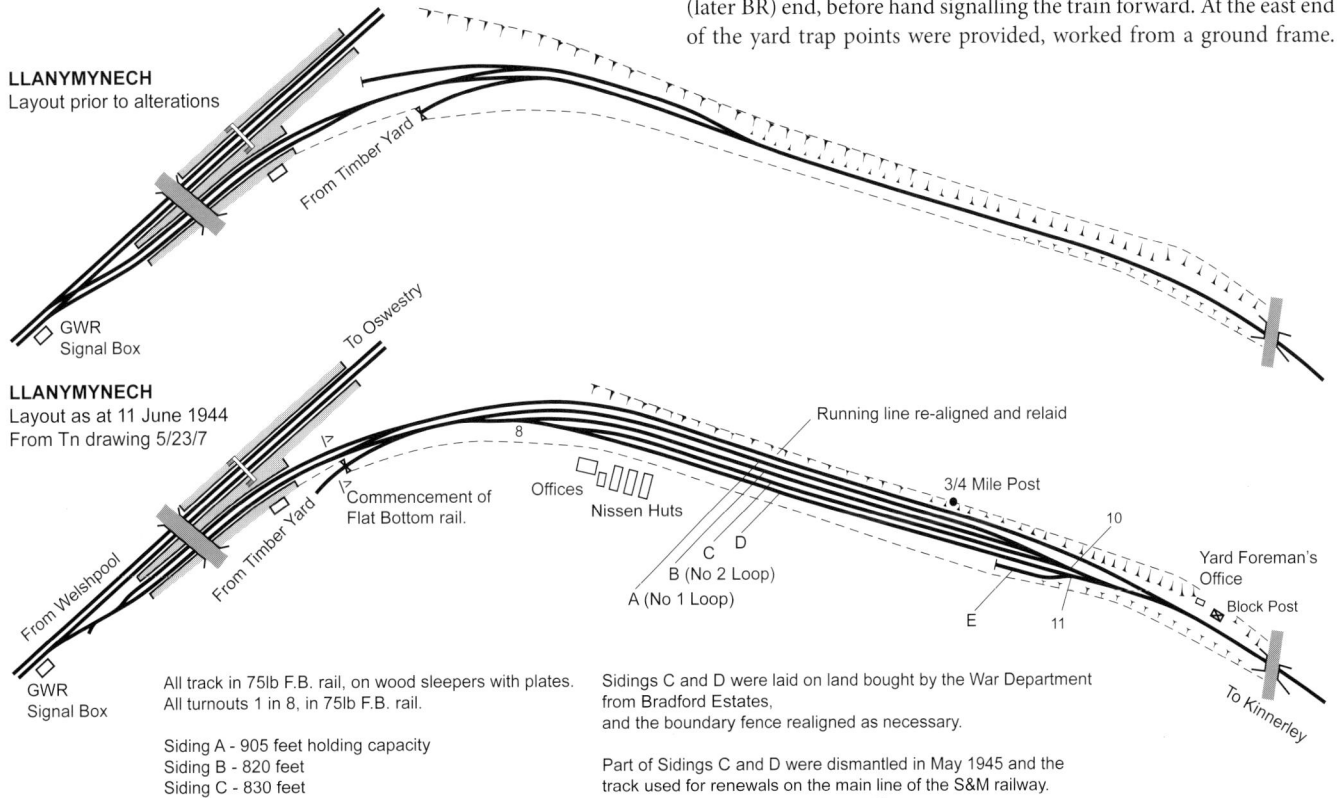

LLANYMYNECH
Layout prior to alterations

LLANYMYNECH
Layout as at 11 June 1944
From Tn drawing 5/23/7

All track in 75lb F.B. rail, on wood sleepers with plates.
All turnouts 1 in 8, in 75lb F.B. rail.

Siding A - 905 feet holding capacity
Siding B - 820 feet
Siding C - 830 feet
Siding D - 825 feet
Siding E - 41 feet

Sidings C and D were laid on land bought by the War Department from Bradford Estates,
and the boundary fence realigned as necessary.

Part of Sidings C and D were dismantled in May 1945 and the track used for renewals on the main line of the S&M railway.
Turnouts 8, 10 and 11 were removed later.

127

The road bridge (Bridge No. 46) at the south end of Llanymynech Station spanned both the BR lines (on the left) and the WD platforms. On 22nd May 1955, locomotive WD 189 waited before running round the coaches of an enthusiasts' special.
Brian Hilton, reference 53/28

The exit from the west end of the station was protected by a ground signal worked from the main line signal box.

The northern line in the platforms (the one nearest to the main line station) was used for placing outwards traffic for collection by the GWR/BR locomotive. This was not to be placed beyond a 'Limit of Shunt' board on No. 46 road overbridge. Because of the severity of the curve, the number of wagons in a single shunt move was to be kept low (but no figure was specified). The south S&M platform was used for receiving traffic on to the WD railway.

The two S&M platform lines were connected by a turnout immediately north of the trap points worked from the main line signal box. Before using this turnout to run round, the WD train crew needed the signalman there to close the trap points and clear the ground disc signal. Running round a train was usually done by backing the train into one of the loop sidings.

The No. 2 siding was in later years allocated to the North Wales Wagon Company, which broke up crippled rolling stock here. The BR locomotive placed these wagons and the maximum number of wagons allowed on this siding was forty-three. The Wagon Company were also allowed to use No. 1 siding for the loading of scrap.

Mason's Timber Yard was served by a dead end siding. This was a private siding maintained by the WD, but traffic was usually worked by a shunting locomotive from British Railways.

On 26th August 1946, one of the J69 locomotives (WD 70084) was paused during shunting when a Whitchurch to Welshpool train arrived on the main line. This train connected at Llanymynech with the branch train to Llanfyllin, which can be seen waiting in a siding in the distance, to follow into the platform as soon as the main line train had departed. The quarries on Llanymynech Hill are a feature of the background.
W. A. Camwell

A view of the WD lines through the platforms at Llanymynech, taken from a westbound train on the main line. The WD treated the outlet to the Depot via Llanymynech as an 'emergency connection' so it was common for there to be no signs of any traffic on the WD side of the station. *Lens of Sutton Association*

By the time that this photograph was taken on 14th February 1959 it was becoming well known that the WD would be giving up its use of the S&M in just over a year's time. The station building at Llanymynech was slowly decaying, and the platform lines were now simply used for stabling wagons awaiting breaking up, or (on the left) outgoing loads of recovered scrap metal. *Photographer unknown*

THE SHROPSHIRE & MONTGOMERYSHIRE LIGHT RAILWAY UNDER MILITARY CONTROL 1940-1960

With the 0-6-0 tank locomotives perforce out of use until bridge strengthening had been completed, the year 1947 saw the Dean Goods still in use. This was WD 180 (GWR 2514) at Kinnerley shed on 21st June 1947. The locomotive carried reminders of the work done to prepare it for work in France (fittings for brake pump, and bolt holes for side chains) and by now the footplate was buckled at the front. Nearly worn out, but still serviceable.
H. C. Casserley, reference 49024

The most outwardly obvious change following the end of the war was the arrival on the S&M of the 0-6-0 saddle tank locomotives built in some numbers for war service, and generally known as the 'Austerity' locomotives. Four arrived early in 1947, and on 1st April of that year they were stored beside the Criggion Loop at Kinnerley, waiting for bridge strengthening work to be completed to allow them to work along the whole length of the line. Early arrivals were painted in 'camouflage green' or a shade of brown, but later arrivals were black.
R. K. Cope (RKC/B307) from the 'Detachment Photograph Album'

Chapter 5
THE POST-WAR PERIOD

Review of operations post-1945

In 1945, the Army had to review urgently its operations on the S&M. It was clear that the rundown of the ordnance factories and storage depots was not going to be very rapid (as it was at the end of the 1914-18 War) and it was envisaged that Nesscliff CAD would be needed for at least another ten years. A meeting on 23rd May 1945 noted, however, that the intention was to allow officers and men to return to civilian life – if they so desired – as soon as their particular release groups became eligible for demobilisation. The manpower requirements were high:

Main line maintenance		66
Depot track maintenance		22
Main line operating		
Blockmen	10	
Railway engine drivers	6	
Firemen	4	
Brakesman/shunter	1	
Crossing-keepers	6	
Main line operating total		27
Depot operating		
Blockmen	2	
TO's	10	
Brakesmen/shunters	12	
Firemen (trainee)	3	
Pointsmen	2	
C&W repairers	3	
Crane drivers	3	
Platelayer	1	
Welder/electricians etc.	13	
Shed sweepers	6	
Depot operating total		55
Grand Total		170

In addition to these there were still seven pre-war S&M employees, of whom four were on permanent way duties, one locomotive driver, one fireman and one fitter.

Post-war WD traffic was expected to be about 100 wagon movements per day, forty-five to and from the various Sub-depots and forty to and from the railhead via Ford marshalling yard. There was also the civilian traffic, much of which was stone from the quarries at Criggion, or to and from Abbey Yard at Shrewsbury. In January 1946, forty loaded fuel tank wagons and thirty other wagons were placed in Abbey Yard. In addition, a passenger train service for WD staff had to be worked. One workmen's train ran in the morning from Maesbrook to Shrawardine Sub-depot station, with a return working in the evening. Similar trains ran daily from Shrewsbury (Abbey) to Shrawardine. The Movement Control HQ was at Nesscliff Camp, with detachments at Shrawardine and Hookagate.

The pre-war survey which suggested that the land beside the River Severn between Shrawardine and Kinnerley (although low lying) would not flood was wrong. In February 1946, the flood levels reached their highest level since 1795. The flood water reached twenty-six Explosive Store Houses, to depths varying from six inches to three feet. All the ammunition in these sheds, amounting to 25,000 tons, had to be moved. This was not easily achieved because the depot was nearly full, so sorting accommodation was not available. Some ammunition had to be dealt with rapidly because it had become dangerous after immersion in water. By September 1946 the task was complete. The level of additional work, and the normal levels of traffic at that time, are shown by these figures for traffic levels in conventional ammunition and explosives (in tons) in the summer of 1946:

	July	August	September
Issues	2,250	3,600	3,000
Receipts	1,350	140	220
Internal*	22,637	9,345	9,330

* tonnage moved for inspection, repair or re-stacking

THE SHROPSHIRE & MONTGOMERYSHIRE LIGHT RAILWAY UNDER MILITARY CONTROL 1940-1960

Above: The locomotives on the system may have been renewed, but the maintenance facilities remained basic. WD 75171 received attention on No. 1 Loco Shed Road, and the locomotive on No. 2 Road carried a board with the message 'Not to be Moved. Fitter at work'.
David Petterson, from the 'Detachment Photograph Album'

Left: Fitters at work indeed. Here the task required that the Austerity be jacked up whilst over the pit. Not for the faint hearted.
David Petterson, from the 'Detachment Photograph Album'

Ingenuity was the watchword of the fitters of the Royal Engineers. A weedkiller sprayer was constructed using the tender from an out-of-use Dean Goods engine – here seen leaving the Criggion Branch line at Kinnerley hauled by one of the Austerity locomotives.
David Petterson, from the 'Detachment Photograph Album'

THE POST-WAR PERIOD

The manpower strength at this time was:

	Officers	Other ranks
17 Coy R.A.O.C.	23	602
'I' Coy A.T.S.	3	168
206 Coy P.C.	3	401
S&M Lt Rly Detachment, R.E.	7	145

The manpower shortage created by constant turnover and demobilisation was expected to be so serious that the Army was forced to consider asking the S&M Light Railway Company to take over the operation of the line again and act as agents for working WD traffic. A number of problems had to be faced, not least the fact that WD pay rates were notably different from the NUR rates paid to S&M civilian employees:

	S&M Rate	WD Rate
Loco driver (steam)	£5 11s 6d	£4 19s 0d (inc 4s shift allce)
Platelayer	£4 2s 2d	£4 9s 0d
Brakesman/shunter	£4 12s 6d	£4 15s 0d

The Director of Tn wrote to Austen (the Secretary of the S&M) on 4th August 1945, but the matter was not followed up at that time. By early May 1946 the position appeared to demand action, for it was expected that by December there would only be 200 men on the complement of the whole camp. A meeting was held with Austen on 8th May, and it was agreed that the S&M should take over operations. However, the military did not take kindly to Austen's statement that the S&M would then 'naturally expect remuneration for their services and the use of their property'. The existing agreement was after all very advantageous to the WD, having been made at a time when the S&M was in desperate financial straits and had a badly run-down infrastructure. It appeared that overall the WD would be losing the close control which it enjoyed over its traffic, and would be paying greater costs. So when in December 1946 it seemed that the manpower situation was much better than forecast and that 600 servicemen were in post instead of the expected 200, and that there were 650 civilians available against an expected 200, the WD wrote politely to Austen saying that the scheme would not be proceeded with.

Closures upon Nationalisation in 1947

The lease agreement of 9th June 1942 thus continued in force until Nationalisation when the S&M line passed to the ownership of British Railways (Western Region) of the Railway Executive (BR). The WD continued to work the civilian traffic for BR. However, it did not take long for BR to realise that receipts did not compare well with staff costs. On 10th February 1949, Keith Grand (by now Chief Regional Officer for the Western Region of British Railways) wrote to the War Office saying that in view of the small amount of traffic handled at them, British Railways proposed closing the stations at Shrewsbury (West); Hookagate; Cruckton; Edgerley; and Wern Las (also Chapel Lane, Melverley, Crew Green, Llandrinio Road and Criggion on the branch which the WD did not operate), and asking whether the WD had any objections. The WD did not, so closure went ahead from 1st May 1949.

The former exchange siding connection at Meole Brace was little used, since Hookagate was the exchange point for WD traffic. The signal box at Meole Brace was formally closed, with the points clipped out of use, on 23rd September 1946. The connections on the BR line were removed in November/December 1949 (Shrewsbury end) and December 1950/January 1951 (Welshpool end). The sidings had been laid in for, and at the expense of, the S&M Light Railway, and BR now looked to the War Department for payment of the costs of removal, as an alternative to continuing costs of maintenance. In the event the value of the recovered materials (£682 10s 7d) more than covered these costs.

Disposal of a veteran locomotive

The rolling stock which had originally belonged to the S&M passed to the Western Region of BR. When **Gazelle** was withdrawn from BR stock in the summer of 1950 it faced being broken up. Some Army officers had, however, expressed concern that such an interesting machine should be scrapped, so on 4th August 1950 Sir Eustace Missenden of the Railway Executive formally wrote to Brigadier R. Gardiner, the Director of Transportation at the War Office, offering the locomotive to Longmoor for preservation in the WD Museum there. Keith Grand was to make the necessary arrangements for transport to Longmoor. After some time at Longmoor and then the erstwhile Museum of Army Transport at Beverley, the locomotive is now (2011) at the Colonel Stephens Museum at Tenterden on the Kent & East Sussex Light Railway.

Pity poor **Gazelle**. By the end of the war the ravages of years of being stored outside (the WD railway was notably very short of covered accommodation for any rail vehicles) had taken their toll. As this photograph, taken on 21st June 1947, showed no-one had even secured the smokebox door or placed a cover on the chimney, so rust was everywhere. At least the historic nature of this locomotive was recognised and shortly after the wartime emergency was over steps were taken to give this veteran a safe home. The locomotive was photographed standing on the Weighbridge Road at Kinnerley. Note the difference in height between the buffers on the locomotive and those of the adjacent wagon on the left.
H. C. Casserley, reference 49027

THE SHROPSHIRE & MONTGOMERYSHIRE LIGHT RAILWAY UNDER MILITARY CONTROL 1940-1960

Bridge reconstruction

The S&M had long been plagued by the weak state of some of its bridges, and the bridge over the River Severn near Melverley (on the Criggion Branch) was out of use after the floods of January 1940 until late in 1941. On 5th June 1942 it was noted that for the previous six months the bridge had been regarded as so weak that no locomotive could safely pass over it, so the quarry locomotive pushed wagons on to the bridge from one side, while the WD locomotive drew them off from the other. The WD was under pressure to ensure that as much as possible of the quarry traffic was handled by rail, thereby saving on petrol and rubber, and the next six months saw detailed planning of work to strengthen the bridge girders. Repairs were made that allowed the quarry company's Sentinel locomotive to cross, but it was only a temporary respite.

The bridge at Melverley was finally replaced by a new structure, but the financing of the work was unusual. The line was not used by the WD, so the government had no reason to pay for a replacement bridge. The post-war roads programme, however, required that the stone be got out from the quarry, and that all the output go by rail. So it was regarded as a matter of national importance that the bridge over the River Severn at Melverley, and a smaller underline bridge near to Kinnerley, be replaced. The solution was that the government made a loan to the S&M company for the costs of the work, the loan to be repaid in equal instalments over twenty years at 2¾ per cent interest on the balance. In all this there was nothing especially unusual, but when the deal was being negotiated it was already known that the S&M company would be taken into national ownership at the end of 1947, so none of the loan would ever be repayable by the Company to which it was made. As early as 12th April 1947, Austen was writing to the officers of the British Transport Commission (BTC) asking for confirmation that the Commission would be taking over the loan. Despite the strange nature of the loan, it was given Ministerial approval on 22nd August 1947.

The work of building the new bridge went to contract, awarded to E. A. Farr & Co. of Westbury, Wiltshire at a price of £10,512 10s 0d. Steel was a commodity in short supply, and it was agreed that the steelwork would come from the Ministry of Supply at a price of £5,830 (delivered) – this cost to be extra to the building of the bridge. By 7th April 1948 detailed drawings had been done, and the cost had gone up to £17,550 10s 0d. It had also been agreed, however, that the River Severn Catchment Board would make a contribution of £6,000 and the British Quarry Company would pay £1,000. The final bill for the Railway Executive was £23,300 less the £7,000 promised contributions.

This was not the only 'extra' expense that the Railway Executive acquired from the S&M company. The Executive also had to pay the compensation (£400) payable to Austen for his loss of office as a Director of the Kent & East Sussex, East Kent, and Shropshire & Montgomeryshire Light Railways.

Reconstruction of Bridge 28

The WD entered into a programme of strengthening the weak bridges between Ford and Hookagate, and eventually had to face the reconstruction of the collapsing bridge (Bridge 28) by which the main line crossed the River Severn south-east of Shrawardine. The bridge had been built for double track, but for the reconstruction of the line as a Light Railway only the upstream spans had been utilised and those on the downstream side stood derelict. In July 1946 plans were drawn up for a new bridge to be made of standard steelwork using the existing stone abutments for the derelict downstream spans, but using new fabricated girder pillars in place of the (by now leaning considerably) original iron-clad piers. On completion of the work the upstream girders were taken out of use. The maximum permissible axle load on the whole system became 16 tons per axle.

Bridge 28 was renewed, but the old upstream spans remained in place. A meeting on site at the bridge on 21st April 1952 concluded that since nothing was being spent on maintenance, the disused spans would be left where they were. Another inspection visit was made on 8th April 1954, and it was discovered that cracks had formed in

The reconstruction of the bridge over the River Severn at Melverley on the Criggion Branch was officially nothing to do with the War Department. The WD did not lease, nor use, the Criggion Branch. Officially the bridge was designed by officers of the Western Region of British Railways and built by their contractors. This was, however, a time of extreme austerity in Britain after the war, and materials (especially steel) were hard to come by. The WD had large stocks of bridging materials, prepared in readiness for the invasion of Europe, and now held at a Transportation Stores depot at Longmoor (and other places). Comparison of this photo of the new viaduct at Melverley with the WD's new bridge at Shrawardine suggests that the steelwork for Melverley was provided from stores of WD materials. It also shows that the WD included a trip to Criggion by Drewry Rail Car in the itinerary of many enthusiasts' visits – even though officially the WD had nothing to do with that branch line.

Brian Hilton, reference 53/33

THE POST-WAR PERIOD

The view through the girders of Melverley bridge is almost 'pure WD', except that the track had been relaid in the S&M company's bull head rail.
R. K. Cope (RKC/B327)

the piers and the bracing. Some cross bracing between the piers had been removed to allow the construction of the rebuilt bridge, and the removal of this constraint appeared to have allowed the piers to move at an accelerating rate. It was therefore decided to demolish the old spans, because although their collapse was not seen as imminent, they would probably damage the new bridge if they did eventually fall over.

Once again the wording of the lease document caused problems – the WD was obliged to hand back the railway assets in the state in which it had leased them. Could it demolish part of the bridge? In addition, the bridge carried a water pipe and a 11,000 volt power cable. So there was a lengthy exchange of letters before demolition could proceed. Photographs show that the old bridge was still standing in August 1955.

A visit to the railway on 1st April 1947 allowed Graham Vincent to record the start that had been made of reconstructing the bridge at Shrawardine. This view, taken from the north bank of the river, shows that the abutments had been cleared and that foundations for one of the new trestle piers were in place.
Graham Vincent

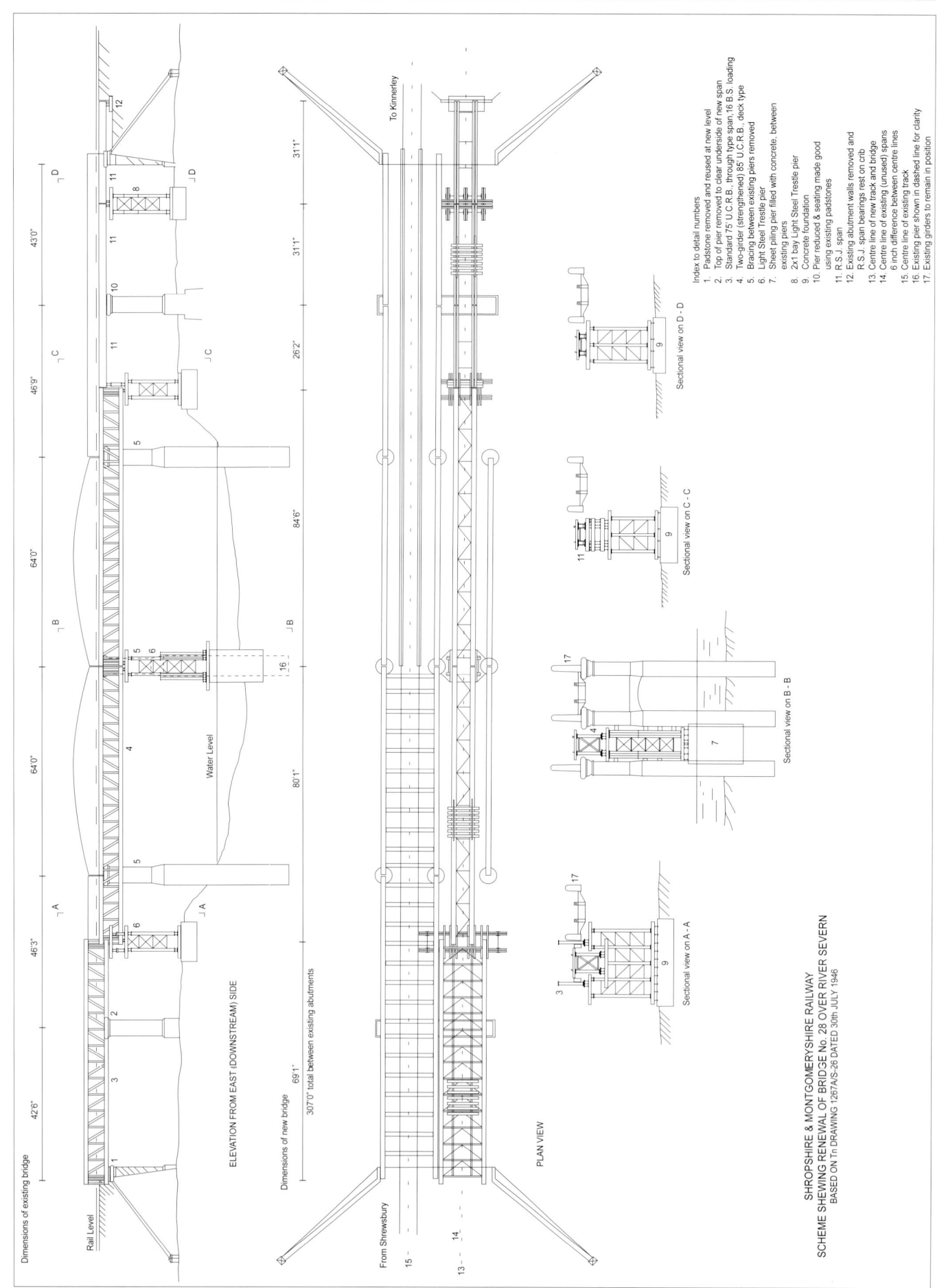

THE SHROPSHIRE & MONTGOMERYSHIRE LIGHT RAILWAY UNDER MILITARY CONTROL 1940-1960

Index to detail numbers

1. Padstone removed and reused at new level
2. Top of pier removed to clear underside of new span
3. Standard 75' U.C.R.B. through type span, 16 B.S. loading
4. Two-girder (strengthened) 85' U.C.R.B. deck type
5. Bracing between existing piers removed
6. Light Steel Trestle pier
7. Sheet piling pier filled with concrete, between existing piers
8. 2x1 bay Light Steel Trestle pier
9. Concrete foundation
10. Pier reduced & seating made good using existing padstones
11. R.S.J. span
12. Existing abutment walls removed and R.S.J. span bearings rest on crib
13. Centre line of new track and bridge
14. Centre line of existing (unused) spans 6 inch difference between centre lines
15. Centre line of existing track
16. Existing pier shown in dashed line for clarity
17. Existing girders to remain in position

SHROPSHIRE & MONTGOMERYSHIRE RAILWAY
SCHEME SHEWING RENEWAL OF BRIDGE No. 28 OVER RIVER SEVERN
BASED ON Tn DRAWING 1267A/S-26 DATED 30th JULY 1946

THE POST-WAR PERIOD

A view through the piers of the downstream side of the bridge, with the load bearing timbers almost completely removed, showing the cast iron ties that connected the piers. When the restraining effect of the girders and the ties between them was removed, the pier in the left foreground of this photograph shifted significantly (enough to break the tie seen in the foreground). *Graham Vincent*

Left: A view of Bridge 28 soon after the new work had been brought into use, with the girders as yet unpainted. The new earthworks on the approach to the bridge – where the formation had been widened – are evident.
Geoffrey Bannister, courtesy Andrew Bannister

Below: The reconstructed bridge on the downstream side, and the original track (now disconnected) on the left, seen on 16th August 1955. This view shows to good effect the short section of UCRB used as through girders, and the absence of hand rails on the downstream side. Sheds 32 and 31 are visible above the temporary wooden fencing on the left.
Brian Connell (Photos/Fifties Ref. B62/1)

137

THE SHROPSHIRE & MONTGOMERYSHIRE LIGHT RAILWAY UNDER MILITARY CONTROL 1940-1960

A view looking south along the old bridge on 22nd May 1955, showing some of the reasons why it was the subject of both speed and weight restrictions. However, the old spans continued to carry electrical cables and pipes, so their demolition was not going to be a simple matter. The spark arrestor on the locomotive was close to complete disintegration.

Brian Hilton, reference 53/17

The bridge, as seen during another enthusiasts' tour on 26th June 1955. The extreme angle of the nearest pier of the old bridge is evident, and the fracture of the cross tie bar is visible. This photograph brings out the three different methods used in carrying the railway – the nearest was rolled steel joists, then UCRB (Unit Construction Railway Bridge) girders used under the track, then UCRB used as through girders. The open doorways on the LT&S coaches serve to emphasise the lack of any footway on this side of the bridge.

Norman Glover (No. 4383) courtesy F. A. Wycherley

This view shows clearly the way in which the pier of the bridge, that stood away from the river and was built of stone, provided the Royal Engineers with a robust support that enabled them to make the northern end of the rebuilt bridge out of simple heavyweight rolled steel joists. The use of a trestle pier to support the junction of the RSJ section to the UCRB (used as an underline bridge) is also well illustrated.

R. C. Riley, Transport Treasury RCR 14539

THE POST-WAR PERIOD

Above: Because of the threat that the leaning piers presented to the new structure should they fall, the WD eventually got agreement that the dangerous piers should be removed. So the whole of the upstream structure, together with the piers on the downstream side (except the centre piers) was removed. It was not a simple task – as this photo shows the cast iron piers had been filled with rubble and mortar. *courtesy of* Soldier *magazine*

Left: The centre piers of the original bridge were retained, since they posed no threat to the new spans and performed a useful function in breaking the flow of water round the piling for the mid-stream pier. This photo, for which the Drewry Rail Car carrying the photographer waited on the new bridge, shows the detail of the construction of the piers using UCRB components. This is the view from the south side of the river, looking towards Shrawardine. The end of Shed 31 can be seen on the left. Note that a handrail had now been fitted on one side of the bridge.

Below: A Drewry Rail Car standing on the new No. 28 Bridge, looking downstream.
Left & below photographer unknown, from The 'Detachment Photograph Album'

THE SHROPSHIRE & MONTGOMERYSHIRE LIGHT RAILWAY UNDER MILITARY CONTROL 1940-1960

A part of the line that the WD decided not to relay was the section from Hookagate (East) to Shrewsbury Abbey. This charming if rather posed photo (possibly by a press photographer) taken near Meole Brace in the 1950s, shows the S&M's original bull head rail to be still in place. The sergeant was probably appointed to act as the photographer's 'minder' – and looks rather bemused as to why the photographer would think that the calf that has halted the progress of his Drewry Rail Car should be worthy of a photograph.
Photographer unknown, from The 'Detachment Photograph Album'

THE POST-WAR PERIOD

Peacetime maintenance by the War Department

With a view to a further ten years of occupation, the WD had to face the cost of continuing the upkeep of the railway. As early as May 1945, under-used track was lifted to provide rails for necessary replacements on the main line, some parts of which still had the S&M bull head rail. The section of the line from Llanymynech to Kinnerley had always been regarded by the WD as an emergency exit route only, to be kept functional in case the bridge at Shrawardine was lost to enemy attack. So as the war ended and that threat was removed, this was the section of line that was 'cannibalised'. Two of the four loop sidings at Llanymynech were removed, as was the western connection in to Maesbrook District. Further, in May 1949 one of the exchange sidings at Llanymynech was leased to the North Wales Wagon Company for an extension of its wagon-repairing facilities, leaving only the running line and one loop siding, plus the two platform lines, for the WD to operate as its exchange siding facility.

Limited use was made of the line between Kinnerley and Llanymynech line so it had never come high in priority for track renewals. By 1954 something had to be done, and on 21st April 1954 the Commandant of the Depot put a proposal to the Under Secretary at the War Office for relaying with concrete sleepers at the very considerable cost of £25,000. Then the question arose as to whether the siding at Wern Las (closed to public traffic on 1st May 1949) had to be relaid or whether it could be removed and the points replaced by plain line. The 1942 Agreement, after all, required that when the WD eventually gave up its occupation of the railway, the line had to be fully restored to its pre-1941 condition, so there was debate as to whether the siding had to be retained even though it had been disused for six years. British Railways accepted that it did not. The situation here was curiously different from that at Edgebold, where the siding points into the milk depot were replaced by plain line during relaying in Summer 1954, because the siding connection there had been laid in by the WD during 1942 (albeit using old S&M rails in the siding), so that the retention of the siding was not required to meet the 'pre-war conditions'.

Level crossings

During the war years, the nature of the 'national emergency' was such that no-one argued with the making of new level crossings across public roads. Post-war, however, the local authorities that had responsibility for roads became very exercised about the dangers presented by level crossings that had no legal authorisation, especially those that did not have the protection of gates. The problem was met using the powers of the Requisitioned Land and War Works Act 1945 as extended by the Requisitioned Land and War Works Act 1948 (and especially Section 3). On 26th November 1951, an Under Secretary of the Ministry of Transport sealed Statutory Instrument 2091 of the year 1951, which authorised the continued use of the level crossings of the Gathering Lines across the public roads at three places in the Argoed and Maesbrook Sub-depot (the locations marked § on the plan on page 121). It is notable that two other level crossings on Withey Lane were not included, which was to cause problems to the WD later. Nor did the Order include the several shed spurs that crossed the road from Kinnerley to Treginford in no less than six places – perhaps because the traffic on that road was so quiet.

In the early 1950s, the WD undertook the relaying of the track from Kinnerley to Llanymynech. In places this amounted to simply lifting out old rail and sleepers and replacing with new. On other parts of the line, the WD did an exercise in completely digging out the trackbed and ditches (and most of the surrounding hedges as well).

courtesy of Soldier *magazine*

An interesting comparison in size between one of the Austerity tank locomotives and a Drewry Rail Car, both standing in front of the block post at Kinnerley. The locomotive carried the number 143. By the end of 1951 the War Department had disposed of many of the older locomotives that it had acquired during the exigencies of the 'wartime emergency', so at the beginning of 1952 it undertook a wholesale renumbering of the remaining locomotive stock. 143, which had previously been numbered WD 75152, came to the S&M from Cairnryan in February 1947. It went away to Donnington around November 1953 and thence to Bagnall's works for repairs. It was back on the S&M from July 1956 until closure, when it went to the Central Ordnance Depot at Bicester. Of the first four Austerity locomotives to arrive at Kinnerley, WD 75152 was the only one of the four that was fitted with the vacuum brake to work passenger trains.

Lens of Sutton Association

THE POST-WAR PERIOD

Additions to locomotive stock

The increased weight allowance permitted the introduction of WD Austerity tank locomotives with their axle loading of 16t 7cwt. At least twenty-one of these are known to have worked on the S&M at various times. Their arrival allowed the withdrawal of the worn-out Dean Goods and 'Collier' engines. The first Austerity tank was received in 1947 and by the end of that year there were five at work on the line. Locomotives 75141, 75152 (fitted with vacuum brake and so suitable for working passenger trains), 75187 and 75191 were all at Kinnerley shed on 1st April 1947, but were stored out of use pending the completion of bridge strengthening. By mid-1948 only one of the Dean Goods was still in use. Others, with the 'Colliers' and the two J69s, were stored in Hookagate Yard.

The new locomotives were not universally popular, despite the fully-enclosed cabs. The tank capacity was only 1,200 gallons, which meant that drivers had to 'run to a water column' more often than with a 'Dean', which carried 3,000 gallons. This could be a problem, because latterly the only water columns were at Abbey, Hookagate, Ford Yard, Kinnerley Loco and Argoed Yard. There were none in Nesscliff, Shrawardine or Pentre Districts. Another point was that the 4ft 3in. wheels on an overall 11 foot wheelbase gave a more lively (a euphemism for 'rough') ride than the 'Dean' class, which had 5ft 2in. wheels and a 15ft 6in. wheelbase.

One Ruston & Hornsby four-wheeled diesel locomotive was tried on the S&M in 1945. It came new from the makers, but went on to Longmoor before the end of the year. Another 0-4-0 diesel shunter was tried in 1955. North British 0-4-0 Diesel hydraulic locomotive WD 8201 (later to become AD 401 in the 1968 re-numbering), came new from the makers (builder's number 27422) on 23rd April 1955, but departed for Tidworth on 15th November. Not for the first time, the operators decided that small 0-4-0 shunting locomotives were not what was required in a Depot where trip haulage over some distance was all part of normal working.

DIAGRAM OF AUSTERITY LOCOMOTIVE.

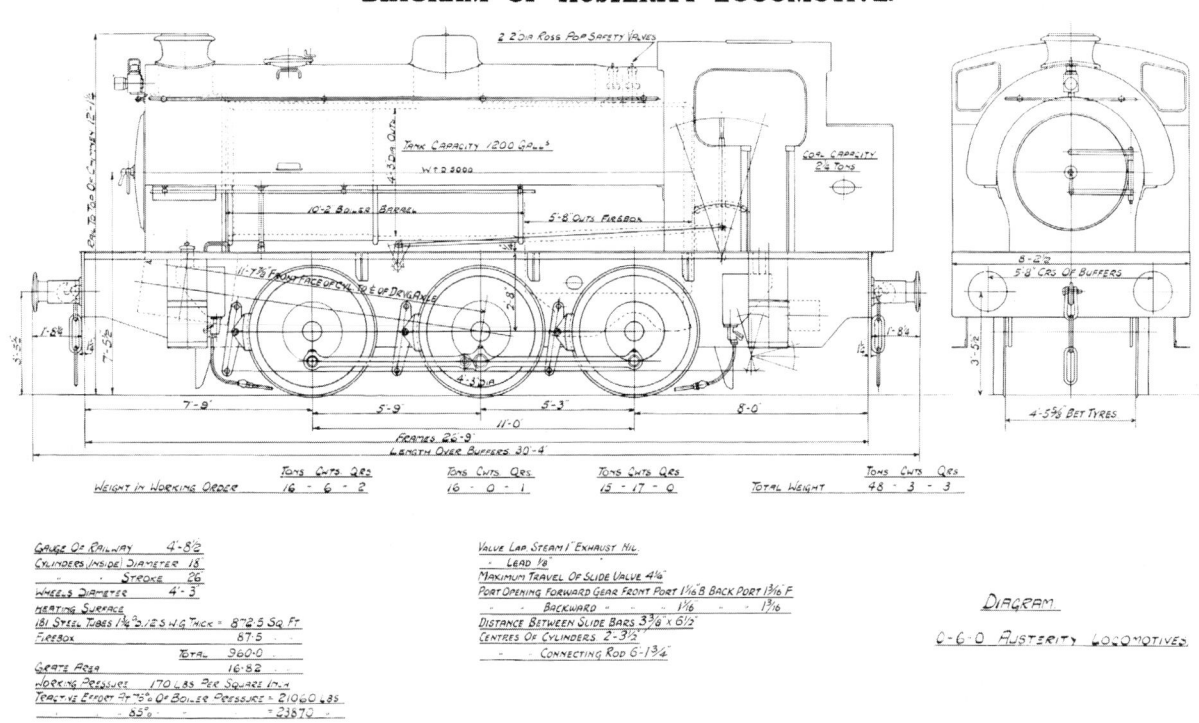

SCHEDULE FOR LUBRICATION CHART.

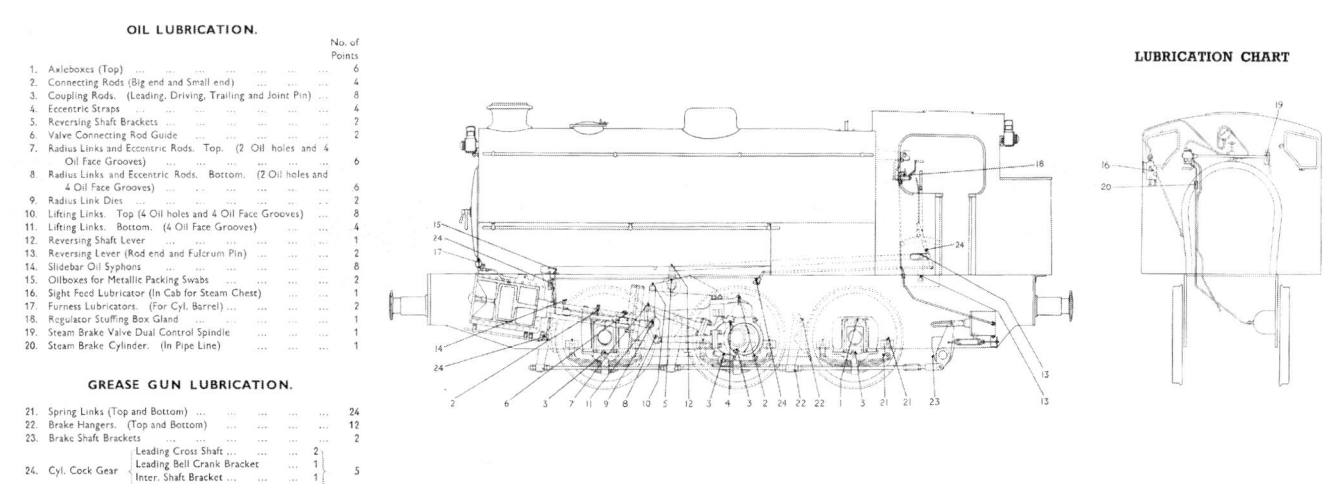

OIL LUBRICATION.

	No. of Points
1. Axleboxes (Top)	6
2. Connecting Rods (Big end and Small end)	4
3. Coupling Rods. (Leading, Driving, Trailing and Joint Pin)	8
4. Eccentric Straps	4
5. Reversing Shaft Brackets	2
6. Valve Connecting Rod Guide	2
7. Radius Links and Eccentric Rods. Top. (2 Oil holes and 4 Oil Face Grooves)	6
8. Radius Links and Eccentric Rods. Bottom. (2 Oil holes and 4 Oil Face Grooves)	6
9. Radius Link Dies	2
10. Lifting Links. Top (4 Oil holes and 4 Oil Face Grooves)	8
11. Lifting Links. Bottom. (4 Oil Face Grooves)	4
12. Reversing Shaft Lever	1
13. Reversing Lever (Rod end and Fulcrum Pin)	2
14. Slidebar Oil Syphons	8
15. Oilboxes for Metallic Packing Swabs	2
16. Sight Feed Lubricator (In Cab for Steam Chest)	1
17. Furness Lubricators. (For Cyl. Barrel)	2
18. Regulator Stuffing Box Gland	1
19. Steam Brake Valve Dual Control Spindle	1
20. Steam Brake Cylinder. (In Pipe Line)	1

GREASE GUN LUBRICATION.

21. Spring Links (Top and Bottom)	24
22. Brake Hangers. (Top and Bottom)	12
23. Brake Shaft Brackets	2
24. Cyl. Cock Gear — Leading Cross Shaft — 2; Leading Bell Crank Bracket — 1; Inter. Shaft Bracket — 1; Operating Handle — 1	5

LUBRICATION CHART

THE SHROPSHIRE & MONTGOMERYSHIRE LIGHT RAILWAY UNDER MILITARY CONTROL 1940-1960

A typical view of the 1950s – in this instance September 1957. WD 193 shunts vans in Ford Yard – note the ESH in the left background. On this locomotive, the W↑D and number were painted on the cab side. A train of British Railways vans at this time betrayed a variety of original owners – standardisation had yet to make a real impact.

M. N. Bland

Right: The Austerity 0-6-0STs have a powerful draught when working hard, and it was decided to fit them with spark arrestors. This photograph (although taken at Kineton) shows how these wire basket spark arrestors were fitted. In practice, the very corrosive exhaust gases, combined with the damp environment, meant that the spark arrestors rusted quickly. The sharp exhaust blast simply blew the fine mesh away. Photographs show that this apparatus was quickly reduced to a wire frame only. No serious attempt was made to keep them in working order.

courtesy Soldier *magazine*

Most of the photographs taken by enthusiasts were inevitably confined to the main line, so views of trains on the Gathering Lines and shed spurs are rare. Brian Connell took this photograph during a tour on 16th August 1955 of a train standing on a Gathering Line for the tour Drewry Rail Car to pass. Driver George Beeston on WD 141 working the 'Civilian Goods' turn, Duty A, waited for the line to become clear. Note the spark arrestor in 'nearly new' condition.

Brian Connell (Photos/Fifties Ref. B62/3)

THE POST-WAR PERIOD

Left, top and middle: The Austerity 0-6-0 saddle tank locomotives that were allocated by the WD to the S&M did not all arrive in pristine condition. Many had seen service elsewhere or had been stored outside for many months after the end of the war. Here WD 75187, one of the 1947 arrivals, was photographed standing at the front of a row of the 'new' locomotives at Kinnerley on 13th April 1947. Note that in the upper view the front coupling had been tied up during transit. The lower rear view was taken later. Note the tank number on the right side of the locomotive had not received the additional leading number 7.

Top, Geoffrey Bannister, courtesy Andrew Bannister
Middle, H. C. Casserley, reference 49025

Below: WD 143, on the No. 2 Coal Road at Kinnerley shed on 20th March 1960. The locomotive carried its number of the tank side, below W↑D in small lettering. The lamp post still carried the white band that had been painted to make it more visible during the blackout days of nearly twenty years before. Even though the railway was closing, the coal stack was as neat as ever. The official story was that the coal stocks had been run down to almost nil to save the trouble of having to load it to take away after the line closed. In reality, it was to prove necessary to continue working the line for a few more weeks, so a reasonable stock of coal was a prudent provision.

R. K. Blencowe Negative Archive, number 51758

145

THE SHROPSHIRE & MONTGOMERYSHIRE LIGHT RAILWAY UNDER MILITARY CONTROL 1940-1960

One of the WD tank locomotives fitted with the vacuum brake, seen approaching Nesscliff level crossing with the Civilian Goods, c1948. Note the pile of parcels on the platform – the handling of civilian traffic was an important (if subsidiary) task for the WD operators. *Geoffrey Bannister, courtesy Andrew Bannister*

In April 1951, WD 75192 was waiting in front of the Traffic Office at Ford Yard with the coaches for the return afternoon workmens train for Lonsdale Camp. Unusually the train was on No. 1 Siding, which was supposed to be kept free at all times as a reception road. The locomotive was not fitted with the vacuum brake – this passenger service would be worked using only the locomotive brake with no brakes on the coaches. The attached brake van would secure the coaches when the locomotive was uncoupled. *J. M. Clayton*

THE POST-WAR PERIOD

Above: The completion of bridge strengthening work allowed the introduction of the Austerity 0-6-0ST locomotives along the whole of the S&M. The older locomotives that had served so well during the war years, but which were worn out, were quickly sidelined to the sidings at Hookagate. This was the scene on 15th May 1948. Nearest the photographer were J69 tank locomotives WD 70084 and 70091 soon to go to John Lysaght Ltd. Beyond that were five Dean Goods locomotives (only one with its tender still attached) and then the out-of-service 'Colliers'. *P. J. Garland*

Left: 'Collier' WD 8236 at Hookagate on 21st June 1947, showing the final scheme of lettering applied to both the locomotive and tender. For a locomotive built in 1881 it had served well, but an appraisal made at Crewe Works on 16th September 1946 was that the boiler was not worth repairing so the engine was back at Hookagate.

R. K. Blencowe Negative Archive, number 37370

The grey-green livery applied to WD 8182 had faded almost to a grey-white by the time that this photograph was taken of the locomotive standing at Hookagate on 6th February 1949. It had been failed with a leaking firebox foundation ring in September 1946 and was not steamed again.

Photographer unknown

THE SHROPSHIRE & MONTGOMERYSHIRE LIGHT RAILWAY UNDER MILITARY CONTROL 1940-1960

WD 8108, the third of the trio of 'Collier' locomotives, was failed in November 1946 with a cracked firebox. As with the other 'Collier' locomotives on loan from the S&M and thereafter from British Railways, it was returned from the WD to BR and went to Swindon Works where it was scrapped in September 1950. Here it is seen on its final journey, photographed at Wolverhampton on 12th March 1949 – WD on the tender painted out but still carrying its LMS and WD number. It was still at Wolverhampton on 4th September. *Photographer unknown*

Also at Wolverhampton on 4th September 1949 were the other two of the trio – 8182 and 8236. The W↑D on the tender of 8236 had been rather crudely painted out with a long cross – these were now British Railways locomotives, not War Department. *L. W. Perkins (No. 3866) courtesy F. A. Wycherley*

The small tank locomotive **Ashford** had remained on the S&M until the end of the war, and was on the 'out of use' line at Kinnerley on 21st June 1947. Although officially renumbered 71872 in the 1944 renumbering scheme, the leading 7 was never added to the side of the locomotive – there was not enough space.

R. K. Blencowe Negative Archive, number 37373

148

THE POST-WAR PERIOD

In the line-up at Kinnerley were (from left to right) WD 70098 (GWR 2415), J69 Class 70084, **Ashford** and WD 70096. On 70096 the WD number had been painted, rather oddly, on the side of the firebox. Note that the locomotive carried a blanking plate where its GWR numberplate would have been.
Graham Vincent

WD 70098, also on the 'out of use' line at Kinnerley on 21st June 1947. The WD number was barely legible, but the locomotive still carried its GWR numberplate – 2415.
R. K. Blencowe Negative Archive, number 3737

By June 1947, some of the other Dean Goods locos had already been transferred to the 'scrap line' at Hookagate. The tender of WD 70095 showed that the letters WD had been applied, painted over, and then repainted again.
R. K. Blencowe Negative Archive, number 37375

THE SHROPSHIRE & MONTGOMERYSHIRE LIGHT RAILWAY UNDER MILITARY CONTROL 1940-1960

At the end of the back siding at Hookagate on 21st June 1947 was WD 70093 – still carrying its GWR number of 2433 on the buffer beam, which bore the holes where side chains had been fitted in readiness for working on the Continent. Behind were two more Dean Goods Class locomotives on which cutting up had already started – WD 70097 (GWR 2442) and 70099 (GWR 2528).

R. K. Blencowe Negative Archive, number 37376

A view of the 'scrap lines' at Hookagate Yard, this time taken on 1st April 1947. In the foreground, work had commenced on removing the lagging from the boilers of Dean Goods 70099 and 70097. In the siding beyond stood Dean Goods WD 70093, 70095 and 'Collier' engines 8182 and 8236. With the Austerity locomotives not yet in use, the train in the background was still hauled by one of the Dean Goods – WD 70196. The composition of the train is interesting, because it included not only two ex-GWR coaches and two of the LT&S coaches, but also some open goods wagons as well. The train may have been engaged in shunting. The locomotive was standing on the running line at the Down direction flagboard for Hookagate West Block Post – the two red flags on the board are just visible above the dome of one of the 'Collier' locos. The small shelter in the left foreground protected a group of fire buckets. There were several of these fire bucket compounds in the yard.

Graham Vincent

WD 70196 on the scrap line, still carrying the fittings on the smokebox to which the air brake pump had once been fitted in the early days of the war when it was expected that the engine would be sent to work in France. France had been occupied and liberated again since those days. Notice also that the handrail had been removed from along the boiler to allow for the fitting of pannier tanks. The inset, below, shows the name **Pretty Polly** painted on the middle splasher of 70196.

Photographer unknown

150

THE POST-WAR PERIOD

The S&M was responsible for the railway operations on the target trolley railway on Harlech Sands. That was a short-lived system, which was out of use before the end of the war in 1945 and was lifted in 1948 (locomotive 75191 was sent to Harlech that year to assist the track lifting, because the small diesel at Harlech was unusable). The year before, in 1947, a vehicle had been transferred from Harlech to the S&M. This was a conversion to rail wheels of a Guy 'Quad Ant' road vehicle, officially known as A 14620 but universally known by the name **Harlech Flyer**. This photograph was taken on 23rd April 1951; it is not known how much longer the vehicle survived.

Photographer unknown

In 1955, the WD decided to conduct trials on the S&M with a small 0-4-0 diesel shunting locomotive. WD 8201 (North British works number 27422 of 1955) was a 275 horse power shunter, weighing 32 tons on two axles. This compared with the Austerity 0-6-0 tank locomotives that were 48 tons (with coal and water) on three axles. With smaller wheels and lesser stopping power (it was not fitted with vacuum brake) than the steam locomotives, this engine was not well suited to the traffic requirements on the S&M, and it was transferred away within a few months. This photograph was taken on 16th August, not long after the locomotive arrived new on 23rd April 1955.

Brian Connell (Photos/Fifties Ref. B62/6)

During the 1950s the traffic of the quarry company continued to be worked between Kinnerley and Criggion by the BQC (British Quarrying Co. Ltd) locomotive. This was a Sentinel vertical boilered, geared drive locomotive built in 1927 (maker's number 7026), in a livery of faded pale green with red buffer beams. It was really a shunting engine – best kept to below 5 mph – and was not well suited to a trip journey of this distance. It took about four hours to do the round trip from Criggion, some six miles each way. However, it had the advantage of light weight and so was able to continue to work over the viaduct at Melverley even when weight restrictions applied prior to rebuilding. Here the Sentinel is seen leaving the WD locomotive yard at Kinnerley. The first three, rather aged, wagons are all lettered 'B.Q.C.'. The quarry only ceased sending out stone by rail when the S&M main line closed.

Photographer unknown, from The 'Detachment Photograph Album'

The BQC Sentinel locomotive had been built at Shrewsbury. Its makers, in need of a test ground to prove their designs, arranged for the testing of a number of locomotives on the S&M. The *Railway Magazine* for February 1928 has two pictures by J. J. Miller of a 'Super Sentinel' steam locomotive (builder's number 6515) on test on the S&M in March and April 1927 – including one rather improbably showing the locomotive on a passenger train. The locomotive, basically just a shunting engine with an enlarged boiler, kept to the timetable for the S&M petrol rail cars – which perhaps says more about how slow the rail cars were than the top speed of the Sentinel. Trials of Sentinel steam locomotives on the S&M continued into the 1950s. Arguably the most memorable trials were in 1955 and 1957. Between 28th July and 11th August 1955, the prototype Sentinel 0-6-0 with rods connecting the wheels (the Sentinel tradition was very much one of using chain drives) – locomotive 9633 – undertook tests culminating with hauling a train of 700 tons from Ford Yard to Hookagate. There was concern about the ability of the locomotive to stop such a heavy train on the falling gradient towards Hookagate, but with sufficient wagon brakes pinned down the journey was completed safely. This photo shows 9633 in the yard at Ford prior to commencement of the trip to Hookagate, with Jack Lee (one of Thomas Hill's drivers) in the cab. In the distance it is just possible to see the station limit board for Quarry Block Post, with the block post beyond.

W. G. Ind, John M. Hutchings collection

THE POST-WAR PERIOD

The feat of haulage by Sentinel 9633 in 1955 was surpassed in 1957, during the testing of the 0-6-0+0-6-0 locomotive No. 9603. On 15th March 1957 this locomotive worked a train of 78 loaded wagons, a load calculated as 1,294 tons, from Ford to Hookagate. The story is told that it took much longer to make up and later dispose of the train than the time taken on the journey. Here Sentinel locomotive 9603 is seen preparing the 78 vehicle train at Ford. Watching was Mr T. A. Hill, whose business had been sales and service agents for Sentinel under an agreement dating from 1947.
W. G. Ind, John M. Hutchings collection

The history of the Sentinel locomotive design and that of Thomas Hill (Rotherham) Ltd is complex. Sentinel (Shrewsbury) Ltd was taken over by Rolls Royce in 1956. It was decided to develop a diesel-hydraulic locomotive with a Rolls-Royce engine. The Thomas Hill business assisted in the design and became the sole distributor. The construction of the pioneer locomotive (builder's number 10001) was commenced in late 1958 and it was on test on the S&M by early 1959 – this photograph shows the locomotive at Kinnerley shed on 14th February 1959. *Photographer unknown*

Sentinel 10001 on test with a train standing on the S&M main line at Hookagate West Block Post. By mid February 1959 it was said to have done around 600 miles on trial runs. Some design features were still being finalised, so the locomotive had a temporary hinged door at the rear of the cab on one side and a window frame made of wood. The prototype was successful, and by the end of the year seventeen locomotives had been ordered. Later developments of this design were adopted as standard for railways in depots operated by the Ministry of Defence – the Thomas Hill designs known as Vanguard (chain drive) and the Steelman Royale (shaft drive).
W. G. Ind, John M. Hutchings collection

Coaches would be needed too

As WW2 drew to its close, it was clear that coaching stock could be spared for repairs, and that repairs were overdue. So in January 1945 the remaining five of the LT&S 'Ealing' coaches were sent to the Wolverton carriage works of the LMS for refurbishment. They were returned in April, still officially on loan.

In 1940 the LMS had strongly made the point that after the war they expected to have the Excursion set coaches back, since every available coach would be needed for the summer holiday traffic. Thus in February 1948, the Director of Transportation (on behalf of the WD) notified the then new British Railways that the WD could now return the coaches off loan and that they were being prepared to go to Hookagate en route to Wolverton. Since only five coaches of the original set were left, and they had been receiving fairly rough treatment, British Railways really had no use for these coaches and suggested that instead the War Office might like to purchase them outright. Despite the years of life that the coaches might expect to give in military service (and indeed in the event did achieve), they were sold to the WD on the basis of one year of useful life plus the residual value (that is, scrap value) thereafter – just £155 for each coach except the Composite, which was valued at £198. The WD got a bargain – the coaches lasted until 1960 on the S&M, and some gave service even after that.

Peacetime traffic arrangements

The number of block posts on the S&M was reduced to six, (Llanymynech and Abbey were not block posts) and the working between them was:

Llanymynech to Kinnerley	One Engine in Steam
Kinnerley to Nesscliff East	Miniature electric train staff
Nesscliff East to Quarry	Telephone and Ticket
Quarry to Ford	Telephone and Ticket
Ford to Hookagate West	Telephone and Ticket
Hookagate West to East	Telephone and Ticket
Hookagate East to Abbey	One Engine in Steam

Although the block posts at Edgerley and Shrawardine had been closed, entry to or exit from the sub-depot lines could still be made at these locations 'in an emergency' (but not at Nesscliff West, where the connection in the main running line had been removed). Updated operating instructions were issued as late as 1st January 1958.

Closure, tidying up the paperwork, and dismantling

On 4th April 1957 the government published a Defence White Paper, reviewing the armed forces in the light of the Suez campaign of the previous year. The paper (Cmnd 230) proposed that the British Army was to be reduced in size and reorganised to reflect the ending of National Service in 1960 – leaving the army with a strength of 165,000 officers and men. The process was to be carried out in two phases, to be completed by the end of 1959 and 1962 respectively. The munitions factory capacity was also to be scaled back, to 'relate capacity to the changed requirements of the Armed Forces resulting from the new defence policy' authorised by the White Paper. Thorp Arch ceased production in April 1958, followed by Swynnerton in May, Poole and Maltby in June, Wigan in December 1958 and Irvine in March 1959.

So the expectation in 1945 that the Nesscliff CAD would be required for about another ten years was very close to the mark. On 18th October 1957, the WD wrote to the General Manager of British Railways (Western Region) to say that CAD Nesscliff would be closed progressively, and completely by March 1960. The WD would then give up its lease on the line, and the working of the civilian traffic would become the responsibility of BR. There was initially some thought that BR might be asked to provide a service for military traffic as far as Ford, but by 23rd December 1957 it had been decided that this would not be necessary. Withdrawal of the civilian freight services by BR would be subject to approval by the Transport Users Consultative Committee, but this was clearly the expected outcome.

There were a number of issues that needed to be considered quickly:

A) The telephone pole route along the line carried wires for the GPO as well as for railway and military phones. The pole route had been rebuilt in 1941/42, with improvements and additional spurs in 1950/51. The GPO circuits, however, were only for GPO telephones in WD buildings, and would not be needed after the Depot closed. The GPO and WD would then remove their equipment, and the British Transport Commission (BTC) would then own the pole route.

B) Some land had been purchased by the WD and incorporated into the estate of the railway. The former owners of the land had a right to purchase it back. The land at Hookagate (where the bungalows had once stood) was wanted by the BTC which proposed to build a rail welding depot on the site. If it was necessary to retain access to the S&M line, it would be through the rail welding depot. The MEB electricity substation would remain to serve the new rail depot. Some land at Ford would simply be sold off. The land at Llanymynech was to prove a much more troublesome issue. The WD had purchased from Bradford Estates two small strips of land on which to lay two of the new loop sidings.

C) There was an 11,000 volt supply cable, some 10 miles long, which was on WD property and was laid along the railway starting at Bridge No. 27 south of the River Severn at Shrawardine and running westwards to Kinnerley. The cable served a number of farms and cottages as well as a number of military installations which would remain in use. Electricity was supplied by the Midlands Electricity Board (MEB), though the area supplied lay within the catchment of the Merseyside and North Wales Electricity Board (MANWEB). MANWEB was expected to extend its supply network to include Nesscliff, and to take over the cable. Shrawardine and Ford would remain supplied by the MEB.

Generally, rails would be lifted as sheds were cleared. Priority would be given to clearance of the sheds served by the railway that crossed Withey Lane, so that the 'level crossing question should die a natural death even before CAD Nesscliff has completely closed down'. The use by the WD of open level crossings had again become an issue, even though the WD had specific rights to use at least some of them. Once the sheds had been cleared and the railway lifted, the right to use the level crossings in the Argoed and Maesbrook Sub-depot – having been formally created by the Statutory Instrument in 1951 – had to be cancelled. This was done by a further Statutory Instrument (SI 1581 of 1960) dated 26th August 1960.

The terms of the original lease required that the WD returned the railway and its assets in good order when the lease came to an end. So questions were asked as to where the rolling stock taken over from the S&M company was now to be found. The answer was that for the rolling stock that had survived to the end of the war, most of it in use as static storage, an agreement had been reached that it should be scrapped. In a letter of 28th April 1952, BR had confirmed the agreement reached with its District Commercial manager at Shrewsbury that those vehicles that were runnable would be removed to Hookagate and broken up there by WD staff. The War Department could have the use of any recoverable timber. The wheels, axles and other metalwork were to be loaded on to wagons and sent to BR's Carriage & Wagon Engineer. This was duly done, and a receipt for the metalwork was sent by the Assistant C&W Engineer of the Western Region on 3rd July 1952. The WD made good use of the bodies from some of the 4-wheeled covered vans. Six van bodies were taken for use as Platelayer's Cabins – at Edgebold, Horton Lane, under Bridge No. 21 at Shoot Hill, one in the triangle leading to Kinnerley

THE POST-WAR PERIOD

Spare but serviceable vehicles were usually stabled in the bay platform line at Kinnerley. In this view, one of the bogie coaches was near the buffer stops. Also on the bay line was the WD's oldest coach. Inherited from the S&M as coach 1A, this was a four-wheeled former Saloon of the London & South Western Railway. Photo taken on 16th April 1949.
R. K. Cope (RKC/B311)

District and two adjacent to Kinnerley Block Post. Most of the other S&M rolling stock had been scrapped in 1943 after agreement with the S&M company at that time. 4-wheeled passenger coach No. 7 had been converted to a flat wagon, which had been scrapped in 1945.

The one notable survivor was S&M coach 1A, a four-wheeled former Royal Saloon of the London & South Western Railway. This vehicle was sometimes known as the 'Adelaide Coach' in the mistaken belief that it had been used for the first journey on the L&SWR by a member of the Royal Family on 15th June 1842, when a special train was prepared to convey the Queen Dowager (Queen Adelaide) from Nine Elms to Southampton. It was one of two coaches from a set built by the L&SWR that were acquired by Colonel Stephens for Light Railway use. The historic nature of this vehicle was recognised, but wartime circumstances

Above right: A close-up view of the L&SWR 'Royal Saloon' revealed its graceful design, though since the coach had no hand brake, it had been chocked using a length of wood to stop it rolling down the siding.
R. K. Cope (RKC/B312) courtesy Roger Carpenter

The 'Royal Saloon' stabled in the bay platform with the tool vans as part of the breakdown train.
R. K. Cope (RKC/B336) courtesy Roger Carpenter

155

THE SHROPSHIRE & MONTGOMERYSHIRE LIGHT RAILWAY UNDER MILITARY CONTROL 1940-1960

Not all of the S&M's ancient vehicles were cut up during the war. Some remained in use as warehouses on wheels, notably in the bay platform line at Shrewsbury Abbey. They survived until the WD had a 'tidying up' of its system in the early 1950s. Here the vehicles pulled out from Abbey, in readiness for scrapping, are seen at Hookagate.
Bob Barnard (Photos/Fifties Ref. 8133)

It is a wonder how even the use of wagon sheets allowed this vehicle to be used for storage. *Bob Barnard (Photos/Fifties Ref. 8134)*

One of these vehicles was the former North London Railway four-wheeled passenger luggage van that had become S&M No. 18. There is a conflict of evidence about the date when these vehicles were taken out for scrapping. A WD paper refers to the recovery of metal from scrapped vehicles in 1952. The photographer, however, noted this photograph as being taken on 25th April 1954, so that date is almost certainly correct. Possibly different vehicles were involved in 1952.
F. W. Shuttleworth, reference AL 66

The cattle wagons, long out of use because of the decline in this traffic, had been converted into stores by the expedient of placing corrugated iron over the openings in the upper part of the vehicles. The arrangement cannot have kept out much of the rain.
F. W. Shuttleworth, reference AL 68

THE POST-WAR PERIOD

meant that it was not immediately set aside for preservation. The vehicle was only on lease to the WD, but since the British Transport Commission was unable to take it into care, it was agreed in September 1953 to send it to Longmoor with a view to permanent preservation there as a static exhibit. On 30th December 1953 the body and underframe were loaded onto Well Trolley No. 41925 (an ex GWR 'Crocodile B') for the journey to Longmoor, together with the wheels, brakes and brake rigging. A receipt from the Stores at Longmoor was duly received on 8th February 1954. Unfortunately after years of storage in the open, the saloon was in much worse condition than at first envisaged. It did not take kindly to being lifted on to the wagon and according to one correspondent was more or less terminally disintegrating by the time it reached Longmoor. There was some consultation about '…what to do next', during which time the saloon was kept under cover. It was still in the diesel shed at Longmoor in the spring of 1956, but in the end the project was beyond the trade skills and resources available at the time even in the Longmoor workshops. In the mid 1950s the skills and resources later taken for granted in the world of rolling stock preservation simply did not exist, and the coach was scrapped.

Another ancient survivor was the Merryweather Manual Fire Engine together with its associated equipment (helmets and hand tools). This had been kept by the S&M at Kinnerely, and pre-war it saw regular use in fighting fires on adjacent farms. The WD took care of this machine during the war, and in September 1951 it was sent to Swindon Works, for the safe keeping of the Works manager. It appears that the panel with the lettering on the side, which is now at the National Railway Museum (object No. 2001-8530), may be all that survives.

In the context of restoring the line to the state in which it was acquired, a question arose as to the state of the locomotive water tanks taken over by the WD. In the post-war era, when the line was worked predominantly by the Austerity 0-6-0 tank locomotive (which had limited water capacity) the availability of water had been an important

The S&M company had maintained this Merryweather hand pump fire engine, more for the benefit of the local community than for any need that the railway had of it. It was kept at Kinnerley. When it was required the S&M men who lived locally turned out – led by 'Carpenter' Jones from the workshops – to crew it with any men from the village who were nearby. They would catch a donkey, kept by a farmer in an adjacent field, to work between the shafts. On at least one occasion the animal refused to be caught and the men hauled the machine to the fire (which was nearby) themselves. In 1951 this historic asset of the newly-formed British Transport Commission was sent to Swindon for safe keeping.

Geoffrey Bannister, courtesy Andrew Bannister

issue. While it might have appeared that the line was well provided with water facilities when the WD took over, by no means all of them worked. A report in 1959 on the state of the water tanks inherited from the S&M showed:

Abbey Station platform – Parachute tank and water crane, connected to the Corporation water supply via a water meter, to be used only in emergency.

Abbey Station, adjacent to Bridge No. 5 over the Rea Brook – Formerly fed from the mill stream of the Rea Brook by hydraulic ram and used to supply the parachute tank. Not used during the WD occupation of the line.

Shoot Hill level crossing – Formerly fed by gravity from a stream running down Shoot Hill cutting. The brick intake still existed but the pipe line was broken. Not used by the WD.

Kinnerley Loop Platform – Resting on the abutment of the road bridge, this open galvanised tank on steel or wooden joists was supplied by pipe from the Kinnerley main water tower. The tank had been removed by the WD as the tender engines in use did not require it – the rusted and broken 1½ inch pipe had been removed in the 1950s.

Kinnerley Down Platform – A parachute tank and water crane, still in situ but not used during the WD occupation of the line.

Kinnerley Loco Yard – The WD had inherited a 3-4,000 gallon open water tower on brick piers. This was used by the WD up to 1945, when a 10,000 gallon Braithwaite water tank and deep well pump were installed. The earlier water tower was demolished in 1950 because the tank and its supports were badly corroded.

Llanymynech – Four connected tanks on cast iron columns, never used by the WD, tanks now badly corroded and in a state of collapse.

The WD also undertook a stocktake of the materials to be handed back when the lease was given up. As might be expected, the stocktake was done in meticulous detail, down to noting '6 x Lock nuts 3 inch, rusty, thread poor'. There were also a number of relics from the pre-1940 era. These included one lubricator for the locomotive **Morus** (which had been transferred to the West Sussex Railway in 1924, and cut up there in the autumn of 1936 after the closure of that line), an injector for **Severn** (locomotive scrapped in 1937), and both nameplates for **Morus**. Clearly Kinnerley stores had become a repository for spares from other railways in the former Col Stephens 'empire'.

Matters connected with land often take a long time to resolve, and the end of the WD lease was no exception. The WD occupied the former station house at Shrawardine, and indeed had rebuilt it after the fire damage of 1st November 1941. From 1st January 1954 this had been deemed to be a dwelling house, for which the WD had to pay separate rent of £19 10s 0d yearly in advance. On top of this, the WD also had to pay to the BTC (as successor to the S&M company) a yearly payment of £16 7s 0d as compensation for rental income lost because the WD had terminated certain rents payable to the S&M by occupying the buildings concerned. Now the WD wished to terminate the lease on the house at Shrawardine. Eventually, it was agreed by a letter of 12th October 1959 that the lease be treated as ending on the previous Quarter Day, and that the WD had given up its tenancy on 29th September. The three keys to the house and one to its outbuilding were duly posted by the WD to the BTC District Surveyor on 19th October 1959.

Rather more quickly resolved was the transfer of Hookagate Yard to BR in preparation for the construction on the site of a new Flash Butt rail welding depot (this was at the time when the introduction of long welded rail on BR was gathering pace). The site was transferred to

Sad days for those who appreciated the unique features of the Shropshire & Montgomeryshire Light Railway. The track in the Sub-depot lines was lifted by the Army using its own men and machines, the recovered rail then being taken out on main line wagons. *Photographer unknown, from the 'Detachment Photograph Album'*

THE POST-WAR PERIOD

Another track lifting gang – a photograph showing nicely the proportions of one of the Sheds.
Photographer unknown, from the 'Detachment Photograph Album'

the British Transport Commission as from 1st January 1959 to allow construction work to commence, on the undertaking that the BR District Engineer would keep a through line on to the S&M – and a run round facility – open until WD traffic finally ceased (at the time envisaged as possibly continuing until June 1960).

By 10th August 1959, application had been made by BR to the TUCC for acceptance of the closure of the line to civilian traffic from Hookagate to Llanymynech and from Kinnerley to Criggion – concurrently with the closure of CAD Nesscliff – as from 31st December 1959. This duly came to pass, and the traffic from Criggion quarries ceased on 31st December. It was anticipated that the section from Hookagate to Abbey would continue to be needed to serve the sidings at Abbey, especially for the traffic in oil tank wagons. The WD would continue to work this traffic. This was, however, a short-lived arrangement, because it was proposed to make a new connection in to the sidings at Abbey from BR's Severn Valley line, after which the section from Hookagate to the new connection would be taken out of use. Closure of the WD operations on the railway by 31st March 1960 was imperative. The railway was run by civilian staff, and there was no provision to pay for any civilian detachment after 31st March.

The construction of the chord line connecting the S&M route to the Severn Valley line was discussed at a joint WD/BR planning meeting on

The fact that the S&M could not survive for ever was obvious, and Major Calder co-operated in arranging rail tours for a number of enthusiast societies in the 1950s. The tour on 22nd May 1955 was hauled by WD 189, with a three coach set (unusually including one of the Composite brake coaches) and a brake van. The train is seen here in Ford Yard. The difference in height between the running line on the right and the yard is apparent. The train was standing on No. 2 Siding. No. 1 Road in the yard was kept clear for through running, and had been laid with concrete sleepers to make it more robust.
Brian Hilton, reference 53/14

The 22nd May 1955 tour included a number of 'photo stops' along the way, including the customary long halt at Shrawardine Bridge to allow participants to climb down to the river bank to take photos.

Brian Hilton, reference 53/15

17th February 1960. In order to keep the gradient of the new curve to 1 in 100, the S&M line would have to be lowered by eight to nine feet at the site where the new line joined it. The work of moving the soil would take about ten days, during which there would be no access to the yard at Abbey. Discussions would need to take place with Esso as to how fuel supplies were to be maintained during this interval. The agreed timetable for the work was that the WD would remove its pole route, which crossed the alignment of the new chord, prior to Friday 26th February. On that day the WD would work the last traffic in to and out of Abbey, and have its train back at Hookagate by mid-day. When that train had cleared, BR men would move in, break the S&M line, and commence on the earthworks. The BR engineers would install the new pointwork on the Severn Valley line on Sunday 6th March. The trackwork on the chord line would be completed on 10th March, and the new line opened on Friday 11th March 1960. The effect of this was that the WD gave up its responsibility for operating from Hookagate to Shrewsbury Abbey on 26th February 1960 (responsibility for maintaining the permanent way on this section had been handed over to BR on 1st January 1959). The WD's responsibility for paying any part of the costs of operating Hookagate signal box ended as from 26th February.

The S&M was officially closed to traffic on 29th February 1960. The Stephenson Locomotive Society ran a farewell trip on 20th March (see Appendix E for the Operating Notice) and on 31st March the line was formally handed over to British Railways (Western Region) for dismantling. One small detail was that the level crossings at Nesscliff and Shoot Hill, which had until this time been protected by pole barriers operated by WD staff, were now no longer so protected. The road signs had to be changed, and 'Crossing. No Gates' signs erected. This was done by the County Council – since road signs were its responsibility – and the WD was on 30th April invoiced for £30 0s 10d for the costs of removing the old signs and providing five new ones.

In practice, the S&M line west of Hookagate was used for a short time after 31st March, 'on an informal basis' and 'solely for the purpose of working away recovered permanent way materials from Nesscliff Depots, this being handed over to British Railways at Llanymynech' – which it had to be since the line was broken just west of the west end of Hookagate Yard. On 20th May 1960, Lt Col Trigg formally confirmed that all WD Tn assets, with the exception of some concrete sleepers (many of these were later sold locally), had been recovered from the Sub-depots of CAD Nesscliff. All unserviceable permanent way materials had been reported to Stores for disposal. The S&M main line was later lifted and Shrawardine bridge demolished, but the bridge at Melverley (for so long a weak link) was converted to road use.

The matter of the land at Llanymynech that had been purchased by the WD turned out to be a long running saga. As Operating Officer, Calder made a report to his Commander at HQ on 20th April 1960 that after the two southernmost loop sidings were removed in 1945, there were no tracks laid on the two parcels of land that the WD had purchased, though this land still lay within the WD boundary fence. Mr A. E. Evans, who had taken over Mason's Timber Yard (purchased by the former proprietor of that business from the Bradford Estate), was interested in buying the land – which was now only accessible via his land or the S&M/BR land. Evans was developing an agricultural business. As to the two lines remaining on the land that had been owned by the S&M company, the North Wales Wagon Co. (NWWC) had reduced its wagon breaking business, but still had a permanent repair depot on the other side of the main line at Llanymynech and wished to retain its use of the two sidings for wagon storage. In fact, the NWWC was using WD land for stacking wagon timbers, for which it was paying no rent at all. Evans was interested in acquiring not only the land that the WD had bought but also the land formerly owned by the S&M – he was interested not so much in the railway track as the area of the platforms and buildings.

The WD naturally had strict rules about the sale by private treaty of land which it owned. So the matter dragged on, unresolved, until 1964. A meeting on 24th February 1964 noted that the lease to the North Wales Wagon Co. had been terminated. The siding in to Mr Evans' yard had been removed, and BR no longer maintained this siding

continued on page 166

THE POST-WAR PERIOD

Above: The tour train on 22nd May 1955 is seen here at Nesscliff and Pentre Station, looking towards Shrawardine. On the left can be seen the station house, built by the first company to build a railway here, the PS&NWR. The WD crossing keeper's hut was on the right. Even at this late date there was traffic in the Civilian Yard.

Brian Hilton, reference 53/18

Left: A view from the roadside at Nesscliff, showing the rear of the station buildings. Of interest is the white painted gate in the station fencing. This allowed a farmer to back his cart up against the tiny shelf on the roadway side of the gate, and unload milk churns straight through on to the station platform – a process repeated all over the country for years, but long since consigned to history.

Brian Hilton, reference 53/19

A further stop was made at Maesbrook. The wooden fencing and cattle grid at the ungated crossing might be rotting away, but the notice about trespassing on WD land was still clear enough. The PS&NWR station house was rock solid (and it is still there to this day, used as a private residence).

Brian Hilton, reference 53/26

161

THE SHROPSHIRE & MONTGOMERYSHIRE LIGHT RAILWAY UNDER MILITARY CONTROL 1940-1960

The tour on 22nd May 1955 worked through to Llanymynech, and is seen here after the locomotive had run round and was ready to depart on the return journey. WD flat bottom rail on the left hand line, original bull head rail on the other platform line where the train is standing.
Brian Hilton, reference 53/32

The special train organised for the Birmingham Locomotive Club photographed standing at Shrewsbury Abbey on 26th June 1955. The locomotive, WD 193, was in notably shiny condition. This engine was a post-war build – it had been constructed as recently as 1953 – and had gone first to Woolmer stores at Longmoor. It had only come from store to the S&M a few months before, on 7th February 1955. After the S&M closed it went back into store at Bicester. Even though closure within a few years seemed probable, maintenance work was still done on the track and some new timbers for spot re-sleepering had been delivered.
Geoffrey Bannister, courtesy Andrew Bannister

The BLC train, photographed at Hookagate Yard. The train consisted of two ex-LT&S coaches (the second one being a Brake Composite), with an ex-LMS coach at the rear before the brake van. Major Calder stood beside the vestibule of the first coach, while a man brought the step ladder forward from the brake van so that passengers could alight.
Norman Glover (4382) courtesy F. A. Wycherley

THE POST-WAR PERIOD

The BLC special also paused at Ford Yard for participants to walk round, whilst some Army personnel and depot staff looked on. Note the two types of concrete sleeper – those in the siding had cast-in slots to reduce the weight, but at the risk of the sleeper cracking if too much ballast was packed under the centre of the sleeper.
Geoffrey Bannister, courtesy Andrew Bannister

THE SHROPSHIRE & MONTGOMERYSHIRE LIGHT RAILWAY UNDER MILITARY CONTROL 1940-1960

The Stephenson Locomotive Society organised rail tours on the S&M in September 1958. On this occasion the train was composed of three LT&S coaches and a brake van, seen here at Kinnerley.
Revd John Parker (Photos/Fifties Ref.3225)

The WD did not officially have running powers from Llanymynech to Criggion, but for some of the enthusiast railtours permission was given for rail cars to go to Criggion, to view both the line and the quarry company's locomotive. It was usual to use two Drewry Rail Cars back to back – it made driving easier. Here such a pair of rail cars is seen approaching Kinnerley from Criggion on 21st September 1958.
H. C. Casserley, reference 94249

WD Drewry Rail Cars 9104 and 9105 forming an enthusiasts' excursion on 21st September 1958, seen in the yard of the quarry company at Criggion. The quarry company's sentinel steam locomotive (Sentinel 7026) can be seen in the background.
H.C. Casserley, reference 94257

THE POST-WAR PERIOD

The very last rail tour of them all was on Sunday 20th March 1960. The empty coaches for this two-coach Stephenson Locomotive Society excursion (which had been propelled from Kinnerley) could only proceed as far as a Stop board just on the Hookagate side of Bridge 15. Here locomotive WD 193 waited while SLS members assembled, having arrived by bus from Shrewsbury. Compare this view with that on page 78.   *R. C. Riley, Transport Treasury RCR 14537*

A view of the final train, looking west from the direction of Hookagate. The railway had been broken just behind where the photographer was standing, as part of the work to build the new rail welding depot. The Stop board erected specially to mark the limit of how far the special train could travel can be seen just to the left of the brake van.   *R. C. Riley, Transport Treasury RCR 14536*

The final day train at Llanymynech. Beside the engine was Driver George Beeston, next to him (in the smart coat and gloves) Elvin Ainsworth – son of Charlie Ainsworth and at this time working on the S&M as an Assistant Yardmaster – and (with a pipe) Charlie Gibbs. Gibbs could do a near-perfect impression on the telephone of the voice of Charlie Calder and was known to use this to play some harmless pranks. *Photographer unknown*

continued from page 160
connection. The WD rails would now be removed by BR. The land belonging to BR would be sold, and the sale of the WD land dealt with at the same time.

In 1961, the WD and BTC were left with the task of reaching a financial settlement – a reckoning of the costs of the WD not completely restoring the line to the state in which it had been leased. This required a judgement of the value of the 'betterments' – the improvements that the WD had made. Should any value be attributed to the fifty-one buildings (all duly scheduled) that the WD had built and would be leaving behind? The answer was no – because they were very specific to the way in which the WD operated the line (block posts for example) and would not be of any value to British Railways. And the WD had to pay for any assets that it had taken over and for which it could not show that it had received agreement to scrap. So the WD agreed to a value of £600 for a petrol driven permanent way trolley for which it could find no records. The WD had taken over 60 tons of coal, and it was expected that it would leave behind 60 tons of coal. The operators explained that it had seemed best to run the stocks of coal down to nil, rather than leave a heap of 60 tons that BR would then have to load up and take away. So the WD paid the value of 60 tons of coal. On the plus side for the WD, it handed over to BR a store of tools and equipment, valued at £2,000 and the betterment value in the track, which BR would recover. So the final balance, set out in a letter from the BTC, British Railways (Western Region) on 10th July 1961 was – credit to the War Department £10,420: credit to Western Region £3,010.

The centre of operations – the Control Office desk at Kinnerley. In front of the Duty Controller are the tools of his trade. His left hand is on the device for selective dialling on the telephone. To dial a particular location, he had only to turn the handle for that location in a clockwise direction to its stop. When he released the handle, it returned slowly to its original position (powered by a clockwork mechanism), during which it sent out the pulses that dialled the desired number. In front of him is the Train Graph that he is maintaining as the record of all events for the day, the latest entry being at 11.30 – which tells us the time of day that the photo was taken. The right hand end of the graph was used to record the details of locomotive working, opening and closing of block posts and other details (for clarity, when making a replica of the Train Graph for this book, these details have been moved to the left hand end of the graph). At the right side of the desk are those vital tools for completing the Train Graph – a selection of coloured pencils and a rubber. In this photo, probably taken in the early summer of 1957, Jack Dubber leans on the telephone concentrator. The controller is possibly J. Barber, who was a Controller in 1951 and was still in the post in 1958.

Photographer unknown, from the 'Detachment Photograph Album'

Chapter 6
A TYPICAL DAY'S TRAIN WORKING IN 1958

The Train Graph kept by the Duty Controller was a key Operating Document, which recorded not only the movements of trains but also details such as the hours worked by the men and the motive power, from which operating and maintenance statistics could be prepared. A copy of the Train Graph for Tuesday 2nd September 1958 has survived and a re-written version is reproduced here. The original document is physically too long to reproduce, and was made out using seven different coloured inks (one for each locomotive or rail car duty), some of which have faded. The following notes interpret the information on the Graph.

Control at Kinnerley was opened by J. Barber at 07.00. He would be on duty until 19.30.

The block posts opened as necessary to deal with traffic – so those further from Kinnerley (except Hookagate) opened last and closed first.

Kinnerley BP	opened 07.05, closed 19.25
Nesscliff East	opened 07.50, closed 19.15 (blockman travelled out and back by train)
Quarry	opened 08.05, closed 17.55 (blockman travelled out and back by train)
Ford	opened 08.10, closed 13.45 (blockman travelled out and back by train)
Hookagate West	opened 08.14, closed 13.10
Hookagate East	opened 08.14, closed 13.25

Three steam locomotives were used during the day, on Duty A, Duty B and Duty C.

THE SHROPSHIRE & MONTGOMERYSHIRE LIGHT RAILWAY UNDER MILITARY CONTROL 1940-1960

S&M LIGHT RAILWAY TRAIN GRAPH   KINNERLEY CONTROL

DATE Tuesday 2nd September 1958

ARMY FORM W 3021

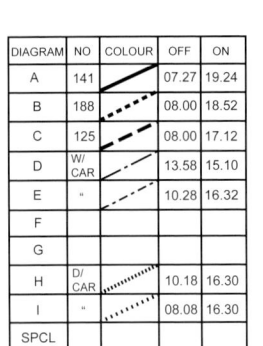

DIAGRAM	NO	COLOUR	OFF	ON
A	141	———	07.27	19.24
B	188	-----	08.00	18.52
C	125	— — —	08.00	17.12
D	W/CAR	—·—·—	13.58	15.10
E	"	—··—··—	10.28	16.32
F				
G				
H	D/CAR	········	10.18	16.30
I	"	········	08.08	16.30
SPCL				

BLOCKPOST	OPENED	CLOSED
KNY	07.05	19.25
NCF.E	07.50	19.15
QUARRY	08.05	17.55
FORD	08.10	13.45
HGW.W	08.14	13.10
HGW.E	08.14	13.25

ENGINE LOCO DUTIES		
A	14.50	15.48
B	14.40	15.58
C	09.55	10.35
SPCL		

CONTROLLER	ON	OFF
J Barber (signed)	07.00	19.30

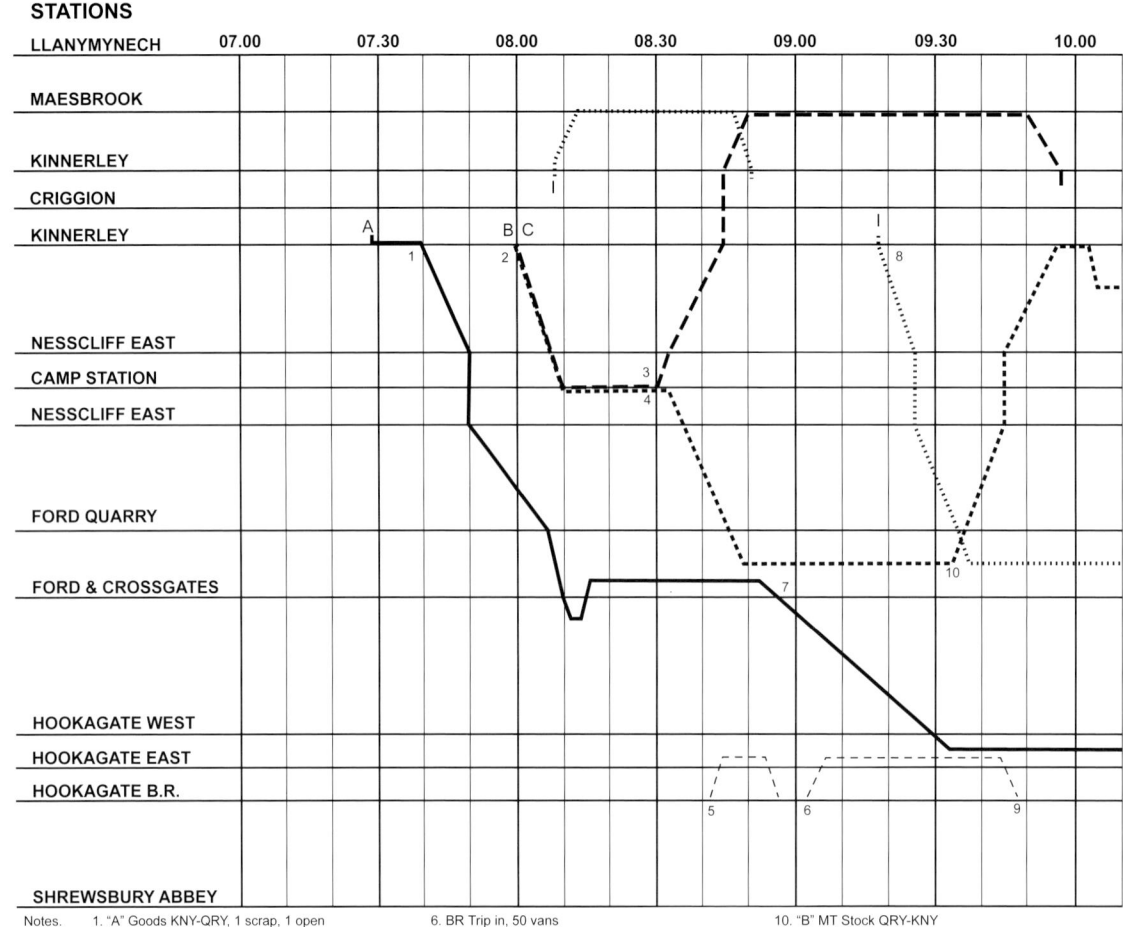

STATIONS: LLANYMYNECH, MAESBROOK, KINNERLEY, CRIGGION, KINNERLEY, NESSCLIFF EAST, CAMP STATION, NESSCLIFF EAST, FORD QUARRY, FORD & CROSSGATES, HOOKAGATE WEST, HOOKAGATE EAST, HOOKAGATE B.R., SHREWSBURY ABBEY

Notes.
1. "A" Goods KNY-QRY, 1 scrap, 1 open
2. "B&C" engines KNY-NCF
3. "C" Pass NCF-KNY
4. "B" Pass NCF-QRY
5. Welshpool Gds in, 2 Gds and 5MTs for Aby, 1 Red
6. BR Trip in, 50 vans
7. "A" Goods FRD-HGT, 23 Issue, 16 Runners, 1 open, 1 scrap, Welshpool gas out
8. "I" D-Car KNK-QRY
9. BR Spl out, 17 Issues, 8 Runners
10. "B" MT Stock QRY-KNY

Duty A

- Locomotive 141 was the first off shed (at 07.27) to take up Duty A, the main goods trip working of the day including the working of civilian traffic, and also the train which 'opened the line'.
- It departed Kinnerley 07.28 with one scrap and one open wagon, paused at Nesscliff East at 07.50 (dropping the blockman off there), passed Quarry at 08.05 (again dropping off the blockman) and arrived at Ford at 08.10, going in to the yard there (again after dropping off the blockman for Ford Block Post, which is why the train worked as far as Ford before going into the yard).
- At 08.52 the trip working left Ford Yard for Hookagate, with a train consisting of 23 'issues' (loaded ammunition wagons going out), 16 'runners' (barrier wagons), 1 scrap, 1 open, and the 'Welshpool Gas' coke wagon. Duty A arrived at Hookagate at 09.34, the slow journey reflecting the weight and nature of the train.
- The 'Welshpool Goods' main line train had already been into the sidings at Hookagate and gone. It had arrived at 08.42 detaching 2 goods wagons, 5 empties for Abbey and 1 Red (explosives), and departed at 08.54. On this day it took no outwards traffic, because a second Special trip was to be worked.
- A short while later, at 09.05, the Special main line trip working arrived with 50 vans. When Duty A arrived at Hookagate at 09.34 the outwards train was soon made up, and the main line locomotive departed with its Special trip at 09.48, taking 17 issues spaced between 8 runners, a total 25 wagons.
- The WD locomotive shunted Hookagate Yard until 10.36, and then departed as the Civilian Goods for Shrewsbury (Abbey) with a load of 5 vans, 2 oil tank wagons, and 1 goods van.
- Abbey was reached at 10.50, and the yard shunted until 11.42.
- With a return load of 4 empty oil tanks and 1 open, locomotive 141 entered Hookagate Yard at the west end at 11.58.
- The locomotive shunted in the yard, making up its train and also another trip for the main line locomotive, which was left ready. The main line locomotive arrived 'engine and brake' at 13.04 and departed at 13.24 with the remaining 6 issues, 8 runners, 1 scrap, 1 open and 4 oil tanks. Hookagate East BP could then close.
- The WD locomotive had already left, at 12.22, with 1 coke, 1 Red and 51 vans for Ford Yard (arrived at Ford BP at 12.52).
- The locomotive then shunted the sorting sidings until 13.42, when it left the yard at Quarry Block Post with 5 vans for Kinnerley.
- This trip working arrived at Nesscliff East at 13.52, but then had to shunt out of the way to allow Duty C with empty passenger coaches to pass and then a Drewry Car on H Duty which followed Duty C after an interval of thirteen minutes.
- The trip resumed at 14.08 and passed through Kinnerley at 14.16 going straight to Maesbrook. Locomotive 141 shunted at Maesbrook from 14.22 to 14.42. It then returned to Kinnerley at 14.50 and went 'on shed' for 'loco duties'.
- After just under an hour's break, the late turn crew brought the locomotive off shed at 15.48. They shunted in Kinnerley District until 16.18 and then stood in the station until 16.30.
- After the arrival of Rail Cars 'H' and 'I' cleared the section, locomotive 141 departed for Nesscliff East with a modest load of 2 issues and 1 other wagon. Having arrived at Nesscliff at 16.38, the

168

A TYPICAL DAY'S TRAIN WORKING IN 1958

S&M LIGHT RAILWAY TRAIN GRAPH   KINNERLEY CONTROL

DATE Tuesday 2nd September 1958

ARMY FORM W 3021

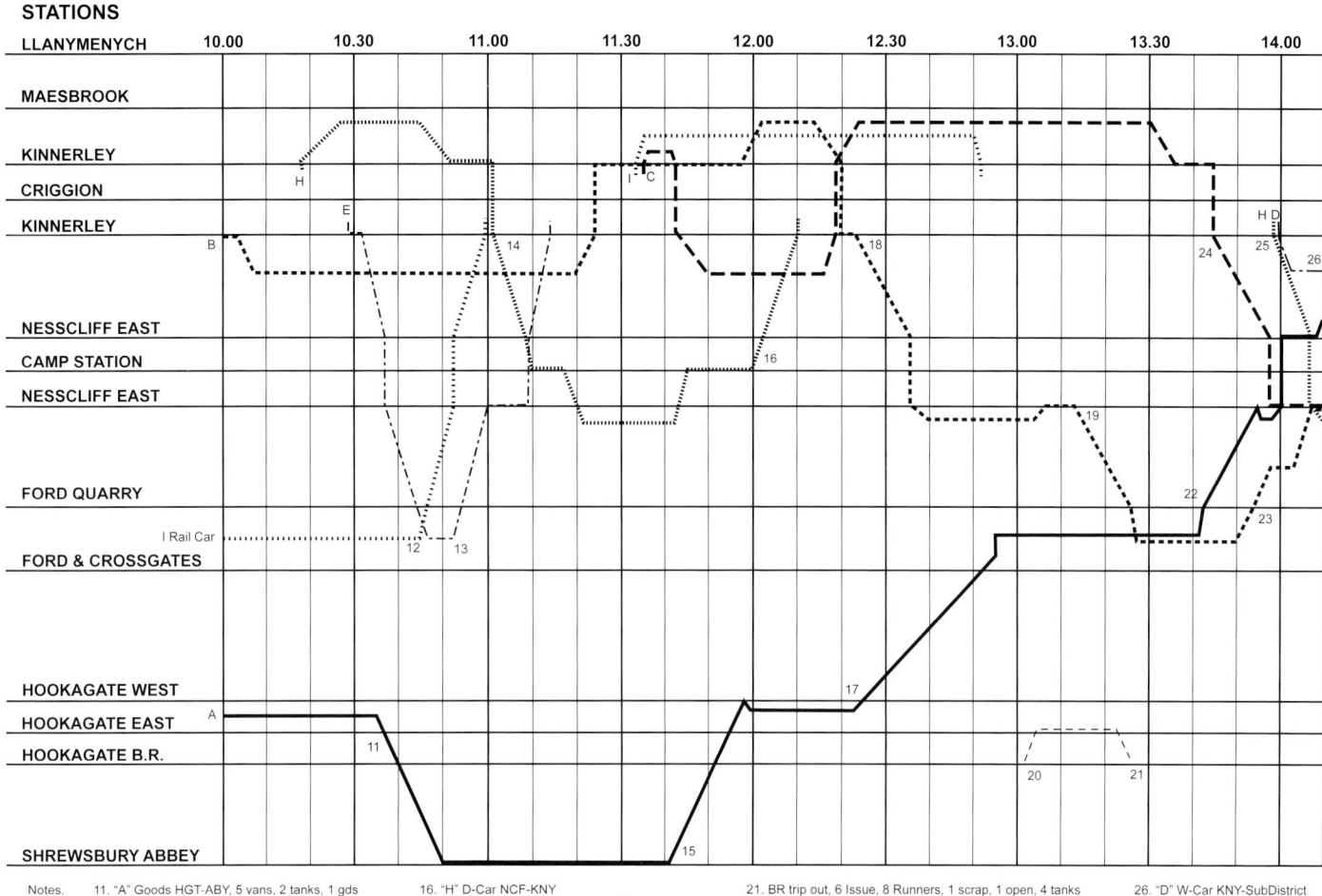

Notes.
11. "A" Goods HGT-ABY, 5 vans, 2 tanks, 1 gds
12. "I" D-Car QRY-KNY
13. "E" W-Car QRY-KNY
14. "H" D-Car KNY-NCF
15. "A" Goods ABY-HGT, 4 tanks, 1 open
16. "H" D-Car NCF-KNY
17. "A" Goods HGT-FRD, 1 coke, 1 Red, 51 vans,
18. "B" Goods KNY-NCF, 8 Issue, 1 38, 1 17
19. "B" Goods NCF-QRY, 14 Issue, 1 17
20. BR trip in, Engine & brake
21. BR trip out, 6 Issue, 8 Runners, 1 scrap, 1 open, 4 tanks
22. "A" Goods QRY-KNY, 5 vans
23. "B" Goods QRY-KNY, 1 123, 1 50, 1 17
24. "C" MT stock KNY-QRY
25. "H" D-Car KNY-QRY
26. "D" W-Car KNY-SubDistrict

locomotive shunted in the Sub-depot there until 17.20.

- It then departed with 12 issues for Quarry, entering the sorting sidings there at 17.29.
- The locomotive departed from Quarry for Nesscliff at 17.55, this time with a train consisting of 34 vans and 1 coke. Quarry Block Post closed with the departure of this train, the blockman travelling back with the train.
- Arriving at Nesscliff at 18.08, the locomotive again shunted the Sub-depot, until 19.15. It then departed light engine for Kinnerley, where it arrived at 19.24. The blockman at Nesscliff closed the block post at 19.15 and travelled back to Kinnerley with the light engine, and the man at Kinnerley closed his block post as soon as the locomotive was on shed.

Duty B

- The locomotives on Duty B and Duty C both came off shed at 08.00, and they ran coupled to Camp Station at Nesscliff (arrived 08.10) to work the two morning passenger trains.
- Locomotive 188 on Duty B departed from Camp at 08.32 (two minutes after Duty C) with a passenger train taking men to all platforms to Quarry, where the train entered the yard at 08.45.
- The locomotive left with empty coaches at 09.36 (after the arrival at Quarry of Rail Car 'I') and arrived at Kinnerley at 09.54.
- Leaving the coaches at Kinnerley, the locomotive went in to Kinnerley District to shunt until 11.22.
- After a short break in Kinnerley Station (until 11.55) it transferred to Argoed District to continue shunting.

- At 12.20 it came out from Argoed and worked a trip with 8 issues and 2 other wagons to Nesscliff (arrived 12.36) where it shunted the Sub-depot until 13.14.
- Locomotive 188 departed Nesscliff East with a load of 14 issues and 1 other wagon, which it took to the outward sorting sidings at Quarry (arrived 13.26).
- The locomotive left Quarry with 3 wagons at 13.50 (having collected the blockman at Ford, who had closed that block post at 13.45) and after shunting en route was at Nesscliff East at 14.08.
- The blockman at Nesscliff East was quite busy at this time, with no less than four trains on hand. Although there was no passing loop on the main line, he was able to shunt trains on to the Dead Road or on to the spur line leading to the Camp Station and the North Balloon. Duty A westbound had arrived at 13.52 and was standing waiting to pass (eastbound) both Duty C (arrived at 13.56) and a following Drewry Rail Car on Duty H (arrived at 14.06).
- Duty A left for Kinnerley at 14.08 and as soon as this train cleared the single line section at Kinnerley, Duty B followed (14.18). After arriving at Kinnerley at 14.24, the locomotive shunted Kinnerley District briefly, prior to going on shed at 14.40 for 'loco duties'.
- Locomotive 188 came off shed again at 15.58 and went to Maesbrook to collect coaches. It left Maesbrook at 16.36 with a passenger train, pausing at Kinnerley at 16.40 before going on to Camp Station, arriving at 16.54.
- The locomotive left its coaches there and (after 125 on the Duty C passenger train arrived at 16.58) locomotive 188 shunted the Sub-depot until 17.30. It then departed with four wagons, passing

THE SHROPSHIRE & MONTGOMERYSHIRE LIGHT RAILWAY UNDER MILITARY CONTROL 1940-1960

DATE Tuesday 2nd September 1958 S&M LIGHT RAILWAY **TRAIN GRAPH** KINNERLEY **CONTROL** ARMY FORM W 3021

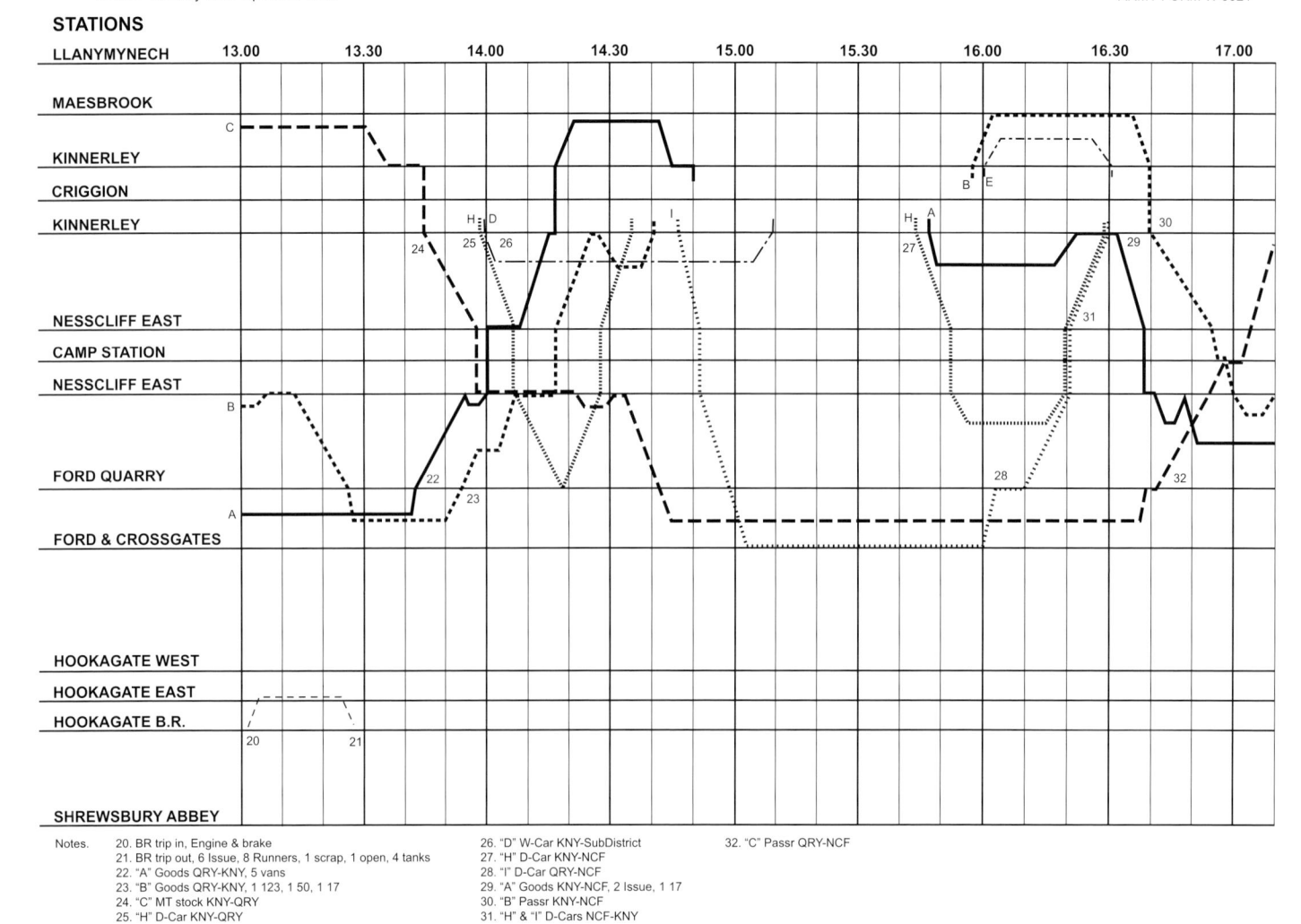

STATIONS

LLANYMYNECH	13.00 – 17.00
MAESBROOK	
KINNERLEY	
CRIGGION	
KINNERLEY	
NESSCLIFF EAST	
CAMP STATION	
NESSCLIFF EAST	
FORD QUARRY	
FORD & CROSSGATES	
HOOKAGATE WEST	
HOOKAGATE EAST	
HOOKAGATE B.R.	
SHREWSBURY ABBEY	

Notes.
20. BR trip in, Engine & brake
21. BR trip out, 6 Issue, 8 Runners, 1 scrap, 1 open, 4 tanks
22. "A" Goods QRY-KNY, 5 vans
23. "B" Goods QRY-KNY, 1 123, 1 50, 1 17
24. "C" MT stock KNY-QRY
25. "H" D-Car KNY-QRY
26. "D" W-Car KNY-SubDistrict
27. "H" D-Car KNY-NCF
28. "I" D-Car QRY-NCF
29. "A" Goods KNY-NCF, 2 Issue, 1 17
30. "B" Passr KNY-NCF
31. "H" & "I" D-Cars NCF-KNY
32. "C" Passr QRY-NCF

Kinnerley at 17.40 and going into Argoed District where it shunted until 18.14.
- It then passed through Kinnerley Station again at 18.20, to shunt in Kinnerley District. This work ended at 18.52 when the locomotive came out of the District and went on to the shed.

Duty C
- Duty C was taken by locomotive 125. This came off shed at 08.00 and ran, coupled to 188, to Camp Station (08.10).
- It left with the first passenger train from Camp (08.30) to run via Kinnerley (08.44) to the platform at the far end of Maesbrook Yard (arrived 08.50).
- Leaving the coaches in the yard for the return workmen's train later in the day, the locomotive did some shunting and returned to shed at 09.55.
- Although locomotive duties were finished by 10.35, the locomotive remained at Kinnerley until 11.35, when it shunted in to Argoed for five minutes, and then went to shunt Kinnerley District.
- It came out again at 12.20 to go back to Argoed, where it shunted until 13.35.
- The locomotive then returned to Kinnerley, to collect the coaches that had been left by Duty B at 09.54. It departed with the empty coaches at 13.45 to take them to Quarry for the return afternoon workmen's train.
- The journey was interrupted by a long wait at Nesscliff East from 13.56 until 14.32, to shunt aside for Duty A and Duty B going westbound, and also the Drewry Car on Duty H which overtook Duty C and took precedence for a round trip to Quarry.
- When Car H cleared the section from Quarry on its return trip at 14.28, Duty C could finally shunt back out on to the running line and proceed (14.32) in to the single line section to Quarry, where it entered the yard at 14.42.
- There was no great urgency to this movement, because the locomotive with its coaches then stood in Ford Yard from 14.42 until 16.36 – indeed a Drewy Car on Duty I came through from Nesscliff and returned back there (at Ford from 15.04 to 16.00) while Duty C was in Ford Yard.
- The return workmens train duly departed from Ford Yard at 16.36, pausing briefly at Nescliff East (16.54 to 16.56) to allow B passenger to clear before proceeding to Camp Station (arrive 16.58).
- Locomotive 125 then departed light engine at 17.02 for the final run to Kinnerley where the locomotive then went on shed at 17.12.

As usual in a Depot where none of the sheds (except those in Ford Yard) were served by roads, rail cars were used to carry men to their places of work, in addition to the workmen's trains. Both the larger Drewry Rail Cars and the smaller Wickham Cars were sometimes used to transfer men between sites, though (since both types of rail cars could haul lightweight trailers) they were more often used for internal transfers (between sheds) of small amounts of ammunition.

A Wickham Rail Car on **Duty D** was out from 13.58 until 15.10, doing a single trip within Kinnerley District.

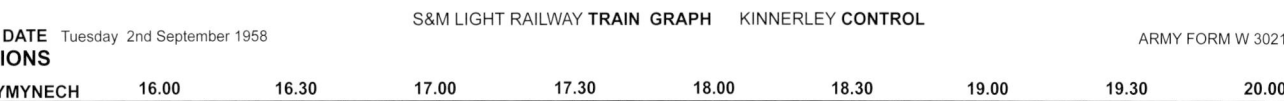

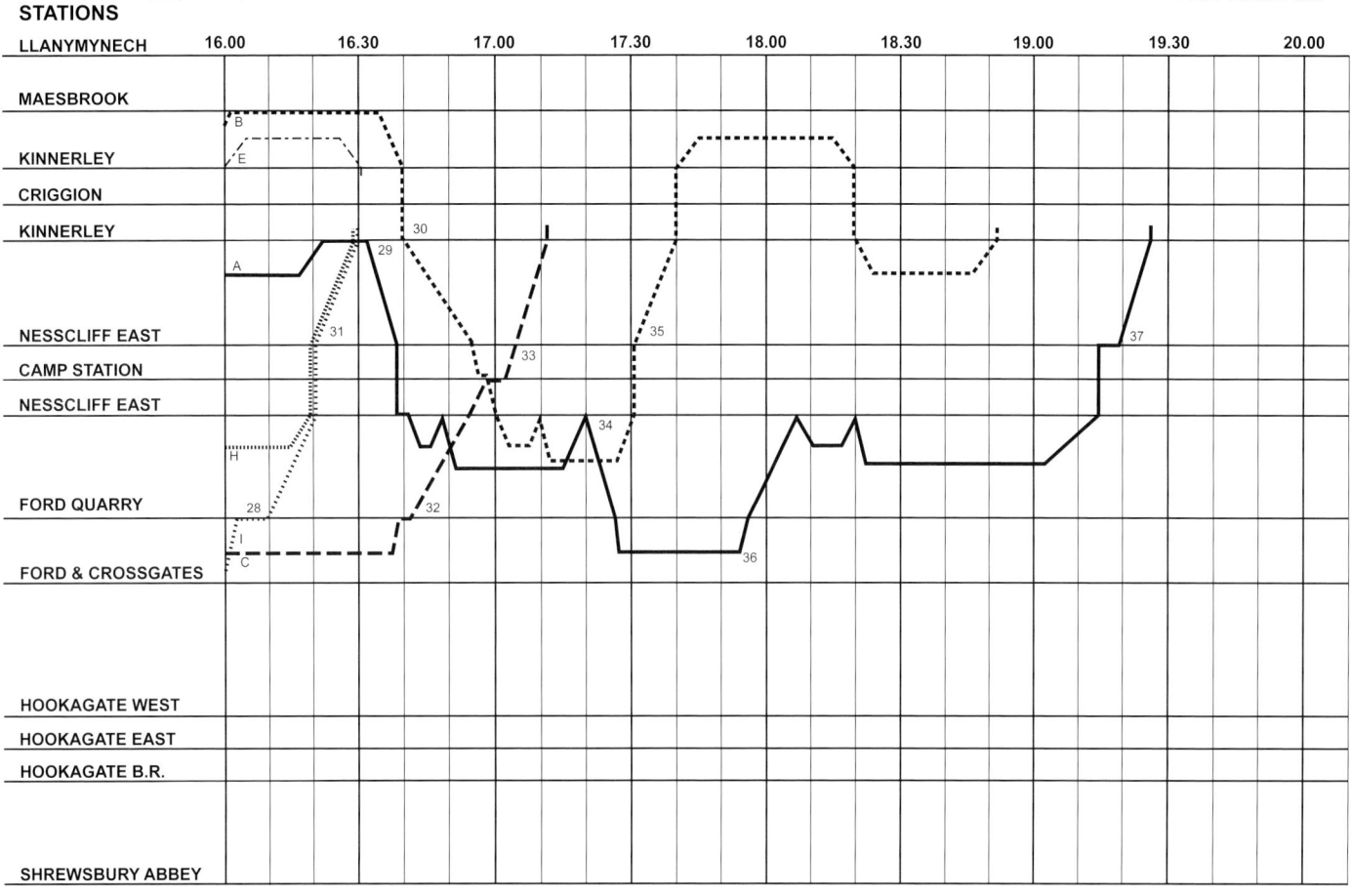

A TYPICAL DAY'S TRAIN WORKING IN 1958

S&M LIGHT RAILWAY TRAIN GRAPH   KINNERLEY CONTROL

DATE Tuesday 2nd September 1958

ARMY FORM W 3021

STATIONS

Notes.
28. "I" D-Car QRY-NCF
29. "A" Goods KNY-NCF, 2 Issue, 1 17
30. "B" Passr KNY-NCF
31. "H" & "I" D-Cars NCF-KNY
32. "C" Passr QRY-NCF
33. "C" Light Engine NCF-KNY
34. "A" Goods NCF-QRY, 12 Issue
35. "B" Goods NCF-KNY, 4 156
36. "A" Goods QRY-NCF, 34 vans, 1 coke
37. "A" Light Engine NCF-KNY

The Wickham Car on **Duty E** did two trips.
- Starting at 10.28 it ran from Kinnerley to Quarry, where it arrived at 10.47.
- It returned from Quarry at 10.54, halting at Nesscliff East from 11.00 until 11.07 to wait while a Drewry Car on Duty H came through from Kinnerley.
- Car E arrived back at Kinnerley at 11.14 and stabled.
- It came out again at 16.00 and did a short trip into Argoed Sub-district (keeping clear of locomotive 188 which had gone ahead of it two minutes before to go to Maesbrook to collect the coaches for the afternoon workmen's train).
- Car E returned to Kinnerley at 16.30 (six minutes before Duty B was due to leave Maesbrook with the passenger train) and finished by stabling at 16.32.

The Wickham Rail Cars on Duty F and Duty G were not needed on this day.

The Drewry Car on **Duty H** was out from 10.18 to 16.30.
- It first went Argoed District, returning to Kinnerley at 10.52.
- It then waited for Car I to clear the section from Nesscliff East. As soon as Car I was in at Kinnerley, Car H departed (11.02) for Camp Station (arrived 11.07).
- After a brief wait until 11.18, Car H then went in to the Sub-depot, returning to Camp Station at 11.48. It then went back (at 12.00) to Kinnerley (12.05) where it stabled.
- Car H came out again at 13.58 to work a return trip to Quarry. This working caused some congestion on the single line. At Nesscliff East, the Empty Coaches train of Duty C was shunted aside for Car H to overtake (at 14.06), and Car H also passed Duty A and Duty B which were proceeding in the opposite direction.
- On reaching Quarry at 14.18, Car H immediately returned, crossing Duty C which was still waiting at Nesscliff East before arriving back at Kinnerley at 14.34 and stabling.
- Car H did one more return trip, leaving Kinnerley at 15.44 to Nesscliff (15.54), into the Sub-depot there, out again to Nesscliff East Block Post at 16.20. Here it coupled to the Drewry Car on Duty I and the two returned to Kinnerley (arrive 16.30 and stable).

The other Drewry Car that day took **Duty I**, out from 08.08 to 16.30.
- The first trip was in to Argoed District (08.08).
- Car I was still in the District when locomotive 125 on Duty C arrived with the morning workmen's train from Camp Station (through Kinnerley at 08.44) and the two passed within the District, Car I returning to Kinnerley at 08.52.
- It then worked to Quarry, departing Kinnerley at 09.18, arriving at Quarry at 09.35 (its arrival cleared the section for B Duty to proceed with its train of empty coaches).
- Car I remained in the yard at Quarry until 10.47, after the arrival of Car E cleared the single line section.
- Car I then returned to Kinnerley, arriving at 11.00 (its arrival cleared the section for Car H).

- After a wait until 11.32, Car I went into Argoed, returning at 12.52.
- It then stabled until 14.46, when it undertook a return trip to Ford (arrival 15.04, departure 16.00). On arrival at Nesscliff East at 16.20 it coupled to Car H, the two arriving back at Kinnerley at 16.30.

Footnotes

1. Two carriage sets were required, both stabled overnight at Camp platforms.
   The first worked by Duty C from Camp Station (08.30) to Maesbrook (08.50) and returned Maesbrook (16.36) to Camp Station (16.54) on Duty B.
   The second set worked from Camp Station (08.32 on Duty B) to Ford Yard. The coaches were then worked empty to Kinnerley where they arrived at 09.54 and were stabled. At 13.45 these coaches were taken by the locomotive on Duty C as empty coaches back to Ford Yard. The return workmens train the left Ford Yard at 16.36 to Camp Station, arrive 16.58.

2. This timetable required that the block posts at Hookagate were opened by men who travelled there by road, so that the trip working from British Railways could be handled before the Duty A locomotive (which opened the line as far as Ford) arrived.

In earlier years, the blockmen at Hookagate were taken there by train. Train Graphs from August 1951 show the two locomotives for the passenger trains leaving Kinnerley at 07.30, and dropping off the blockman at Nesscliff East at 07.43 before going in to the Camp Station. The workmens trains then departed from Camp Station at 08.04 and 08.09 – earlier than in 1958. Nesscliff East Block Post opened after the light engines had passed clear of the running line on their way to the Camp Station, and the blockman immediately accepted (07.45) an engine and brake van, which ran from Kinnerley through to Hookagate East (08.30) to drop off blockmen at Ford and Hookagate (the blockman for Quarry arrived later, with the Civilian Goods). The engine and brake van then went 'light' all the way back to Kinnerley, to begin shunting in Argoed. The Civilian Goods (the only trip through to Shrewsbury) was worked by the locomotive off the morning workmen's train to Maesbrook after it had left its coaches at Maesbrook West Yard – so it departed from Kinnerley at about 09.15 not 07.30 as in 1958.

3. The times of the main line trips serving the Hookagate exchange sidings varied a little over the years.

   Hookagate Signal Box could switch out of circuit, and was shown in the WTT (Working Time Table) as open as follows:

WTT 2 October 1944 UFN	Open continuously
WTT 1 October 1945 UFN	Open 06.00 am to 22.00
WTT 16 June to 5 October 1946	Open weekdays (i.e. not Sundays) 06.00 until 20.00
WTT 31 May to 26 September 1948	Same
WTT 26 September 1949 UFN	Open Weekdays 08.00 to 15.20

Then open Weekdays 08.00 to 15.20 until WTT 12 June to 10 September 1961.
UFN (Until Further Notice)
In the summer of 1947, the trains serving the exchange sidings at Hookagate were:

- Up direction, 06.30 from Welshpool (Conditional, runs only if required) called if required en route to Coton Hill, Abbey Foregate or Harlescott (as required).
- 09.15 from Shrewsbury Coleham Yard arrived at 09.42, departing back to Coleham at 10.20.
- 11.30 from Coleham, arrived at 11.40, departed back to Coleham at 12.20.
- 13.40 from Coleham, arrived 14.07 and departed back to Coton Hill Yard at 14.45.

In the summer timetable for 1948, the early morning conditional train from Welshpool did not appear again, and the trips serving Hookagate were reduced from three to two with the 09.15 now working as far as Hanwood.

- 09.15 from Coleham, called at Hookagate from 09.25 until 09.45, thence to Hanwood. This trip returned from Hanwood at 10.10, calling at Hookagate from 10.17 to 10.35 to collect outwards traffic, thence to Coleham.
- 13.40 from Coleham, arrived 13.50 and departed back to Coton Hill Yard at 14.45.

The summer 1948 timetable brought changes to the afternoon trip,

- 09.15 from Coleham, called at Hookagate from 09.25 until 09.45, thence to Hanwood. This trip returned from Hanwood at 10.10, calling at Hookagate from 10.17 to 10.35 to collect outwards traffic, thence to Coleham.
- Except on Saturdays, 13.40 from Coleham, arrived 13.50 and departed back to Coton Hill Yard at 14.50. On Saturdays the train ran about an hour earlier, 12.40 from Coleham, arrived 13.00 and departed back to Coton Hill Yard at 13.35.

The 1949/1950 winter timetable was the same, but Hookagate box now switched out as from 15.20. The 1950/1951 winter timetable was the same, except that the Saturdays only train now ran as required and to even earlier timings,

- 11.10 from Coleham, arrived 11.20 and departed back to Coton Hill Yard at 11.45.

The timetable from 15th September 1952 saw further changes, with the first trip running earlier to allow it to work through to Minsterley.

- 08.50 from Coleham, called at Hookagate from 09.00 until 09.20, thence to Minsterley. This trip returned from Minsterley at 12.00, calling at Hookagate from 13.02 to 14.00 to collect outwards traffic, thence to Coleham (on Saturday it departed at 13.30 and ran to Coton Hill).
- Except on Saturdays, 13.40 from Coleham, arrived 13.50 and departed back to Coton Hill Yard at 14.50. On Saturdays the train ran only if required, 11.10 from Coleham, arrived 11.20 and departed back to Coton Hill Yard at 11.45.

The timetable from 21st September 1953 was the same, but the timetable from 18th June 1955 saw further changes (which set the pattern through to the closure of the S&M), with the first trip now working to Welshpool instead of down the Minsterley Branch, and in consequence starting earlier still.

- 08.35 from Coleham, called at Hookagate from 08.45 to 09.00, thence to Welshpool.
- The afternoon trip (except Saturdays) was now 12.30 from Coleham, arriving at Hookagate at 12.40 and returning to Coton Hill at 13.40. The Saturday only, runs as required, timings remained unchanged at 11.10 from Coleham, arrived 11.20 and departed at 11.45 back to Coton Hill Yard.

4. As early as 1951 it was unusual for a train to work through to Llanymynech. If it did, then it was usually the sort of trip undertaken by engine 187 on B Goods on 24th August 1951, when the engine spent half an hour on a return trip to bring in one wagon of locomotive coal.

The 24th August 1951 also saw an unusual working. A Special, engine number 531, left Kinnerley at 15.17 to run to Llanymynech and back light engine, taking a full hour for the journey. Quite regularly the S&M was used for testing locomotives from the works of Sentinel, and this trip has the appearance of being a locomotive testing journey. The Controller could allow a locomotive on test to run to Llanymynech, knowing that if it suffered any sort of failure it was not going to be in the way of any other traffic. The identity of 'engine 531' however is something of a mystery. There was no WD locomotive of that number, nor any Sentinel locomotive that would be an obvious match. The only possible contender is Sentinel 9538, a 200hp machine ordered for stock on 1st January 1951, reallocated for demonstration use on 23rd August 1951 and completed towards the end of the year. It is possible that the mystery locomotive was not a Sentinel, but from some other manufacturer.

The SLS final day railtour on Sunday 20th March 1960 took a break (from 14.30 to 15.30) at Kinnerley. Here the train locomotive (193) was seen beside the coal stage on shed in the company of 188 – a contrast in cleanliness.
R. C. Riley, Transport Treasury RCR 14542

THE SHROPSHIRE & MONTGOMERYSHIRE LIGHT RAILWAY UNDER MILITARY CONTROL 1940-1960

The coaches inherited by the WD from the S&M were inadequate for the numbers of construction workers that had to be conveyed to their work sites. Additional coaches were needed. Changed operating requirements on the Melbourne Military Railway meant that the ex-London, Tilbury & Southend coaches on the MMR became surplus to requirements and could be transferred to the S&M. By 1945 they were in very poor condition, and they were sent to Wolverton Carriage Works for essential repairs – the coaches were after all still officially on loan from the LMS. Despite this work, WD 3069 appeared to be in a rather sorry condition when photographed on the Criggion Branch at Kinnerley on 21st June 1947. 3069 was the LMS number for this coach, which at this time was not owned by the WD.
H. C. Casserley, reference 49034

The state of LT&S corridor Composite WD 4784 (LMS 4784) was no better. It was completely missing two windows on this side. *H. C. Casserley, reference 49033*

APPENDICES

To meet growing demand, the WD hired coaches from 'main line' companies whatever coaches these companies could spare. Inevitably the coaches that could be made available were well past their prime. That did not matter, because the WD rightly anticipated that they would get rough usage at the hands of the soldiers and labourers – as evidenced by the request that all light fittings be removed and any toilets sealed up before the coaches were handed over. By the end of the war the coaches displayed signs of the rough treatment that they had received. This ex-GWR coach 8-compartment Third had by 21st June 1947 completely lost half of the droplight windows one side – including some on the doors labelled 'Ladies', 'WOs and Sgts' and 'Officers'. *H. C. Casserley, reference 49046*

Appendix A
PHOTOGRAPHS OF SOME OF THE ROLLING STOCK

A considerable volume of the traffic on the S&M (and in other rail-served ammunition depots) was internal traffic between sheds. Wagons released after unloading incoming traffic could not, as a rule, be used. The WD had to pay demurrage, a charge for retaining a wagon after a specified time allowed for unloading. Indeed, the days allowed ran from when the numbertaker noted that the wagon had been handed over to the WD (at Hookagate or Llanymynech), so the time taken to get the wagon to the shed where it was to be unloaded came out of demurrage time. Thus the WD needed to own a fleet of 'internal user' wagons. These were bought as cheaply as possible, and so were usually wagons beyond further use on the 'main line'. That was acceptable on the S&M, where the internal journeys would be for short distances. The result was that the S&M became home to a remarkable collection of vintage wagons.

Despite their great age, the WD internal user wagons were not simply scrapped when the S&M line was closed. Many were transferred to other depots. It is known, for example, that brake van WD 49016 arrived at the Central Ordnance Depot at Didcot on 29th April 1960.

Some of these wagons, now really beyond reasonable maintenance, were still in use into the early 1980s – many of them at the Central Ammunition Depot (CAD) at Kineton. One incident illustrated just how fragile the wagons had become. During a shunt involving pulling a number of wagons out of a shed, the buffer beam was pulled completely off one van, allowing the frames to spread, so that the van body and its contents were deposited on the track.

Wagons 47481, 47482 and 47483 were amongst a large number offered for sale at CAD Kineton in December 1981 as Lot 9 of Tender 5399, but were unsold. They then appear in another report dated 2nd April 1982 – together with another 118 items of rolling stock – with a note 'All disposals to Birds Commercial Motors Ltd'. The Army undertook a major 'clear out' of obsolete rolling stock and these wagons were scrapped by Birds (who operated from part of the former WD depot at nearby Long Marston) during 1982.

This view shows LMS 19463 as the nearest vehicle in the bay platform line at Kinnerley on 21st June 1947, no longer in regular use. In 1943 the WD requested more coaches for some of its depots, and allocated to the S&M were two LMS Lavatory Composites – 19406 and 19463. These had been built by the London & North Western Railway a long time previously – indeed when 19463, a 45ft 0in. vehicle, was built at Wolverton in 1896 it was almost the last of its class. The vehicle arrived on the S&M from the LMS in August 1943, and was returned to the BR in March 1948. BR had no use for such an old and now rather abused coach. It almost certainly saw no further service prior to its formal withdrawal from traffic in May 1951. *H. C. Casserley, reference 49037*

175

THE SHROPSHIRE & MONTGOMERYSHIRE LIGHT RAILWAY UNDER MILITARY CONTROL 1940-1960

At the end of the war, the S&M had on loan the five LT&S coaches that remained after accident damage. In 1948 the WD offered to return them to British Railways, despite the fact that after their overhaul at Wolverton in 1945 these were the best coaches on the line. BR really had no use for coaches such as these – a fact that must have been known to the WD – and BR offered to sell them to the WD at a bargain price. Passing into WD ownership in December 1948 they were later painted in a dark olive green livery and maintained in smart appearance until the closure of the line. This was the renumbered WD 3202, seen on 21st September 1958.

H. C. Casserley, reference 94260

This view of Saloon Third WD 3203, photographed at Kinnerley on 21st September 1958, shows the arrangement of the sliding doors on the LT&S coaches, originally designed for through trains on sub-surface routes of London 'Underground'. *Bluebell Railway Museum Archive – J. J. Smith Collection, reference 6-87-6*

APPENDICES

Composite coach WD 3204 at Kinnerley. At some stage a handbrake column had been added in the passenger vestibule. The coach was by now also fitted with vacuum brake instead of Westinghouse air brake. It seems possible that modifications to the brakes were one of the reasons why the LT&S coaches went through Wolverton Works in 1945. This coach carried a hand painted sign lettered 'Officers, Civilians and Guard' by the doorway. *H C Casserley, reference 94262*

Internally, the original seating of the LT&S coaches had been removed, and replaced by some basic but robust longitudinal wooden slatted seats.
Photographer unknown, from the 'Unit Photograph Album'

THE SHROPSHIRE & MONTGOMERYSHIRE LIGHT RAILWAY UNDER MILITARY CONTROL 1940-1960

The man responsible for the smart turn-out of the WD's coaches on the S&M, although his working conditions were far from ideal. Sadly, his name was not recorded on this photograph.
Photographer unknown, from the 'Detachment Photograph Album'

APPENDICES

It was common for passenger trains on the S&M to include one of the standard SR pattern brake vans. The arrangement ensured that when the vacuum brakes finally leaked off – as they always will when the locomotive has been uncoupled for a while – there was a vehicle with a handbrake to prevent the coaches from moving. The workmen's trains were sometimes worked by locomotives that were not fitted with the vacuum train brake at all. It was convenient to have a brake van at each end – this saved walking when uncoupling from the locomotive – but in this photograph of the workmen's train set stabled during the day on No. 2 Siding at Ford Yard on 16th August 1955 there was a third van as well.
Brian Connell (Photos/Fifties Ref. B63/12)

Happily at least some of the LT&S coaches survived to give service after the S&M closed. This photograph of an internal train at Long Marston Engineer Stores Depot, believed to have been taken in 1960, shows locomotive WD 160 (not an S&M engine) hauling two of these graceful coaches. Not bad for vehicles sold by British Railways in 1948 at a price calculated on the basis that they had only one year of working life left.
Roy Miller, courtesy Roger Carpenter

THE SHROPSHIRE & MONTGOMERYSHIRE LIGHT RAILWAY UNDER MILITARY CONTROL 1940-1960

An example of the SR design of brake van that was adopted by the WD as its standard vehicle. The vacuum brake cylinders are prominent at the end of the van, with the substantial sand box between them and the end of the veranda. WD 11030 was photographed at Kinnerley on 21st June 1947. *H. C. Casserley, reference 49039*

The Drewry Rail Cars were rather larger than those built by Wickham & Co., but as this photograph shows, they were quite lightweight vehicles. Nonetheless, they became the preferred vehicles for moving small montmers of passengers, or small loads of ammunition, around the system – and they were used for many of the enthusiasts' trips in the early 1950s. Here 2324 was photographed at Shrewsbury in April 1951. 2324 was the builder's number – the WD later allocated number 9104. WD 9103-6 (builder's numbers 2323-6) came to the S&M from the builders in 1950. *J. M. Clayton*

APPENDICES

Above left: One of the aged wagons that the WD had acquired was this ex-Great North of Scotland Railway van, WD47482. This was a GNoS 8-ton Covered Wagon to diagram 14S (LNER series) with a 16ft body on a 10ft wheelbase and wooden underframe. These wagons had been built by the GNoS over the period from 1902 to 1912 and 127 were in service at 1923. The GNoS rated these as 8 ton capacity (and they are shown as that on the LNER diagram book) but the WD marked them to carry up to 10 tons.

Above right: By coincidence, the GNoS Van WD 47482 was photographed stabled attached to WD 47483. The photograph shows some of the maintenance issues on these old wagons. The buffer beam on 47482 was splitting, and on 47483 the spring behind the buffer had collapsed, so that the buffer was fully depressed. From the appearance of these vehicles, it would seem unlikely that they would survive to the closure of the railway, let alone beyond that. However, WD 47482 and 47483 were amongst the vehicles offered for sale at Central Ammunition Depot at Kineton as late as December 1981.

both C. C. Green

Another ancient vehicle, photographed at Kinnerley, was this low-roof van with wooden wheel centres – WD 47507. Note that the adjacent wagon is bereft of one of its buffers. *C. C. Green*

WD 47544 was a former Lancashire & Yorkshire Railway van, with a long overhang beyond the axles, and brake gear with two V hangers. It is also the vehicle seen above with the missing buffer head. The close-up view of one end of WD 47544, shows another common problem with the older wagons. The buffer centre line was very much below that of the adjacent WD brake van. Such misalignments increased the risk of buffer lock on sharp curves – of one buffer head sliding behind the other. Derailment would often follow. *C. C. Green*

WD 47481 was a van of Midland Railway origins. The War Department had more freight vehicles of Midland Railway build than from any other company. The fledgling Woolmer Instructional Military Railway (later known as the Longmoor Military Railway) acquired wagons from this source as early as 1905-08.
Right: A close-up view of the end of WD 47481. This was a robust design, which had stood up well to the test of being used in Army railway service. *both C. C. Green*

WD 47483 was one of the several thousand vans built by the Midland Railway to this design, with the door 'off-centre'. Despite having a damaged buffer spring when this photograph was taken in the early 1950s, it was to survive until the large-scale scrapping of older vehicles in 1981/82.
C. C. Green

WD 47487, seen here in the Civilian Yard at Kinnerley, was another of the MR vans to the same design. The WD rated this vehicle to carry 10 tons – in common with its other vans – but the MR had designed them to carry 8 tons (in a vehicle weighing just over 5 tons when empty) on a 9 foot wheelbase. *C. C. Green*

APPENDICES

WD 47568 was to a later Midland Railway design, fitted with vacuum brakes, with steel underframes and steel body frames. Construction of this type of 'Covered Goods Wagon' had begun on the MR in 1911 to Drawing 3557. The 10 foot wheelbase design was to carry 10 tons in a vehicle with a tare (empty) weight of 7 tons 10 cwts.

C. C. Green

WD 47529 had originated with the North Eastern Railway. Notably taller than the van to the left, it was rated to carry 10 tons. There was access to the inside both through the side doors and through an opening centre panel in the roof – but this arrangement was difficult to keep watertight under 'minimal maintenance' conditions.

C. C. Green

Some wagons received more regular maintenance attention than others, especially those used in the Breakdown Train set. It is not possible to read the WD number on this 12 ton rated van ex-GER, but it had additional lettering 'RAOC SITE 136', which suggests that the vehicle had been used at another Royal Army Ordnance Corps depot before arriving on the S&M. Photographed in the Civilian Yard at Kinnerley on 21st June 1947.

H. C. Casserley, detail from negative 49039

THE SHROPSHIRE & MONTGOMERYSHIRE LIGHT RAILWAY UNDER MILITARY CONTROL 1940-1960

Numbered SMR Nº 1 as part of the W↑D Breakdown Train kept at Kinnerley, this steel framed vehicle had been built by the Great Eastern Railway. The other van (below) in the Breakdown Train in 1947 was lettered differently with SMR in large letters and the words Breakdown Train on a white panel on the door mostly obscured by the Stop board (see also page 60). Notice also the Stop board had been relettered, the original wording had been the more common 'Stop until authorised to proceed'. Photographed in the Civilian Yard at Kinnerley on 21st June 1947.　　　　　　　　　　　　　　*H. C. Casserley, detail from negative number 49020*

Not all the WD internal user wagons were vans. There was also a requirement for open and low-sided wagons, especially for carrying materials for track repairs. WD 45127 was a drop-side wagon. Faded paintwork dating to its former use revealed that it had been relegated to internal use only, for building sand, and for 'site work only'.
C. C. Green

WD 45126 was a fixed-side wagon designated for use by the permanent way (track) maintenance teams. Its age is demonstrated by the fact that the handbrake operated on only one wheel. The former Great Eastern Railway van behind (WD 47485), was being fitted with a new roof.
C. C. Green

Appendix B
SUMMARY OF LOCOMOTIVES AND ROLLING STOCK AS SET OUT IN WD RECONNAISSANCE REPORT OF 4/5 NOVEMBER 1940

Locomotives. Total 4 in number, three ex-L&NWR tender 0-6-0 and one ex-L&SWR tender 0-6-0

No. 2 L&NWR 0-6-0. Seen in steam and appears to be in fairly good order. This is the engine working the line. Approximate age 56 years.

No. 3 L&SWR 0-6-0. This engine is laid aside and would require a considerable amount of money to put into working order. In view of the age of the engine (probably 60 or 70 years) expense would not be justified.

8182 L&NWR 0-6-0. Understand that two new half sides are required in the copper firebox and boiler requires re-tubing. Age approx 56 years.

8236 L&NWR 0-6-0. This engine requires 110 tubes to completely re-tube it. 86 of the old tubes have already been replaced. The tubeplate and firebox generally are in poor condition. Approx age 56 years.

Before deciding whether these engines should be taken over, a competent Boiler Inspector should examine the fireboxes and remove a few tubes for inspection. In any event it is doubtful whether these engines would stand up to heavy work, and if the line is taken over it is considered necessary to provide engines which have had a recent railway workshops overhaul.

Author's Note. The survey party seem to have got some of the details of the rolling stock incorrect – see the table below. The list of locomotives (perhaps understandably, since it was concentrating on the resources available to work the Depot) omitted to mention the diminutive locomotive **Gazelle**.

Rolling stock. The following rolling stock is on the books of the S&M Railway Company:

Goods stock

1	5 tons capacity hand travelling crane. New jib required.
14	Open wagons, low sided, 8 ton. Bodies in poor condition generally, wheels and frames on good order, would need new floors.
9	Covered goods wagons. Wheels and frames in fair condition, bodies developing defects, now being used as store vans.
7	Cattle wagons. In poor condition, now being used as stores.
6	Bolster wagons. In fair order.
2	Brake vans. One brake van in use, the other in Carriage & Wagon shop.
1	Stores van. In poor condition.

The stock generally is in poor condition but could be made serviceable within the Depot.

Coaching stock
Nine coaches, consisting of:

Two North Staffordshire Railway 4-wheel coaches
Four Midland Railway 4-wheel coaches
Three Caledonian 8-wheeled bogie coaches.

The coaching stock is in a very bad state of repair. Some of the coaches could be cleaned up for military use on the line but would require new roofing canvas. Subject to roofs being repaired and interiors removed, some coaches could be used in the Depot for temporary offices.

A SUMMARY FROM GRAHAM VINCENT'S DIARIES:

1A 4-wheeled former Royal saloon from the London & South Western Railway, painted blue.

1 4-wheeled brake, from Midland Railway in 1911. Painted green.

2 4-wheeled brake, from Midland Railway in 1911. Painted brown. Believed scrapped by the end of 1941.

3 Bogie, seven compartment 3rd Class, from MR in 1911, painted brown.

4 Bogie, seven compartment 3rd Class, from MR in 1911, painted blue.

5 Bogie, Brake First/Third Composite, from MR in 1911, painted blue.

6 Bogie, Brake First/Third Composite, from MR in 1911, painted brown.

7 4-wheeled vehicle from London & South Western Railway, scrapped, details not known.

8 4-wheeled 5-compartment 3rd Class, from London & South Western Railway, painted brown, later used as an office at Kinnerley.

9 4-wheeled 5-compartment 3rd Class, from London & South Western Railway, painted brown, later used as accommodation at Nesscliff.

10 4-wheeled 4-compartment Brake/3rd Class Composite, from L&SWR, painted brown.

11 4-wheeled vehicle from London & South Western Railway, scrapped, details not known.

12 4-wheeled 3-compartment Brake Third, from North Staffordshire Railway, repaired, repainted in 1940, in regular use in 1941.

13 4-wheeled 4-compartment Composite (2 First, 2 Third), from NSR painted brown.

14 4-wheeled 4-compartment Composite (2 First, 2 Third), from NSR painted brown.

15 A vehicle from the Great Eastern Railway, scrapped, no details known.

15 4-wheeled horsebox, painted blue, lettered S&MR 15. Used as a tool van.

16 5-compartment vehicle, used as store at Shrewsbury Abbey Bay Platform, origin unknown.

17 5-compartment 3rd Class, used as store at Shrewsbury Abbey Bay Platform, origin unknown.

18 4-wheeled passenger van, ex-North London Railway, painted brown, used as store at Shrewsbury Abbey Bay Platform.

Appendix C
STEAM LOCOMOTIVES ALLOCATED TO THE S&M AS AT 31 DECEMBER FROM 1941 TO 1948

	Allocation as at 31st December	1941	1942	1943	1944	1945	1946	1947	1948
0-6-0 Tender	Dean Goods ex GWR		2425 (96)	2425 (96)	2425 (96)	2425 (96)	2425 (96) *	2425 (96) *	Scr 9/48
		2442 (97)	2442 (97)	2442 (97)	2442 (97)	2442 (97)	2442 (97) *	Scr 6/47	
		2552 (200)							
			2415 (98)	2415 (98)	2415 (98)	2415 (98)	2415 (98) *	2415 (98) *	Scr 9/48
			2511 (175)	2511 (175)	2511 (175)	2511 (175)	2511 (175)	2511 (175)	Scr 8/48
			2558 (176)	2558 (176)	Scr/44				
				2433 (93)	2433 (93)	2433 (93)	2433 (93)	2433 (93)	Sold
					2528 (99)	2528 (99)	2528 (99) *		
					2479 (169)	2479 (169)	2479 (169)	2479 (169)	2479 (169) *
					2536 (170)				
							2576 (196)	2576 (196)	2576 (196)
							2540 (197)	2540 (197) *	Scr 9/48
							2399 (94)	2399 (94) *	Scr /48
							2470 (95) *	2470 (95) *	Scr 9/48
							2514 (180)	2514 (180)	2514 (180) *
	Coal Engines ex LNWR	8108	8108	8108	8108	8108	8108 *	8108 *	8108 *
		8182	8182	8182	8182	8182	8182 *	8182 *	8182 *
		8236	8236	8236	8236	8236	8236 *	8236 *	8236 *
	On loan from LMS	28204							
	J15 ex LNER		7825 (212)	7825 (212)	Scr /44				
			7541 (221)	7541 (221)	Scr /44				
0-6-0 Tank	Bagnall, new to S&M in 1941	WD 73	WD 73	WD 73					
	'Ashford', built 1920		WD 1872	WD 1872	WD 71872	WD 71872	WD 71872	WD 71872	WD 71872 *
	Manning Wardle 654, built 1877		WD 92	WD 92	WD 92				
	'USA' Tank				WD 1395				
					WD 1399				
					WD 1427				
	J69 tank, ex LNER					7388 (70084)	7388 (70084) *	7388 (70084) *	Sold 5/48
					7088 (70091)	7088 (70091)	7088 (70091) *	7088 (70091) *	Sold 5/48
	Austerity tank							75141	75141
								75152	75152
								75171	75171
								75187	75187
								75191	75191
									75131
0-4-0 Tank	Ex LNER (NER)	982	982						
	Ex LMS (LNWR)		3014	Sold 1943					
			3015	Sold 1943					
	'Tartar' Avonside of 1899		WD 202						

Notes: WD numbers of ex-main line locomotives is shown in brackets. All three figure WD numbers were converted to 70XXX series during 1944. 8108 was carrying the number S&M No. 2 when the WD took over the line. 2558 (WD 176) was scrapped in January 1944, after an accident. The 0-4-2 locomotive 'Gazelle' was on the line thoughout this period. Locomotives 'Victory' and 'Yeovil' arrived and were disposed of within the year 1942. * indicates withdrawn and out of use. At 31st December 1946 there were a total of 11 locomotives withdrawn from use, 7 at Hookagate and 4 at Kinnerley. At 31st December 1947 there were 13, all at Hookagate.

Appendix D
DESCRIPTION OF THE DEPOT
AS SET OUT IN REPORTS OF MARCH AND NOVEMBER 1946

Shropshire and Montgomeryshire Light Railway

Six Districts have been established on this railway, as under:

Name	Number of sheds	Average amount of wagons dealt with per week
Maesbrook	64	126
Kinnerley	26	42
Nesscliff	28	76
Shrawardine	22	50
Pentre	46	60
Ford	10	82

There is also a passenger station in Shrawardine Sub-depot serving Nesscliff Camp.

Military traffic is exchanged with main line railways at Hookagate Exchange Sidings. The railway operating service is required to work wagons between the Exchange Sidings and the shed at which the loading and unloading is performed, in accordance with the requirements of Movement Control staff. There is also a certain amount of internal transfer traffic between sheds.

A workmens train runs from Maesbrook to Shrawardine Sub-depot passenger station every morning and back in the evening. Similar workmens trains run daily between Shrewsbury (Abbey) and Shrawardine Sub-depot passenger station.

A motor trolley and trailer has to be manned and placed at the disposal of the RAOC daily for the internal movements of small quantities of ammunition.

To deal with present traffic five engine shifts are required.

All communications with the Depot Authorities or the main line railways regarding military traffic or empty wagons are made through Movement Control staff only. A rigid adherence to this rule will be found to be of advantage to the railway operating service as well as to Movement Control.

The headquarters of Movement Control are at Nesscliff Camp, with detachments at Shrawardine and Hookagate. Inwards loaded wagons are marked for disposal by Movements Control staff on arrival at Hookagate, giving the number of the shed to which they are to be worked.

Movement Control staff advise the railway operating service daily at 16.00 hrs
a) Outward Loaded wagons waiting dispatch giving shed number in each case.
b) Empties required for loading at each shed the following day, 'outwards' and 'internal' separately.
c) Orders (if any) regarding interchange of empty wagons with main line railway.

Movement Control staff deal ordinarily with the Control Office at Kinnerley Junction in all matters.

S&M Railway, Staffing as at March 1946

Military

1. Main Line Maintenance
    45 men of 1028 P.O. Coy (Port Operating)
    21 men S&M Detachment (S&M Det.)

2. Depot Track Maintenance
    10 men 1028 P.O. Coy
    12 men S&M Det.

3. Main Line Operating
    3 men 1028 P.O. Coy (stevedores working as level crossing keepers)
    24 S&M Det, made up as follows
    - 10 Blockmen
    - 1 Brakesman/Shunter
    - 6 R.E.D. (Railway Engine Driver)
    - 4 Firemen
    - 3 Pioneers working as level crossing keepers

4. Depot Operating
    11 men 1028 P.O. Coy, made up as follows
    - 1 Coalman
    - 2 Firemen loco } trainees
    - 1 Boilermaker
    - 1 Crane Driver
    - 6 Pioneers, Shed sweeping

    44 men S&M Det, made up as follows
    - 2 Blockmen
    - 2 Welders
    - 1 Stoker S.E.
    - 3 Brakesmen/Shunters
    - 2 Pointsmen
    - 1 Riveter
    - 4 Fitters
    - 1 Crane Driver
    - 1 Excavator Operator
    - 10 T.O.s
    - 9 Brakesmen/Shunters
    - 1 Storeman
    - 2 Coppersmiths
    - 1 C&W repairs
    - 2 C&W Joiners
    - 1 Platelayer (odd man in depot)
    - 1 Electrician

Civilians

1. Civilians Employed by S&M pre-war
    7 men, made up as follows
    - 4 Plate Layers
    - 1 Fitter
    - 1 R.E.D.
    - 1 Fireman

2. Main Line Maintenance — 4 men

3. Depot Track Maintenance — Nil

4. Main Line Operating — 2 men

5. Depot Operating — 1 man

Appendix E
OPERATING NOTICES

11th September 1958

Operating Notice No 12/58

<u>Special Train Working for The Stephenson Locomotive Society's Visits</u>
<u>Sundays, September 14th, 21st and 28th</u>

1 (a) On the above three consecutive Sundays a Special Passenger train will be provided, at the above Society's expense, and will run as under:-

	Dep	Arr	Remarks
Kinnerley	10.15		Engine off shed 10.10 hrs
Abbey Station		11.30	
Abbey Station	11.45		Stop as required on-route
Kinnerley		12.45	Stable stock in platform
			Engine to Loco until 15.30 hrs
Kinnerley	15.45		Propel stock to Llanymynech
Llanymynech		16.10	Stop at Maesbrook Station 3 minutes on-route
Llanymynech	16.25		
Kinnerley		16.50	
Kinnerley	17.00		Direct to Abbey Station
Abbey Station		17.45	
Abbey Station	17.55		Return stock to Camp Station
Kinnerley		18.40	Brake van No. 49013 and engine to Loco

1(b) Maesbrook 3 Coach set to be used with two Brake Vans, Nos 49013 and 49017, one front and rear.

1(c) Rule 97 M.R.R.B. will be carried out at all level crossings, as laid down in S&M Light Railway Working Instructions.

2. Drewry Rail Car Runs to Criggion
There will be two Drewry Rail Car trips to Criggion, both cars being coupled together, and will run as follows:-
1st Trip.   Dep. 13.00 hrs from Kinnerley and return by 14.10 hrs
2nd Trip.   Dep. 14.15 hrs from Kinnerley and return by 15.25 hrs.
Mr W. Jones, Station Agent, will accompany each trip as Pilotman

3. Yard Master and Loco Foreman to provide staff as verbally instructed. Namely:- 1 Brakesman/Shunter, 1 Travelling Blockman and 2 Rail Car Drivers, One Engine Crew and Loco No. 188. Engine crew to come on duty at 07.30 hours to light up and prepare engine.

Signed
(C. H. Calder)
Operating Officer
S&M Light Railway Detachment
Western Division, 1 Railway Group RE.

Kinnerley Station
Nr. Oswestry
Salop.

Footnote (not part of the Notice)
Railtour participants divided into two parties for the trips to Criggion. While one party was en route, the other inspected the sheds at Kinnerley and took refreshments in the Army Canteen.

Shropshire & Montgomeryshire Rly.
STEPHENSON LOCOMOTIVE SOCIETY
(MIDLAND AREA)
SPECIAL TRAIN TOUR
21st September, 1958
Shrewsbury (The Abbey), Kinnerley, Llanymynech and return, also Kinnerley-Criggion Branch.
Second Class.   Fare 10/-
Conditions as per itinerary.

THE SHROPSHIRE & MONTGOMERYSHIRE LIGHT RAILWAY UNDER MILITARY CONTROL 1940-1960

LAST TRAIN ON THE S&M LIGHT RAILWAY
SPECIAL TRAIN – THE STEPHENSON LOCOMOTIVE SOCIETY

Sunday 20th March 1960

1. A Special Train comprising Engine 193 with two passenger coaches with a brake van front and rear, will run to the following timings:-

	Depart	Arrive
Kinnerley (propelling stock)	11.45 hours	
Bridge No. 15 (Stop board)		12.40 hours
Bridge No. 15 (Stopboard)	13.00 hours	
Kinnerley		14.30 hours
	Break for lunch etc.	
Kinnerley	15.30 hours	
Llanymynech		16.00 hours
(Run round in Platform)		
Llanymynech	16.15 hours	
Kinnerley		16.45 hours
Stable coaches, engine to Loco.		

2. All concerned to note that a Stop board 'STOP LIMIT OF SHUNT' has been erected 3 rail lengths short of where the track has been broken on the West end of Hookagate Yard.

3. This train will stop as required from Hookagate to Kinnerley and on the outward journey to Llanymynech.

4. Loco crew come on duty to prepare engine at 10.30 hours
   Mr Funnel will light engine at 06.00 hours Sunday morning
   Controller, Guard and Blockman come on duty at 11.00 hours

                                                                       Signed
                                                                        (C. H. Calder)
                                                                        Operating Officer
                                                                        S&M Light Railway Detachment
                                                                        Western Division, 1 Railway Group RE.

Kinnerley Station
Nr. Oswestry
Salop.

                                         Distribution:-   Operating Officer
                                                                    Control
                                                                    Driver of Special Train
                                                                    Guard of Special Train
                                                                    Blockman
                                                                    File

Footnotes (not part of the Notice)
A) Even though there was only one train operating, a Controller was required to be on duty.
B) The aptly named Mr Funnel generally 'looked after' Kinnerley Shed.
C) SLS members made their own way to Abbey Station. At 11.30 they made an inspection of the new connection with the Severn Valley line at Bridge No. 7 near Abbey Station, after which they were transported to Hookagate by bus. After inspecting the new works at Hookagate, they walked up the line to the train which was waiting at the new Stop board just on the Hookagate side of Bridge No. 15. After the rail tour, SLS members returned from Kinnerley to Shrewsbury by bus.
D) The SLS produced a special ticket for this rail tour, on white card edged in black. Mr T. R. Perkins obtained ticket numbered 000.

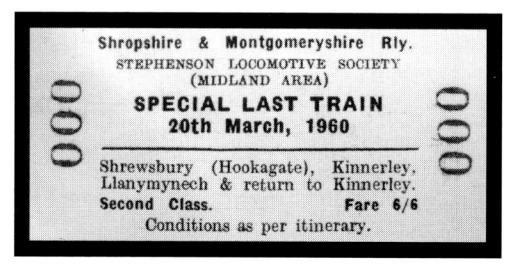

```
Shropshire & Montgomeryshire Rly.
    STEPHENSON LOCOMOTIVE SOCIETY
              (MIDLAND AREA)
         SPECIAL LAST TRAIN
            20th March, 1960
    Shrewsbury (Hookagate), Kinnerley,
    Llanymynech & return to Kinnerley.
    Second Class.          Fare 6/6
        Conditions as per itinerary.
```

ACKNOWLEDGEMENTS & SOURCES

Much of the inspiration for this work, part of which was originally available in 1994 as a slimmer volume (Publication No. 1 of the World War Two Railway Study Group), came from members of the Royal Engineers and of the now defunct Army Railway Organisation – some of who have sadly passed away since the first edition was published. I am most grateful especially for the assistance of Major G. A. Robins of the erstwhile Museum of Army Transport at Beverley, Col D. Ronald, Iain Pardoe, Mike Polglaze, Captain Joe Platt, Eric Fardoe, Alan Pugh, Des Ainsworth, Garth Tilt, John McCrickard, David Giddins and Cliff Shepherd of the Industrial Railway Society.

For many years the S&M was in the charge of Major C. H. (Charlie) Calder. Major Calder had been the Technical Officer In Charge at the Melbourne Military Railway in the War years, and in the post war era was the Operating Officer (equivalent to Operating Superintendent) on the S&M. Favourably disposed to those with a genuine interest in railways, Calder supported R. C. Riley's application to move from an Infantry unit on to Army railway work in 1943. After the war his assistance made possible a number of visits to a railway, which was otherwise 'off limits' to visitors because of the nature of the materials stored in the Depot. Without those visits, many of the photographs in this book would not have been possible. The men on duty for the many rail tours also deserve thanks for their tolerance and patience.

Someone as yet unidentified kept what amounted to a Photographic Album for the Railway Detachment – a personal scrapbook of photographs that were given to him by his visitors as well as a few photographs taken by himself. This scrapbook has been the source of a considerable number of the illustrations used in this publication.

Special thanks are due to:
Sue Whitehouse who has freely allowed access to the papers and photographs of her father Graham Vincent. Graham was a senior boy at Shrewsbury School in the early years of the war. He found that he had considerable freedom to cycle around the area west of Shrewsbury. The notes that he kept, and his letters to R. C. Riley, provide great insight into the early days of the WD take-over and confirmation of the dates of some key events.

If this book were to be dedicated to just one person, it would be to the man seen here on 5th March 1960 standing beside a photographic display of some of the history of the line – Major [retired] Charles Henry (Charlie) Calder MBE. His wartime service, which included supervision at the Melbourne Military Railway, led to him being awarded the MBE in the June 1944 Honours List. He became the 'Operating Officer' for the S&M in November 1947 (following the death of the previous Operating Officer, Mr W. Proctor) and remained in charge until the line closed. Calder personally authorised the access permit for Geoffrey Bannister's work on Geoffrey's thesis. He allowed and arranged several enthusiast's rail tours on his system, without which many of the photographs in this book could not have been taken. To him goes a considerable vote of thanks. Calder went to work at Kinnerley as usual on 3rd May 1960, still busy with concluding the paperwork after the closure of the line. A caller later that day found that he had died (of natural causes) at his desk. Truly a servant of the railway to the last.
Photographer unknown, from the 'Detachment Photograph Album'

Andrew Bannister – for making available the photographs taken by his father Geoffrey, and also the text of Geoffrey's BA thesis (written in 1949) which covered the history of the S&M Railway up to that date. Geoffrey was allowed research facilities on the S&M, and also access to figures held by Mr Anstey (then District Goods Manager, BR, Shrewsbury) and by Mr N. K. Stuart who was then the Assistant Manager at British Quarrying Co., Criggion Quarries. The data that Geoffrey assembled has been the source of many of the traffic figures in this book.

The late Geoffrey Balfour provided considerable assistance in sorting out the history of the London, Tilbury & Southend coaches.

For photographs I am also much obliged to Roger Carpenter and F. A. Wycherley (whose photo business allows us access to many valuable collections, including those of H. F. Wheeler, Norman Glover, P. J. Garland, Roy Miller, Patrick Whitehouse (Millbrook House Ltd and R. K. Cope), Mike Bland, Brian Hilton, the Bluebell Railway Museum Archive which now has the collection of the late J. J. Smith, Colin Betts, Hugh Davies (plus Bob Barnard, Brian Connell, Revd John Parker and Mike Esau) of 'Photos from the Fifties', Barry Hoper at The Transport Treasury, Rod Blencowe, Paul Bolger of Stations (UK) and the photographic section of *Soldier* magazine for their ready permission to use photographs as illustrations.

Sources

Primary sources have been

A) War Office and other files in the National Archives (formerly the Public Record Office):
   WO32/19181 (formerly 120/HOME/4470 and 120/HOME/4329) (the early WD railway papers)
   WO271/139 (CAD Nesscliff quarterly report for July to September 1946)
   WORK26/161 (formerly 120/HOME/4343)
   WORK13/1389 (copy of the contract for the construction of the CAD)
   WORK32/17165 (formerly 120 HOME 6095) (closure of the railway)
   AN2/167 (Railway Executive Committee files, 1939-1945)
   AN13/1373 (reconstruction of the bridge at Melverley)
   RAIL1057/363/subfile 8 (the Pulpit at the Abbey)
   MT78/51 (retention of level crossings at Kinnerley)
   ZSPC11/376 (a scrapbook of newspaper cuttings, photos and train graphs, one of a series of four)

B) Working Instructions, Shropshire & Montgomeryshire Light Railway, issued by 1 Railway Group RE.

C) The diary of Graham Vincent, which has provided evidence of key dates.

D) Notes made by R. C. Riley of a discussion with W. J. Thorne (which formed the basis of an article in *Railway World*, October 1960 under Thorne's name). Thorne had been a Station Foreman at Waterloo. In December 1939 he answered the call for experienced operating men to go as War Department Instructors at Derby. He moved to the S&M to be a Sergeant Line Inspector there in July 1941, staying for some 18 months before moving to Marchwood to become involved in the Mulberry Harbour project.

The principal secondary source is *The Shropshire and Montgomeryshire Light Railway* by Eric S. Tonks (published by the Industrial Railway Society in 1972), an excellent account of the whole of the complex history of this railway, which was opened as a double track line in 1866, largely converted to a single track line in 1867, closed in 1880, the subject of a failed attempt at re-opening during 1890-91, derelict for 31 years, and re-opened as a Light Railway in 1911 by the redoubtable Colonel Stephens – all prior to the coming of the War Department.

The history of WD locomotives is comprehensively covered in *War Department Locomotives* by R. Tourret (Tourret Publishing, 1976). The working of Sentinel locomotives on the S&M is described in an article by John Hutchings in the *Industrial Railway Record* (the journal of the Industrial Railway Society) issue Number 202 (September 2010).

Left: Another long serving member of the railway's staff was George Beeston, seen here in a characteristic pose in the cab of an Austerity locomotive while working the Civilian Goods, handing the keys for the Shrewsbury section of the line back to the blockman at Hookagate East in exchange for a paper Line Clear ticket to allow him to proceed to Hookagate West. Born in August 1910, George had joined the railway on 11th March 1926 and he was working as an assistant fitter when the WD took over the railway. On the retirement of the one and only civilian driver, George took on that role – which he fulfilled until he worked the last passenger train on 20th March 1960. *Photographer unknown*

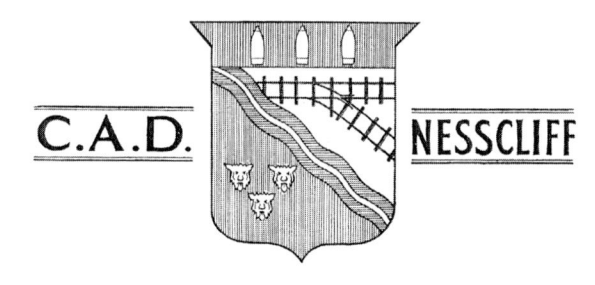

C.A.D. NESSCLIFF